The ADD Brain

Diagnosis, Treatment and Science of Attention Deficit Disorder (ADD/ADHD) in Adults, Teenagers and Children

THE ADD BRAIN

DIAGNOSIS, TREATMENT AND SCIENCE OF ATTENTION DEFICIT DISORDER (ADD/ADHD) IN ADULTS, TEENAGERS AND CHILDREN

MONROE A. GROSS, MD

NOVA SCIENCE PUBLISHERS, INC.
Commack, New York

Art Director: Maria Ester Hawrys
Assistant Director: Elenor Kallberg
Graphics: Susan Boriotti and Frank Grucci
Manuscript Coordinator: Phyllis Gaynor
Book Production: Gavin Aghamore, Joanne Bennette, Michelle Keller
Christine Mathosian and Tammy Sauter
Circulation: Iyatunde Abdullah, Cathy DeGregory and Annette Hellinger

Library of Congress Cataloging-in-Publication Data
available upon request

ISBN 1-56072-430-7

Kroshka Books. A division of
Nova Science Publishers, Inc.
6080 Jericho Turnpike, Suite 207
Commack, New York 11725
Tele. 516-499-3103 Fax 516-499-3146
E Mail Novascil@aol.com
Novascience@earthlink.net

Printed in the United States of America

DEDICATED TO

My brother, Paul Alton Marshall Gross, who,
in spite of ADD,
graduated from Harvard College magna cum laude, and
graduated from N.Y.U. medical school as a physician,
but who committed suicide at the age of forty
after being treated with only psychotherapy.

Table of Contents

Chapter Four: The Neurobiology of ADD

Chapter Five: The Clinical Picture of Attention Deficit Disorder Neurology in Children

Chapter Nine: Attention Deficit Disorder and Criminality

Chapter Ten: Clinical Findings And Analysis - A Study of 1377 Patients with Attention Deficit Disorder

PREFACE

Even as we enter the second half of the 1990's, most health and education professionals have only limited skill diagnosing and treating individuals with Attention Deficit Disorder (ADD). Moreover, those who are identified as being ADD people are too often only recognized because they are troublesome or so dysfunctional that they have a very limited ability to succeed in society. This "tip-of-the-iceberg" recognition of people with ADD is not good enough.

Without a correct diagnosis and proper medication, all individuals with ADD move through life with more difficulty than they should and often only with great effort. Because of the way their brain is programmed to function, they struggle longer and harder to complete academic work than they would if treated ..... have difficulty getting even simple chores and tasks done ..... are likely to be periodically violent ..... frequently feel negative ..... and sometimes are chronically depressed. For far too many, the ultimate consequence of living with untreated ADD neurology is repeated failures at home and work as well as interpersonal and social inadequacy which lead not infrequently to personal and social ills such as illicit drug use, alcoholism, periodic acts of violence, crime, and murder.

This book, hopefully, will serve two major purposes. The first is to help professionals and nonprofessionals feel confident in their ability to identify individuals who have ADD neurology. Like many other clinical conditions, ADD can be recognized with amazing accuracy even by nonprofessionals when the dysfunctional behaviors that are strong clues to its diagnosis are appreciated for what they are.

The second purpose is to describe precisely what ADD neurology is so that, whether the clinical presentation is classical or atypical, severe or mild, those with ADD can be easily diagnosed. It is only after the diagnosis is established that ADD individuals can be safely treated with medication.

Accordingly, this book provides an enlarged, up-to-date, full detailed description of the spectrum of neurological dysfunctions which are clues to the ADD syndrome, not just the three research criteria of hyperactivity, impulsivity and inattentiveness that are listed in the 1994 *DSM-IV (Diagnostic and Statistical Manual*, fourth edition).

The ability of clinical professionals to diagnose and treat those with Attention Deficit Disorder is less than ideal. There are several reasons for this. The formal medical education of many physicians now in practice was completed well before ADD was first described in the 1980 edition of the *DSM-III* (*Diagnostic and Statistical Manual*, third edition). Few physicians are familiar with the psychiatric literature in general and with the contents of the Diagnostic and Statistical Manuals in particular. A significant number of pediatricians continue to believe that many of the problems that ADD children experience are not diagnostic of ADD and are unimportant because they disappear with maturity. Most physicians who care for adults fail to read either the pediatric or psychiatric literature where most of the research on ADD is published and do not understand that ADD continues into adulthood.

For a long time, I, too, knew little about the ADD syndrome. As a physician whose initial training was mainly in adult medicine, all too often I would choose diagnostic labels for ADD individuals who came to me for medical care which reflected little more than their presenting complaints. For example, it used to seem logical to me to diagnose a periodically violent person as having the Intermittent Explosive Syndrome [1], and it seemed equally reasonable to do little more than refer such an individual for psychotherapy. Now, I am aware that episodic explosiveness is but one of the ten major neurological dysfunctions of the ADD syndrome, and its definitive treatment includes medication even if psychotherapy and counseling are needed.

In this preface, I would like to describe the evolution of my own understanding of and approach to the ADD syndrome. I hope that this will illuminate why many professionals today have difficulty understanding that

ADD is a neurological disorder and why they are often reluctant to prescribe medication for those who suffer from it. After all, it took me years to realize the extensiveness of the clinical picture of the ADD syndrome, stop believing that people with ADD are always inattentive as the name implies, and become aware that so-called antidepressant drugs and not stimulant medications are usually the treatment of choice.

As a physician trained in internal medicine, an endocrinologist by virtue of postgraduate study, and a neuroendocrinologist because of basic research experience and personal interest, I now realize that a rather strange sequence of events led to what is my present understanding of the ADD syndrome.

Although then unknown to me, my exposure to ADD people began in my postgraduate hospital training years of internship and medical residency. During that period, I was extremely fortunate to have had two particular mentors, Dr. Bud Levy, Chief Neurologist, and Dr. Ed Massie, Chief of the Cardiology Division, both professors at Washington University School of Medicine, St. Louis, Missouri, and Physicians at the Barnes Hospital in St. Louis. They had an informal but very interesting and challenging clinical collaboration to which I was fortuitously exposed.

Dr. Levy and Dr. Massie often worked cooperatively trying to determine whether or not patients referred by community doctors because of atypical chest pain had underlying cardiac (heart) disease or a disorder called atypical depression as the underlying cause of their complaints of recurring chest pain.

Atypical depression is a diagnostic term which has been applied to individuals who deny feeling "depressed" but have symptoms that occur commonly in depressed individuals including waking with difficulty, excessive tiredness, loss of interest in sex, altered appetite and, for some, somatic (body) pain. Differentiating between organic heart disease with atypical chest pain and atypical depression with somatic pain was not an easy task in the 1960's when the sophisticated tools we now have for diagnosing cardiac disease and the present-day choice of antidepressant medications did not exist.

I am not aware that this cooperative venture was formally documented, but Dr. Levy once told me that approximately half of the adults whom he was asked to evaluate by Dr. Massie for chest pain and possible heart disease turned out to be suffering from the syndrome of atypical depression. Their pain disappeared after treatment with antidepressant medication and heart disease was never documented as the causative factor.

Atypical depression is a variant of what used to be called "biological depression" and is now one of ten psychiatric classifications of "depression." The basis for categorizing atypical depression along with other kinds of depression is the observation that individuals with these diagnoses usually respond to treatment with antidepressant medication.

Later, about twenty-five years ago, I first began to treat adults who were suffering from what at that time I was calling atypical depression. Then, I too believed that atypical depression was merely a kind of psychiatric depression. More recently, my view of atypical depression has undergone a drastic metamorphosis. This change came about after adults with atypical depression, whom I had treated successfully with antidepressant medication, told me about scholastic and behavioral problems in their children that were "just like" what they had experienced when they were young. Interestingly, many of the children of these patients were hyperactive, inattentive at school, and impulsive but not clinically depressed. As such, they fit the *DSM-III*, *DSM-III-R*, and *DSM-IV* criteria for Attention Deficit Hyperactivity Disorder, commonly called simply Attention Deficit Disorder.

When I treated these children with antidepressant medications, the same class of drug that had helped their parents who had been labeled as having atypical depression, the ADD dysfunctions of the children, including hyperactivity, impulsivity and inattentiveness, disappeared or dramatically lessened in intensity and school performance immediately improved. It thus became clear to me that these children with ADD could respond to treatment with antidepressant medication.

At the same time, the fact that children labeled as having ADD could be successfully treated with antidepressant medication suggested that perhaps the adults whom I had diagnosed with atypical depression should be thought of as having an adult version of ADD. It was then that two almost heretical thoughts entered my mind. First, antidepressant medication can do more than treat depression, typical or atypical. Second, depression itself is a second-order, reactive or psychological phenomenon, and as such a consequence of negativity which is one of the ten major neurological dysfunctions of the ADD syndrome.

Contrary to what my earlier medical training had taught me, I came to realize that the diagnostic designation, atypical depression, useful as it had been, did not appropriately direct my attention as a physician to the full range of neurological dysfunctions that in fact exist in ADD adults whether depressed or not. In addition, the atypical depression diagnosis did not encourage me to explore for the possibility of ADD, a genetic disorder, in other members of the same family. The diagnosis of atypical depression in adults had not been "wrong," but it was less useful diagnostically and therapeutically than the diagnosis, Adult ADD.

As I began to search carefully for and find ADD neurological dysfunctions in the medical history of adults who would otherwise have been labeled as having atypical depression, it become clear why so few adults were being diagnosed with ADD, and why medical thinking even today teaches that the ADD syndrome often "disappears" with adulthood. The reason is that adults rarely volunteer information about those dysfunctions that are strong clues to the diagnosis of ADD, and physicians almost never ask about them. As a result, the diagnostic clues to ADD are commonly not identified and largely ignored as such.

After learning to properly identify the ADD syndrome in adults, I noticed that many ADD patients came to me having been previously labeled as suffering from a variety of traditional psychiatric diagnoses including agoraphobia, alcoholism, anorexia nervosa, bulimia, chronic pain syndrome, chronic fatigue syndrome, compulsive eating, compulsive gambling, compulsive sexuality, criminality, dystonia musculorum deformans, episodic explosiveness including family violence and child battering, hyperventilation syndrome, hypoglycemia syndrome, hysteria, illicit drug dependence, major depressive episode, panic syndrome, Tourette's syndrome and the workaholic syndrome. These individuals typically sought my medical care because they had not yet been successfully treated. Many had received only psychotherapy.

When treated with the proper antidepressant medication, individuals with the various dysfunctions and diagnoses listed above dramatically improved whether or not they felt chronically "depressed," that is, "low," "sad most of the time," "blue," "hopeless, or "down in the dumps." In particular, treatment reduced or even eliminated poorly controlled urges, impulsive behaviors, cravings, and excessive responses to stress and temptation, important factors contributing to their dysfunctional behaviors. These individuals were also dramatically more able to focus mentally, perceive more accurately, and better handle frustrations and difficult social situations that had formerly entangled their lives.

Now, let's change to a related but slightly different topic. Many of those who have benefited from so-called antidepressant medications have asked me why I chose to prescribe "antidepressant" medication when they were not depressed. Even though I explained that the medication was effective treatment for their particular disorder, some patients were confused and even refused to continue taking antidepressant medication because they were uncomfortable with what they believed was an unconventional therapeutic approach.

This concern of patients prompted me to ask myself if it is reasonable to label a class of drugs as "antidepressants" when these same drugs also help individuals who are not "depressed?" I now think it is not! In fact, I usually say that antidepressant medications are really "neurotransmitter hormone potentiators" to try to help reduce terminological confusion as well as help patients understand something about the underlying mechanism of action of this class of drugs. There should be a search for a more generic and physiological name for the class of drugs called antidepressants. Even a class name such as "synapse modulator" would be suggestive of the biochemical action of these drugs and an improvement over the antidepressant nomenclature.

A name change would also help to stress that ADD has a neurological rather than psychological basis. In addition, such a change would alert doctors, insurers, parents and teachers to the fact that what are now called antidepressant medications can be helpful in people with a variety of complaints, not just those who feel depressed.

By way of example, propranolol, a beta-adrenergic receptor-blocking medication, used to be referred to simplistically as a "blood pressure" pill even though it can be effective for the treatment of headache and hyperthyroidism. Prescribing "blood pressure" medicine for the treatment of an overactive thyroid gland has, in the past, been as confusing as the dispensing of antidepressant medication to ADD individuals who are not depressed. Today, propranolol is generally recognized as a beta-adrenergic receptor blocking agent with multiple uses, and antidepressant medication should be recognized as a synapse modulator rather than as medicine that only treats depression.

At this point, let's tackle the problem of the disorder nomenclature. The term, Attention Deficit Disorder, does not properly describe those with satisfactory school grades and no obvious "attention" or "learning" problems. Nor does it focus attention on the broad spectrum of nine other neurological dysfunctions that affect those with ADD. Should ADD be renamed at this time? Probably not right now. The ADD syndrome is now commonly known to health professionals, teachers, school administrators and many in the lay public. Until a name that reflects its biochemical basis can be invented, it is reasonable to continue its use. On the other hand, it is essential that knowledge of the full spectrum of dysfunctions associated with ADD be disseminated as much as possible to both professionals and the lay public.

Finally, it is my hope that this book will encourage others to investigate the association between the Attention Deficit Disorder syndrome and violence, criminality, illicit drug dependence and alcoholism, to name a few of the problems for which ADD is a known risk factor. Untreated, ADD can lead directly to problems which carry momentous consequences for society. Untreated ADD individuals who gravitate toward violence, crave excitement, have a prolonged negative attitude, and hold on to grudges and anger rarely find peace with themselves nor contribute peaceful solutions to human conflict.

Reference

1. **Editorial,** *Diagnosis of Intermittent Explosive Disorder.* Mayo Clinic Proceedings, 1987. **62**: p. 205-207.

ACKNOWLEDGMENTS

This book is full of information from my medical patients, not just research articles and books. Accordingly, I very much want first to thank my patients with Attention Deficit Disorder who have been open with me about their medical history and who have taken time to tell me how various medications helped or did not help to correct their ADD complaints.

In addition, I want to thank several people who very generously contributed material which was incorporated into this book: Patricia Churchill, Susan English, Richard Epstein, Rick Huebsch, David Paterson and Areta Stadler.

I am grateful to my wife, Winifred T. Gross, J.D., M.S.W.. She was a constant inspiration to me and a helpful critic of my writing. She also helped gather and interpret information about the relationship between ADD and criminality.

Marianne Nevins, medical staff librarian at The Good Samaritan Hospital, San Jose, California, was repeated helpful and cheerfully provided requested references as well as access to the hospital computerized medical reference database.

Professor Evelyn Neufeld and Mrs. Elaine Brett unselfishly took time to meticulously review the manuscript and offer helpful, meaningful comments.

Finally, I wish to thank the staff of my private medical office and especially Ms. Lia Oeschey, my nurse for many years.

Monroe A. Gross, MD

1

Think of ADD as a Medical Problem

The ADD Brain is about people born with Attention Deficit Disorder (ADD) neurology. It is about children, teenagers and adults who feel alert and alive only when involved in high adventures or emergent, outrageous, and sometimes life-threatening situations. It is about people who, for biological reasons that are still unclear, do not function well in routine, ordinary, so-called boring circumstances. When seeking thrills, those with ADD all too often exceed ordinary societal limits and even cause harm to themselves and others. As they struggle to function and cope in the modern, complex world in which we all now live, those with ADD commonly find the challenges of ordinary living unexciting and dull, experience repeated episodes of personal failure, and, as a consequence, develop low self-esteem. The ultimate result: ADD is a major cause of human suffering and tragedy.

Lots of people have ADD. As you learn more about the disorder, you will almost certainly become aware of ADD individuals all around you, at work, in the classroom, even living in your very home. You might even discover that you have ADD neurology.

For many, ADD is still a confusing, uncertain, almost mysterious term. Some doubt it exists other than in the minds of a few professionals. A few erroneously believe that ADD is just the consequence of transient psychological problems. Whether you are a nonprofessional with an interest in trying to understand ADD, an educator who is confronted with ADD students, or a health professional helping ADD individuals cope with the consequences of their dysfunctional behavior, you will soon learn that ADD is a very real, neurologically determined pattern of behaviors and, equally importantly, you will learn that you can identify ADD individuals because the disorder is no more than a clinical syndrome which anyone can come to understand and recognize.

Think of how many grandmothers can identify chickenpox, another clinical disorder. You do not need a scientific background to diagnose ADD because there are no specific diagnostic laboratory or psychological tests any more than there are for chickenpox.

The ADD neurological syndrome is often missed by professionals and nonprofessionals because the clinical clues to the diagnosis are simply not known or are erroneously considered merely passing problems, so-called developmental difficulties, or environmentally-induced inflictions. Dyslexia, bedwetting, tantrums, even hyperactivity, are often attributed out of ignorance to "slow development" or "delayed socialization." Even school teachers sometimes assure parents that their children will outgrow the writing reversals of dyslexia and physicians insist that hyperactive behavior and tantrums are just temporary aspects of the maturing process without encouraging parents to be aware of the possibility of underlying ADD neurology.

It is true that, as most children progress toward adulthood, they have less trouble with certain ADD dysfunctions such as dyslexia, bedwetting, tantrums and gross hyperactivity. But, this is not always the case, and it is not true with respect to most of the other dysfunctions of ADD. If the dysfunctions of ADD are not recognized for what they are then, later, when they become less tolerable and academic and social failure becomes overt, dysfunctional behavior is commonly and incorrectly attributed not to ADD but to the hormone changes of puberty, teenage turmoil or the stress of early adult life. When this happens, ADD teenagers are frequently labeled by parents, teachers, physicians and others as being lazy, undersocialized, stupid, unmotivated, consciously obstreperous or intentionally oppositional. Even adults with moderate to severe ADD may experience similar criticism from their spouses, friends and work associates.

This is all possible because very few people, whether they are professionals or nonprofessionals, understand the full spectrum of ADD diagnostic clues, and even fewer know how the expression of these clues is influenced by age, sex and other factors.

I wrote *The ADD Brain* to deal with just these issues. This is a book with a modern view of the ADD syndrome. It contains basic information about what ADD is and detailed descriptions of the clinical clues that establish the diagnosis. Moreover, based on a review of the medical literature and personal research on 1377 patients diagnosed and successfully treated by the author, this book documents that the clinical criteria for diagnosing ADD are more than just hyperactivity, impulsivity and inattentiveness as is commonly described in the psychiatric literature.

ADD is a neurological, not a psychiatric, disorder that can and should be treated with medication. It is important that the neurological criteria of ADD be clearly understood not only for making the correct diagnosis but also because these criteria should serve as a guide to whether or not medication treatment is effective.

Of course, not everyone with a problem has ADD. Making a correct diagnosis is very important because ADD medication should not be prescribed for people who do not have ADD. They will not benefit from it and are likely to be harmed by inappropriate medication treatment.

This book will be of value to both professionals and nonprofessionals. While the ultimate responsibility for confirming the diagnosis of neurological disorders rests with physicians, others should be confident at suspecting the diagnosis of ADD and in taking the necessary steps for seeing to it that a diagnosis is established in a timely fashion.

If not properly understood, ADD is often confused with a multitude of other problems. Failure to diagnose usually means denial of proper medication treatment and, for many as they enter their teens and adult years, severely dysfunctional lives. It is an act of kindness to the ADD individual and it is in the interest of society that people with ADD be identified and offered medication treatment as early in life as is possible.

Testing Your Knowledge of the ADD Syndrome

Take a moment and look at how much you know about ADD and some ADD issues you should be up-to-date on. Try answering the following questions.

If you have trouble with any of these questions, do not be discouraged. Just realize why you are bothering to read this book.

Even most professionals in the fields of health and education still do not have a clear understanding of the Attention Deficit Disorder (ADD) syndrome. This is why many ADD children and most ADD adults are not recognized as such even though ADD is one of the most common and devastating medical disorders in our country today.

The good news is that what you cannot answer now, you will be able to answer after you have read this book.

THE "ARE-YOU-CURRENT" QUIZ

1. Does everyone in the world have Attention Deficit Disorder?
   Yes ____ No ____

2. Do more people have ADD neurology than is generally recognized?
   Yes ____ No ____

3. Is it reasonably safe to start medication treatment for ADD at an early age?
   Yes ____ No ____

4. Are Attention Deficit Disorder (ADD), Attention Deficit Hyperactive Disorder (ADHD), and the Hyperactivity Syndrome different names for the same medical syndrome?
   Yes ____ No ____

5. Do you know the ten major neurological dysfunctions that define the ADD syndrome?
   Yes ____ No ____

6. Is the behavior of children and teenagers with ADD little more than a reflection of their obstinacy, stupidity, laziness and bad manners?
   Yes ____ No ____

7. Is it almost certain that a child with ADD will become an adult with ADD?
   Yes ____ No ____

8. Is ADD an important cause of "learning disability" in children and adults?
   Yes ____ No ____

9. In a family with more than one ADD individual, do those with ADD always have the same pattern of ADD neurological dysfunction?
   Yes ____ No ____

10. Are ADD adults more likely to be fidgety than grossly hyperactive?
    Yes ____ No ____

11. Is it likely that those who grow up with ADD and are not treated with ADD medication will develop important psychological dysfunctions as adults?
Yes ____ No ____

12. Is the behavior of ADD individuals truly painful and dysfunctional or just charming, engaging, and really no more than a creative variant of "normal?"
Yes ____ No ____

13. Is ADD behavior always inherited from one or both parents, without skipping generations?
Yes ____ No ____

14. On a reverse note, does having ADD neurology often offer personality advantages such as an enhanced ability to deal with highly stressful situations?
Yes ____ No ____

The medical criteria for diagnosing ADD and evaluating treatment success are defined in detail in future chapters. With this information, you should be able to tell whether or not you, members of your family, friends, or people you work with have ADD. ADD people often think as well as cope with emotional problems in ineffective ways. Trying to communicate and work with them is dramatically easier if you understand the nature of ADD and why people with ADD think and behave the way they do.

ADD is a problem that can now be readily diagnosed, and its treatment with medication is simple and very available. ADD individuals no longer have to live out their lives needlessly suffering.

By the way, if you had trouble answering the questions in "The Are-You-Current" quiz, do not feel that you *should* have known the answers. Not very long ago, I, too, would have answered a lot of the questions incorrectly.

2

WARNING: "ADD MAY BE HAZARDOUS TO YOUR HEALTH"

ADD DYSFUNCTION: CATALYST FOR TRAGEDY

The brain chemistry of people with ADD is just enough out-of-kilter to limit their ability to cope maximally with the world around them. Some ADD people, however, are so dysfunctional that they unfortunately cope minimally.

Whether moderate or severe, the neurological dysfunctions of untreated ADD teenagers and adults cause a variety of cognitive, emotive and behavioral disabilities. Not only do these disabilities reduce the ability of those with ADD to cope with the stresses of ordinary living, they are important risk factors for many of the common illnesses and tragedies that modern society is struggling to combat today.

Down-the-road learned (psychological) behaviors of people with ADD who grow into their teens and adulthood without the benefit of medication treatment all too often include the use of illicit drugs, the excessive consumption of alcohol, aberrant dietary practices, inadequate exercise, reckless driving, noncompliance with medical regimens, and maladaptive responses to stress.

In the more extreme cases, these unhealthy behaviors can have especially costly and socially destructive consequences. Escapism can turn into drug addiction. Impulsive eating can lead to heart disease. Inappropriate responses to stress can perpetuate smoking and cause cancer. Inattentiveness and the search for high adventure are factors leading to automobile accidents and death. Episodic explosiveness can be expressed as life-threatening violence directed inward (suicide) or toward others (child or spousal abuse).

ADD people often do not have a sense of well-being. They function effectively only with great effort. Many feel a lot of stress much of the time. Medically untreated, they have difficulty gathering, organizing and expressing thoughts. Their feelings are excessively intense and often distorted by incorrect perceptions. Demands on their cognitive function are a strain which leads to untoward anxiety as they attempt to perform even the ordinary tasks of life.

Not every untreated ADD individuals will eventually develop a host of unhealthy ways of living. But, many do, especially if they live with a stressed and dysfunctional family or in an environment that has little understanding or allowance for their particular disabilities. Interactions with family members in particular tend to be tense and explosive. Simple life situations such as studying in a room with other people, watching television with the family, or dealing with other automobile drivers in traffic are typical circumstances that repeatedly irritate and fray the nerves of those with ADD for little or no reason.

Because of how their neurology works, ADD individuals are driven toward unhealthy behaviors. They have a propensity for seeking high-thrill activities to relieve excessive feelings of boredom. They often succumb to ritualistic and addictive behaviors because of feeling impulsive, compulsive, frustrated and anxious. They frequently act impulsively, unable to slow their rush of thoughts and effectively process individual ideas. Many feel negative much of the time. Too many are victimized by offers of pleasure and fun that may ultimately lead to tragic, even fatal, outcomes, and thus they become easy prey to momentary gratifications that may have long-term negative consequences.

The tragic consequences of ADD neurology often are cause of severe pain for the individual. For example, ADD children who have been disruptive in the classroom and underachievers academically are likely to end up feeling like outcasts and failures. Children and adults suffer when they think they are disliked and rejected by others because of their ineptness, irritability, and/or violent antisocial behavior. Many ADD individuals who experience a lot of pain when interacting with others attempt to deaden these feelings with drugs such as alcohol and marihuana or escape from them by withdrawing and isolating themselves from other people.

Adults with ADD neurology can end up destroying their families as they escape from what is boredom to them by being involved in activities that they find extremely exciting. "Turning-on" may mean, for example, seeking out extramarital affairs. Driven by an ADD brain chemical imbalance, the ADD person does not understand the reason for his or her need for adventurous or driven behavior and is stunned when disaster strikes and divorce ensues.

Commonly, ADD children and adults are episodically explosive. A major reason young children are dismissed from school is their explosive behavior. Explosiveness in adults can be the cause of failure to advance at work, lost jobs, and physical injuries. Rage exposes family members of all ages to repeated verbal and sometimes physical episodes of abuse. Living with explosive individuals is especially frustrating because the episodes of rage often occur in unpredictable circumstances and, strangely, are inexplicably provoked by varied and only minimally adverse stimuli. Both the children and the spouse of an ADD adult with episodic rage are likely to become unfortunate and helpless victims because of their physical and emotional ties to the dysfunctional adult with whom they live. Dealing with violence in the family can be frustrating. Much too often, family members who are the target of explosive people are mistakenly accused by them, other family members, and outsiders of being the cause of the anger and deserving of the abuse they receive.

Medically untreated ADD people, almost regardless of the intensity of their dysfunctions, suffer much more than they let on to others. Let's turn for a moment to a true story told by Patricia. She describes in her own words how she was trapped by handicapping and painful dysfunctions of ADD until she discovered medication that changed her life:

Case Study

"Stupid! Stupid! Stupid! How can you be so dumb? You are such an ass that you can't do this!" I raged at myself both inwardly and outwardly when something in my life, that I perceived should have worked easily didn't. My self-esteem was at an all time low because I was ruthless with myself when I couldn't accomplish things that other people seem to take for granted and could complete with ease. Reading, spelling, organizing, finding something, following a map, fixing something, or following directions, any one or all of these were enough to send me over the edge into a morass of self-flagellation.

Daily life was difficult, frustrating, and generally unmanageable in every area. I lived in continual frustration from my failures and as I watched others succeed, my anger and self-worth continued to plummet. My mind couldn't filter out the constant clutter to focus on whatever I was attempting to do at any given moment, and my mind felt like a spinning top I couldn't shut off. I felt pushed all the time, even when I was doing the simplest of tasks. If there were other pressures on me while I was trying to focus on a single task, and I couldn't complete the chore, I would lose control and find myself in a rage. Daily life had become a zoo for me and my family.

A typical example of this was getting dinner fixed and served for my family of four. For me, preparing a meal was not one simple task, but a whole series of tasks requiring memory, coordination, organization and timing. This chore tested all my focusing abilities, from the first step of deciding what to prepare to finally getting the meal on the table. Remembering to remove pork chops from the freezer on time was merely the beginning, because the concept of time isn't really nailed down in my mind. This simple step was often enough to stop the whole process and require a trip to the store or eating a meal out. If I passed this stage unscathed, the tension usually escalated as dinner was coming to the final stages requiring my juggling the potatoes, final touches with the salad, the chops, and the vegetable so that it all landed on the table at the same time instead of winding up on the floor. Setting the table, answering a kid's question, listening to my husband recount his day, and then, in the final minutes having the broccoli coming out of the microwave looking like petrified wood, would touch off one of my explosive rages.

When explosions like these occurred, my family, often caught off guard, would look at me wide-eyed and, one by one disappear until my rage was spent. My fear and shame felt overwhelming. How could I be so out of control? My guilt and shame were so intense that I could not accept the love and support my family offered to me. It was awful for all of us. I couldn't forgive myself for not being able to do everything efficiently and remain inwardly calm.

These feelings of low self-esteem and especially, my feeling stupid, had their origins during my school years when I had continuing difficulties with reading, spelling, simple math, and tests of any kind. Education was almost worshipped in my family, and we children regularly heard about how important reading was. I always was in remedial reading labs in order to learn how to read faster and to help comprehend what I'd read. In spite of this, I still found reading to be nearly an insurmountable barrier. I was the child who didn't enjoy reading the cereal boxes at breakfast or the comics in the Sunday paper.

Later on, in high school, I spent hours sitting cross-legged on my bed, studying. I would read sentences over and over again in order to comprehend their meaning. I would read paragraphs again and again because I couldn't remember the beginning of one paragraph by the time I reached the end of it. When I finally finished a chapter I wouldn't be able to answer the questions at the end of it, because I wouldn't have discerned what was important while I was reading. The obscure pieces of information, such as how people dressed, or what kinds of houses they lived in, would grab my interest and attention, instead of the important situations, people and dates. I struggled to learn the information the teacher required, in order to try and remember it for tests. The resulting C's and D's were a clear reflection of my, then, unknown learning disability.

In spite of these difficulties, I still loved to learn and found that I learned best in discussion classes or hands on classes where I had the freedom to ask questions, which I often blurted out. My social skills were good, even though I often embarrassed myself by my outspokenness. My hunger to learn, my curiosity, and my wanting to succeed drove me to endure in all my study efforts. Finally all my perseverance in studying was rewarded when I landed on Dean's List my last semester at LaSalle Junior College. It felt wonderful to finish my formal education with a B average, but I still felt stupid and believed I was unable to go further in college.

When I was thirty-five, an intelligent and trusted friend of mine told me I was intelligent too. For the first time in my life I heard and believed that I might not be stupid. It was still hard to believe, because why couldn't I do simple things easily without so much effort and stress? This was the beginning of my search for answers, but I was still ten years away from discovering why I struggled so hard to accomplish anything and had become very discouraged and depressed.

Eventually, I reached the point of wishing I didn't have to wake up in the morning to repeat another frustrating day. I felt "down," frustrated, hopeless, and afraid, with a very low self-esteem. My search for solutions from the medical profession had led me down a trail of wrong answers and given me false hopes, so when the opportunity to see the author of this book in 1984 came, I nearly turned it down. Dr. Gross explored my history and, as I was able to articulate my symptoms adequately, I learned I wasn't alone in experiencing life as difficult and overwhelming. My symptoms pointed to a Neurotransmitter Disorder, which the author explained as a brain chemistry dysfunction, that for some people improves with medication.

Taking the medication the author recommended produced such a change in my life that I can only describe it as being reborn and this new life allowed me the ability to begin to focus easier and think more clearly. The "down" feeling disappeared overnight and I began to look forward to waking up in the mornings again. I was forty-five years old and for the first time someone had given me an answer for the confusion and frustration I had been feeling my entire life. I was flooded with relief. I also felt consumed by a need to learn everything I could about my disorder. I discovered this disorder was also called Attention Deficit Hyperactivity Disorder but in 1984 there was a shortage of information on this subject. In spite of this, I continued to read everything I could find. Yes, I read and read and read!

In spite of the medications and increased awareness of ADD, the rages and self-loathing continued. I sought cognitive therapy hoping to adjust my way of thinking about myself. The nearest psychologist who understood ADD in adults was four-and-a-half hours away. My husband and I made the journey in order to find someone to help us differentiate between ADD traits and other issues we were having within our marriage relationship. My marriage and my life began to turn around as I started to implement the tools I was given. These enabled me to positively re-parent myself. I learned to give myself permission to make choices, to reward myself positively, and challenge my intelligence. I gradually became better at being kind to myself, communicating my moods out loud, cultivating a sense of humor, and reaching out to others. My medication allowed me to focus during my therapy sessions and, later to follow through with what I learned.

As my self-worth improved I began to feel empowered to do things I never imagined I would do. I was motivated to follow an old dream of graduating from a four year university. In therapy I realized I learn best in a hands-on setting, so I searched for a university which teaches that way. I returned to college, but even with medication, therapy and an enlightened institution, I still had to spend hours studying and I still feared tests. In spite of these difficulties I had been given the tools and confidence I needed to succeed. I graduated with honors in June of 1993 and am now working towards my Masters in Clinical Psychology. This will allow me to become a licensed MFCC therapist, counseling others struggling with ADD.

Another goal I had was to start a self-help support group. I was able to fulfill this goal five years ago when I began facilitating meetings for adults struggling with ADD. Working with the members of this group has confirmed the need for therapeutic support in addition to medication for adults who are diagnosed in adulthood. This gives families a way to have support and learn strategies for successfully managing ADD issues.

Starting and working with this ADD Support Group gave me a hunger for additional training and networking opportunities. I have had a strong desire to be better equipped in order to help facilitate our group and provide a caring, and growing environment. My excitement accelerated when I learned about the first Adult ADD conference in Ann Arbor, Michigan.

This first Adult ADD Conference held in May of 1993, was a wonderful opportunity to meet and network with others in this growing field. I benefited from the experience and learned more about available medications being used to treat ADD. I learned there are a variety of medications and combinations that work successfully for many suffering with ADD symptoms. The doctors who lectured at the conference discussed advances in medications being used to treat ADD symptoms. Talking with other ADD adults helped me to decide to add Ritalin to my own medication regime.

I believe a combination of strategies contribute to my ability to cope with my ADD symptoms. Medications handle the cognitive fuzziness, helping me to think clearly and make productive, healthy choices. My own combination consists of Prozac and Ritalin working in concert. The Prozac controls my mood swings, while the Ritalin allows me to think logically, concentrate, read my assignments faster with better comprehension, and to complete my daily school and work tasks with plenty of energy.

I continually exercise positive self-talk when I make mistakes and am still working to develop a sense of humor about my ADD symptoms. I exercise in an attempt to expend the pent up energy I seem to carry inside. I program stimulating recreation may range from sewing a garment to painting a picture or going on an outing to the city. In a self-help group I allow others to see me vulnerable in my own areas of struggle, while I work to manage my own ADD symptoms. I reach out in an attempt to educate others and to grow myself as a part of my way to live with this challenging disorder. I enjoy my creative abilities, my desire for challenges and my growing opportunities to work with others, helping them to develop a sense of hope and to believe in their own dreams.

But just the other day, I became enraged over the difficulty of finding a new store, because I read the paper advertisement incorrectly. I drove for 50 minutes rather radically around a two miles radius, in which we passed the store at least three times. My patient husband sat quietly beside me, occasionally suggesting we stop at what turned out to be the store we were looking for. After I finally took his suggestion and stopped, he told me how long our search had taken. Later we both laughed as we recounted the humorous event to our children.

* * * *

Many of the psychological dysfunctions evident in ADD individuals such as Patricia are alleviated when the root neurological causes are ameliorated. For example, low self-esteem because of academic failure diminishes when academic inattentiveness, hyperactivity and impulsivity are properly treated with medication and the individual begins to encounter success and praise instead of repeated criticism. But, as the story of Patricia points out, this is not always what happens when the start of medication treatment is delayed until adulthood.

It is difficult to overstate the importance of starting medication treatment as early as a diagnosis can be made. Early treatment prevents exposure to repeated failures of one sort or another, constantly recurring negative social experiences, and the development of the health-harming, compensatory psychological dysfunctions.

The dimensions of the ADD health tragedy are enormous when translated into the number of individuals affected, the degree of suffering experienced by individuals and their families, and, in the case of those with severe dysfunction, the high cost to society from the variety of dysfunctional and harmful behaviors that are common to those who do not receive medication treatment.

Compensatory Learned Behaviors Can Turn into Addictions

The compensatory, dysfunctional psychological behavior of individuals with ADD can persist in spite of medication treatment and long after the brain chemical imbalance of ADD and the neurological dysfunctions which fostered the addictive problems are corrected. These self-perpetuating, harmful psychological behaviors are generally referred to as addictions.

It is unlikely that only ADD individuals are susceptible to being addicts. On the other hand, ADD neurology predisposes people to become the victim of addictions. Illicit drug use, alcoholism, compulsive gambling, binge eating, bulimia and anorexia nervosa, for example, are behaviors that have positive as well as negative consequences for ADD people. Thrilling, violent, sexually aberrant and even criminal behaviors can also be addicting. Even though any of these behavior patterns might begin as an attempt at "self-treatment" such as the search for high-adventure, they can be reinforcing and pleasurable enough to turn into addictions.

Friendships and lifestyles around which addictive activities are formed often strongly reinforce these harmful behavior patterns and make them difficult to replace. Avoiding the abuse of alcohol, for example, often is a struggle because its use is generally very much interwoven and intermixed with an individual's lifestyle, that is, self-image, self-control, social behavior, and response to stress. To maintain abstinence from alcohol, even after the institution of proper medication treatment for ADD, clearly requires psychological willpower and self determination to resist recurrent temptations to drink again.

For those with addictive behavior, attention to lifestyle issues is critical. It is for this reason that Alcoholics Anonymous, for example, an organization which often helps recovering alcoholics fight their addiction, stresses the value of a healthy environment for each individual as it supports the coping efforts of those who are trying to avoid alcohol abuse.

When medication correction of ADD neurological dysfunctions is not sufficient by itself to rectify all of the dysfunctional, health-harming, compensatory behaviors that may have developed, the additional support of ancillary educational and psychological services including participation in support groups and individual psychotherapy is not just helpful but essential.

When addicted ADD individuals seek help, professionals are likely to focus only on stopping the addictive behaviors. When this happens, the addictive behaviors, unfortunately, get all the attention and the underlying ADD neurological dysfunctions are ignored or missed.

This diversion of professional attention away from the causative role played by ADD neurological dysfunctions in addictions is always unfortunate when it delays the start of medication treatment. Even when psychological dysfunctions and educational deficits require non-medicinal treatment approaches, it is only after the institution of proper medication treatment that substantial and permanent progress toward eliminating the frustration of repeated failures, the inability to cooperate with professionals, and recidivism will dramatically diminish.

3

CONTROVERSY GALORE

"Doctor, should I get a second opinion?"
"Why not? Come back tomorrow."
Milton Berle [1]

It is an old story. Put ten doctors in one room, ask them to solve one problem, and it is likely that they will arrive at ten solutions.

Even doctors look at challenges from their own, individual perspective and, given the same set of facts, often come to very different conclusions. Professionals still have difficulty agreeing about very much when it comes to the ADD syndrome.

ADD is variably described as a mental illness and a psychiatric disorder, as a neurobehavioral disorder that is a cross between a neurobiological disease and voluntary rebelliousness, as a learning disability which interferes with cognitive function, and, in this book, as a neurological disorder that often has adverse psychological consequences for the individual and often for society as well.

There is even disagreement about the cause of ADD. Some nutritionists believe that ADD is due to dietary imbalance. An occasional physical therapist will say that ADD can be corrected by manipulation of muscles. Rarely, even physicians express the belief that ADD is the consequence of an adverse environment and will disappear when the environment changes for the better.

There is also a lack of agreement about how common ADD is in the population. This is not surprising, however, because professionals do not yet agree about which neurological dysfunctions belong to the syndrome. That Attention Deficit Disorder is being diagnosed more often than before, as it should be, has fueled controversy about the possibility that physicians are overzealous in their efforts to identify ADD people. A number of professionals continue to warn that there is an ADD diagnostic "epidemic" that they feel is not justified. In my opinion, professionals are finally starting to play catch up with a disorder that has long been underdiagnosed.

ADD has several different diagnostic labels. Which name is most correct is still being actively debated in academic circles.

It is safe to say that ADD remains shrouded in professional controversy.

Updating the ADD Syndrome: The Number of Neurological Dysfunctions Has Expanded

Do people who stay awake because they have difficulty falling asleep at night have ADD or are they simply "night people?" Is dyslexia just a developmental problem that disappears with maturity, or is it an important clue to the existence of ADD neurology? Is periodic explosiveness merely an expected behavior of flaming redheads and hotheaded executives or is it indicative of ADD?

The American Psychiatric Association continues to define ADD as only hyperactivity, impulsivity and inattentiveness. Yet support for enlarging the spectrum of ADD neurological dysfunctions is now emerging even from some involved in psychiatric research. For example, nocturnal enuresis (bedwetting), episodic explosiveness and dyslexia have recently been described as comorbidities of ADD, that is, neurological disturbances that occur very commonly in people with ADD.

In my experience, ADD people always have more neurological dysfunctions than just inattentiveness, hyperactivity and impulsivity, the three recognized by the American Psychiatric Association. Typically, they have at least five and sometimes all ten neurological dysfunctions. To avoid missing the diagnosis of ADD in many individuals requires that professionals and others know the full spectrum of dysfunctions possible as well as the variability of intensity that each dysfunction can have from individual to individual and in different age groups. If the intensity of dysfunction is minimal, treatment may not be indicated. People do deserve to know, however, if ADD neurology is affecting their behavior so that they can decide for themselves whether or not they want to choose the option of medication treatment.

Even though the American Psychiatric Association has not yet recognized more than three ADD neurological dysfunctions, it is clear that these criteria have nevertheless been of great value to professionals because they promoted medical recognition and established the authenticity of the syndrome as well as helped to stimulate ADD research.

Based on my clinical experience which is detailed in Chapter Ten, the following list of neurological dysfunctions now defines the ADD syndrome, and all dramatically diminish or disappear in those who are properly medicated.

1. (*)**Inattentiveness**, especially **Academic Inattentiveness** resulting in **Underachieving** due to difficulty processing and understanding information

2. (*) **Hyperactivity** or excessively **Fidgety Behavior** of varying intensity, and/or **Tics**

3. (*) **Impulsivity**

   Verbal i.e., blurts out or interrupts others

   Physical i.e., acts before thinking or shifts from one activity to another excessively

4. **Falling Asleep With Difficulty** (even if tired)

5. **Coming Awake Slowly** (unless excited)

6. Frequent **Irritability and/or Easy Frustration**

7. **Episodic Explosiveness, Rage** or **Tantrums** especially in response to minor issues

8. **Negative** Thought and Feelings with or without focus

   Holds on to anger

   Holds on to negative feelings and attitudes

9. Primary Nocturnal **Enuresis** (bedwetting)

   Age of five or older

   With or without dreaming of the act of urinating

10. Dyslexia

a) Spatial reversals in writing letters or numbers and number sequences; difficulty with left-right discrimination

b) Verbal inverted meanings: "I want to invite *me* to *your* birthday party" rather than "I want to invite *you* to *my* birthday party" (inverted meaning)

(*) Diagnostic criteria in the *DSM-IV* (*Diagnostic And Statistical Manual of Mental Disorders*, fourth edition)

* * * *

It is important from both a diagnostic and therapeutic point of view that ADD be recognized as possibly consisting of the ten neurological dysfunctions listed above. Not only does this approach facilitate diagnosis of ADD in the largest number of afflicted individuals, it allows professionals to evaluate the effectiveness of medication treatment. Proper medication treatment should always be assessed in terms of how many of and how completely the ten possible ADD neurological dysfunctions are corrected.

Based on this treatment criteria, the most successful type of medications that are now available belong to the so-called antidepressant class of drugs, not the stimulant drugs which are most commonly prescribed. Only antidepressant medications can correct all ten ADD neurological dysfunctions, and they are effective whether or not an individual is depressed.

What is the True Prevalence of ADD in Our Population?

The percent of the population that has ADD neurology has not been unequivocally determined. Certainly, ADD affects more than the common claim of 3% to 6% of the population if the diagnostic criteria discussed in this book are used.

In fact, while not generally cited, research by Shaywitz concluded that 10-20% of children have ADD [2].

Additional support for an incidence of at least 20% can be deduced from my data on primary nocturnal enuresis (bedwetting), a neurological dysfunction which, in my experience, is diagnostic of the ADD syndrome and rarely if ever occurs in people who do not have ADD. Approximately 50% of ADD males and females have at one time suffered from primary nocturnal enuresis. Bedwetting is reported to occur in the "general" population of the United States in about 10% to 11% of children age 4 to 14 [3]. Based on these statistics, at least 20% of the general population has ADD neurology.

Does ADD disappear with maturity? How many adults have ADD? While psychiatrist Weiss states that about 70-75% of ADD children continue to have ADD as adults, it is important to remember that his diagnosis of ADD was based on the limited psychiatric diagnostic criteria of the *DSM-III-R* [4]. Whether it is only 70% or really 100%, however, the incidence is startlingly high. It is certainly higher than would be gleaned from the office practice of many physicians, whether medical or psychiatric, who rarely ever diagnosis ADD in adults. Some professionals today do not even know that adults can have ADD.

My clinical experience is that the syndrome never disappears with maturity. When the diagnosis of ADD is based on the spectrum of ten neurological dysfunctions, it is found as commonly in adults as it should assuming that it does not disappear with maturity. However, ADD adults often avoid notice. They do not seek the help of health or education professionals for ADD-related problems and many function well enough to maintain interpersonal relationships and not experience psychological disintegration.

In fact, some ADD neurological dysfunctions are almost always absent in adulthood while others are minimally evident. Adults rarely continue to be bedwetters. Gross hyperactivity is hardly ever seen in adults, and fidgetiness often causes so little concern or discomfort to adults or their families that it is seldom defined as a problem in need of a solution. The impatience of impulsivity is commonly masked by social finesses and subterfuges such as interjections of "being in a hurry," of course "for good reason," or of "needing" to interrupt others because of a "very busy work schedule." Inattentiveness may not be evident because adults often avoid "boring" academic pursuits and find a niche in society into which they can fit and function reasonably well. Even explosiveness may not cause major disruption of interpersonal relationships because some ADD adults can voluntarily minimize its intensity and expression.

Whether their ADD neurology is severe or only mild, many ADD adults, from shyness, fear of being "discovered," concern for their social acceptance, difficulty embracing new ideas, or unawareness, choose to constantly fight the ill-effects of their ADD neurology, ignore medical help, and remain undiagnosed.

Many are not identified as having ADD for another reasons. Even those who do seek professional help often present with pressing psychological and social complaints that are a consequence of their ADD neurology, but neither they nor the professional from whom they seek help make the extra effort to identify whether or not there is underlying ADD neurology. Psychological dysfunctions and the perceived stresses of everyday living are generally of more intensity and immediate concern to ADD individuals and professionals than long-standing ADD neurological dysfunctions themselves tend to be.

Treatment of ADD neurology commonly takes second place, if it happens at all, when the presenting problem to professionals is the pain and suffering of a spouse seeking divorce, court hearings for charges of shoplifting, illness resulting from overeating and obesity, an elevated blood cholesterol and subsequent heart problems, headaches from unresolved tension, loss of employment because of alcoholism, or physical harm to one's children because of explosiveness. When confronted with these kinds of situations, and others like them, it is not likely that ADD individuals will complain bitterly about long-standing ADD dysfunctions such as impulsivity, irritability, or emotional outbursts with which they have lived since childhood.

Yet Another Controversial Area: What is the Best Name for the ADD Syndrome

Over the past century, medical and psychological professionals have used at least the following diagnostic names for what is now called simply the ADD syndrome: minimal brain damage, postencephalitic disorder, minimal brain dysfunction, minimal cerebral dysfunction, minor cerebral dysfunction, hyperkinesis, hyperkinetic impulsive disorder, hyperkinetic reaction of childhood and hyperactive child syndrome. Each of these medical names reflected what was thought to be the etiology or the dominant clinical characteristic of the disorder at the time.

Because precise knowledge of its neurochemistry and anatomy is still not known, ADD is a clinical syndrome, a disorder, perhaps a disability, but not a "disease." At this time, only three names are in current usage: ADD (Attention Deficit Disorder), ADHD (Attention-deficit Hyperactivity Disorder), and Hyperactivity. All of these names describe the same clinical disorder.

Professionals involved in university-based ADD clinical research prefer to establish the diagnosis of ADD in patients by documenting a history of hyperactivity, clearly a unique neurological sign of and strong clue to the ADD syndrome. Understandably, academic medical centers want maximum diagnostic accuracy and certainty even if some ADD individuals are unfortunately excluded from study or medical care as a consequence. It is for this reason that they prefer the term, ADHD.

Community physicians who specialize in treating people with the ADD syndrome commonly use the more inclusive diagnostic term, ADD, and do not require a documented history of hyperactivity to make the diagnosis. This approach ensures that fewer ADD individuals will be denied effective treatment. There is no therapeutic value in distinguishing between ADD individuals with and those without a history of hyperactivity because all respond equally well to proper medication treatment.

Agreement over a single nomenclature for the ADD syndrome still is not in sight. The *DSM-III-R* and the *DSM-IV*, published by the American Psychiatric Association, favor the research term, ADHD, which requires a documented history of hyperactivity. An earlier edition of this tome, the *DSM-III*, included hyperactivity as a diagnostic criteria but did not require its documentation.

Information about the ADD syndrome is increasingly available through a variety of professional sources. While this heightened awareness of ADD is making cooperation among professionals easier, it is nevertheless imperative that a single name be adopted so that nonprofessionals, healthcare professionals, educators and others can work together most effectively in recognizing and treating ADD individuals.

References

1. **Berle, Milton,** *Milton Berle's Private Joke File.* **Milt Rosen,** Editor. 1989, Brown Trade Paperbacks, New York. p. 1951.
2. **Shaywitz, S.E. and B.A. Shaywitz,** *Attention Deficit Disorder: Current Perspectives.,* in *Learning Disabilities: Proceedings of the National Conference,* J.F.K.&.T.J.T. Jr., Editor. 1988, York Press: Parkton, MD. p. 369-567.
3. **Adams, R., MD and M. Victor MD,** *Chapter 27. Normal Development and Deviations in Development of the Nervous System,* in *Principles of Neurology.* 1985, McGraw-Hill Book Company: New York. p. 446.
4. **Weiss, G.,** *et al., Psychiatric Status of Hyperactives as Adults: A Controlled Prospective 15-Year Follow-Up of 63 Hyperactive Children.* Journal of the American Academy of Child Psychiatry, 1985. **24**: p. 211-220.

4

The Neurobiology of ADD

ADD is a neurological disorder. It is a complex of clinical dysfunctions which, at the neuroscience level, are associated with reduced effectiveness of neurotransmitter hormone action and/or synaptic abnormality in various centers of the brain. The chemical imbalance is not the same in every individual which is why no one medication or single combination of medications is effective for everyone with ADD.

It is more precise to define ADD as a neurological disorder of the brain than as a mental illness, a disturbance of the "mind" which is treated primarily with psychotherapy. ADD neurological dysfunctions define the syndrome, are presently correctable with the proper use of medication in over 95% of instances, and serve as the guideposts by which the effectiveness of medication treatment should be judged.

All of the ten major neurological dysfunctions of the ADD syndrome listed below, if present, are eliminated, or at least dramatically diminished in intensity, within hours (not days) after the start of an effective dose of the proper ADD medication treatment:

1. (*) **Inattentiveness**, especially **Academic Inattentiveness** resulting in **Underachieving** due to difficulty in processing and understanding information

2. (*) **Hyperactivity** or excessively **Fidgety Behavior** of varying intensity, and/or **Tics**

3. (*) Impulsivity

Verbal i.e., blurts out or interrupts others

Physical i.e., acts before thinking or shifts from one activity to another excessively

4. Falling Asleep With Difficulty (even if tired)

5. Coming Awake Slowly (unless excited)

6. Frequent **Irritability and/or Easy Frustration**

7. Episodic Explosiveness, Rage or **Tantrums** especially in response to minor issues

8. Negative Thought and Feelings with or without focus

Holds on to anger

Holds on to negative feelings and attitudes

9. Primary Nocturnal Enuresis (bedwetting)

Age of five or older

With or without dreaming of the act of urinating

10. Dyslexia

Spatial reversals in writing letters or numbers and number sequences; difficulty with left-right discrimination

Verbal inverted meanings: "I want to invite *me* to *your* birthday party" rather than "I want to invite *you* to *my* birthday party" (inverted meaning)

(*) Diagnostic criteria in the *DSM-IV* (*Diagnostic And Statistical Manual of Mental Disorders*, fourth edition)

Thus, ADD individuals are typically not only hyperactive or fidgety, cognitively unfocused, and impulsive, but they are hard to arouse in the morning, up late at night because of difficulty falling asleep, cranky, sometimes explosive, negative about school and social activities, and dyslexic. Fifty percent are still bedwetters after they have turned five years old.

Without medication treatment, people with ADD almost always develop psychological dysfunctions or negative, harmful, learned behaviors as they attempt to cope with a world that does not accommodate to their neurological dysfunctions. Many ADD teenagers and adults need and benefit from psychotherapy to deal with their psychological dysfunctions. Psychotherapy, however, does not correct the underlying neurobiological abnormality of ADD and should not be thought of as treatment of the ADD syndrome.

ADD is an Inherited, Genetic Disorder

Evidence is building that ADD, usually called ADHD by psychiatrists and sometimes merely Hyperactivity by researchers, is a biological disorder of genetic origin [1-6]. My clinical experience over the past two decades supports that ADD is a genetically determined disorder which is inherited in a fashion consistent with autosomal dominant transmission.

In more simple language, one gene from one parent is enough to cause ADD in a child. Both sexes are affected equally. Statistically, this means that if one parent has ADD, 50% of the children will have ADD. If both parents have ADD, 75% to 100% of all offspring can be expected to have ADD.

Conversely, and this is sometimes difficult for parents to accept, if one child has ADD, at least one parent must have ADD neurology. ADD does not skip generations.

If half of the children in a family have ADD and half do not, one parent has ADD and the other does not.

I first became aware that ADD is transmitted in an autosomal dominant fashion in 1980 when I studied eighteen families in which one parent had ADD and the other did not. All of the ADD parents were treated successfully with medication as were 22 of the 48 children of these families. It was apparent from this pilot study that autosomal dominant genetic inheritance was likely because approximately half of the boys and girls of these eighteen families had ADD. Since then, my clinical analysis of ADD families has consistently confirmed the autosomal dominant pattern of ADD inheritance.

Additional support for the autosomal dominant transmission of ADD comes from two other kinds of evidence. First, Tourette's syndrome, a behavioral disorder characterized by verbal tics, is the psychiatric name for a disorder that occurs only in ADD people. This particular expression of an "ADD disorder" is clearly transmitted to offspring in an autosomal dominant fashion [7].

Second, the results of my own study of 1377 adults and children with ADD shows that ADD occurs equally in males and females as it should if transmission is governed by autosomal dominant genetics.

The old idea that ADD is not transmitted in an autosomal dominant fashion is derived from studies published in the pediatric literature in which boys are diagnosed more often than girls. What is the basis for this diagnostic skewing? In part, the reason for this skewing is that boys are more likely to act out, behave violently, misbehave, and be disruptive in school and in various social and family settings than are girls. Because of their overt misbehavior, boys are more likely to be brought to professionals for help and are thus more commonly identified as having ADD.

Also, at least by past tradition, parents have been more concerned about "helping" their sons function and succeed in society than their daughters. Sons are generally expected to carry on the family name and "family tradition," be the "bread winner" in adulthood, and take over the family business, if one exists. These expectations of parents usually are intermixed with the assumption that to succeed in this world their sons must achieve a reasonable degree of academic competence. Accordingly, academic failure can attract more family attention in boys than in girls who may not even be encouraged to attend college and, in some cases, may satisfy parental requirements for academic achievement with nonacademic pursuits such as cooking, sewing and typing.

Knowledge of the genetics of the ADD syndrome is especially important because it discredits claims that psychological factors are the *cause* of the ADD syndrome. Environmental factors do affect children and adults in many ways, but they do not cause ADD neurology. Even exposure *in utero* to alcohol (fetal alcohol syndrome) or cocaine (cocaine babies), while potentially very toxic to the body chemistry, are not causes of ADD. Because parents, however, who are alcoholics and drug abusers are likely to have ADD neurology, it is reasonable to expect that their offspring will have ADD for genetic reasons. Toxic exposure does not cause ADD but is an additional handicap for those with ADD neurology.

It is vital that research into how biological and psychological factors affect each other and influence human decision-making be continued. Family, social, and cultural factors certainly play an important role along with genetic determinants in the psychological and intellectual behavior of people. Individuals with ADD neurological dysfunctions not infrequently develop specific devastating psychological dysfunctions and make behavioral choices that lead to alcoholism, illicit drug use, tics, sexual promiscuity, bulimia, depression, compulsive gambling, and even criminality for reasons that are not yet totally clear.

It is to be hoped that this kind of research will lead to a better understanding of the neurobiology of the ADD syndrome and improve the ability of professionals to predict which psychological dysfunctions are likely to develop in specific ADD individuals. Professionals will then be more able to intervene and prevent negative and destructive outcomes before they start.

Nurture vs. Nature: What Role do Environmental Factors and Learned Behaviors Play in the Expression of ADD?

The causes of aberrant, troublesome or maladaptive human behavior has been the subject of psychological research and speculation for a long time. Various theories have achieved such high levels of popularity as to now be cultural myths. One of these myths which has evolved from psychoanalytic theory lays causation for the dysfunctional behavior of ADD children at the feet of the parents. But, medical research is continually uncovering underlying chemical abnormalities which lead to cognitive errors and deficiencies as well as emotional excesses and distortions that have been associated with many behaviors that are popularly blamed on poor parenting and dysfunctional rearing.

The ADD issue of nurture versus nature should finally be put to rest. ADD is a biological disorder, not the consequence of inadequate and incompetent parenting. The most direct and obvious "proof of the pudding" of this is that ADD neurological dysfunction can be reversed in just hours with proper medication treatment, not weeks, months or years as learned behaviors usually require. Moreover, ADD neurological dysfunctions return when medication is stopped.

Nurture is always important in child rearing, but nature is the biological cause of the ADD syndrome.

What And Where Is the Chemical Imbalance in the ADD Brain?

When first recognized medically about a century ago, the dysfunctions now known as the ADD syndrome were considered the consequence of "mental" disorder because there was virtually no biochemical understanding of brain function. The syndrome included only children with adequate intelligence who had difficulty learning in the classroom setting and whose conduct in school was unacceptable because of disruptive behavior.

Consistent with the little that was then known about brain physiology, a child's poor academic achievement and disruptive, nonconforming behaviors were interpreted to be a reflection of bad character, inadequate upbringing or, at the least, a lack of manners and training. Some even believed that ADD was due to deviant behavior which was best modified with punishment.

By the 1930's, the medical profession began to consider that ADD might be a mental disorder that was due to brain damage, similar to that caused by the newly discovered illness, Economo's viral encephalitis lethargica. Fortunately this thinking rapidly gave way to our modern concept of ADD as a syndrome of brain dysfunction rather than brain damage because it could be at least temporarily reversed by the use of amphetamine stimulant medicine.

Exactly how the brain chemistry of people with ADD differs from those without ADD is still not known. In addition, no one is sure what specific chemical imbalance exists in the ADD brain or where the chemical dysfunction or dysfunctions are located. What is now clear, however, is that the positron-emission tomographic measurements reported by Dr. Zametkin and associates show definite brain metabolic differences between hyperactive adults and adults without hyperactivity [8] as well as hyperactive teenagers and teenagers without hyperactivity [9]. Unfortunately, there are no studies yet that specifically differentiate between the brain metabolism of ADD individuals without hyperactivity and individuals without ADD who, of course, are not hyperactive.

On the other hand, there is now at least general agreement by most experts that people with ADD have a chemical abnormality and that the abnormality is in the neurotransmitter synaptic mechanism of the brain, the dominant pathway by which nerve cells communicate with each other. This conclusion is supported by the fact that medications which diminish ADD neurological dysfunctions have measurable actions on the neurotransmitter synaptic mechanism.

There is no evidence that the ADD syndrome is in any way related to nerve cell death or destruction.

What is the Neurotransmitter Synaptic Mechanism?

Communication between different brain cells and sometimes between various parts of the same brain cell takes place across synaptic spaces and is dependent on chemicals which are called neurotransmitter hormones. This is not the only way but it is the most common way by which one nerve "talks to" or effects other nerves in the brain. Important steps in how the synaptic mechanism works include:

1. For a communication to take place, there must be intracellular vesicles or walled-in packets containing neurotransmitter hormone (a chemical) in a nerve axon (or arm which reaches out) that is in contact with another nerve. To be usable, vesicles must be in an active state and those in the inactive state must be changed by a chemical process to the active state. As the process of chemical communication proceeds, vesicles move to the most distal end of the axon of the stimulating (presynaptic) nerve. It is from there that they are released into the synaptic space between two nerves.

2. When nerves are stimulated chemically or electrically, vesicles open and the stored neurotransmitter hormone is emptied into the synaptic space.

3. The released neurotransmitter hormone moves across the synaptic space to terminals on the receptor nerve. The unused neurotransmitter hormone is subsequently taken back (re-uptake) into the presynaptic nerve.

4. To have an effect on the post-synaptic nerve or receiving nerve, neurotransmitter hormone must combine with a chemical on the receiving nerve called a receptor.

5. The neurotransmitter hormone-receptor complex activates or, in scientific jargon, causes gating (opening or closing) of ion channels (passages in the cell wall through which ions such as calcium, sodium and potassium can move) in the receiving nerve cell. This process is modulated by recently discovered G-proteins.

6. Finally, the movement of ions into the receiving nerve cell body stimulates additional chemical activity in that nerve by post-ion channel mechanisms completing the message transfer from one nerve to another.

The neurotransmitter/synaptic on-off communication process usually takes place between a large number of brain nerve cells for short but measurable periods of time. It is a complex neurobiological process which is not fully understood and is under intensive study today.

Thoughts, feelings and body movements due to brain activity are complex expressions of what start out merely as neurotransmitter activity. The end result of this activity can also be something quite different such as the regulation by the brain of water retention by the kidney and other activities that do not become part of an individual's thoughts and feelings. Regardless of the specific end result, most neurological brain functions depend on the presence of neurotransmitter/synaptic activity.

Researchers are still actively searching for the exact anatomical areas in the brain where ADD abnormality resides. While there is some support for involvement of the frontal lobes in hyperactive ADD individuals, especially after the studies of Dr. Zametkin and associates, inferential evidence from both animal and human clinical studies suggests that the dominant anatomical area of the brain responsible for the neurological dysfunctions of ADD is the limbic system or "primitive" part of the brain.

The limbic system is an anatomical area that is located near the center of the brain and is defined as the medial part of the mesencephalic reticular formation (the so-called midbrain limbic system), hypothalamus, hippocampus, septum, amygdala, and cingulate, orbitofrontal, and pyriform cortex area [10].

The clinical picture of ADD is consistent with the known consequences that result from abnormality and/or artificial manipulation of the limbic system. This part of the brain has a profound influence on such basic brain functions as those involved in learning and memory, wakefulness and attentiveness, hunger and thirst, impulsivity, explosiveness and rage, stress, sexuality, and negative social behaviors such as belligerence, uncooperativeness and anger [11].

While the limbic system is a dominant brain area for many of the types of functions that go awry in individuals with ADD, only further research can confirm these tentative suppositions. Moreover, it is very possible that multiple centers of the brain have various roles in the total ADD picture even though the limbic system area may be dominant.

Scientists, using modern tools such as Positron Emission Tomography (PET), Single-Photon-Emission Computed Tomography (SPECT), Brain Electrical Activity Mapping (BEAM), X-ray Computerized Tomography (CT) and Magnetic Resonance Imaging (MRI), hopefully will soon define precisely the anatomical areas of physiological dysfunction in individuals with ADD.

ADD is Only One Example of Hormone Dysfunction that Can Cause "Mental" Problems

The ADD syndrome is only one of several examples of chemical imbalance that can lead to disturbances of thinking and feeling. When the source of the chemical imbalance is outside of the central nervous system, the mental disorders that result are called somatopsychic disturbances.

Well known somatopsychic disturbances resulting in brain functional impairment such as depression, aggressiveness, irritability, and psychosis are imbalances of calcium, testosterone ("male hormone"), estrogen ("female hormone"), cortisol ("adrenal hormone"), and thyroid hormone. These imbalances can be measured by blood testing. The initial, most effective, and preferred therapeutic approach for each of these somatopsychic disorders is the proper use of medication to correct the underlying chemical imbalance.

Blood Calcium Elevations Can Cause Severe Depression

An elevated blood calcium level can lead to excessive brain calcium which can cause neurological dysfunction and severe mental depression. Failure to understand the etiological importance of a high blood calcium concentration as a possible cause of depression can result in overlooking a significant chemical disorder of the body and delaying the use of effective treatment. When depression is a consequence of hypercalcemia, the treatment indicated is the immediate correction of the high blood calcium level. A bias which rejects or neglects a biochemical cause of depression typically leads to unsuccessful treatment with psychotherapy or antidepressant medication and leaves the underlying calcium disturbance medically uncorrected.

Testosterone Hormone Deficiency Affects Mental Aggressiveness

Testosterone hormone deficiency also is a cause somatopsychic disturbance. Testosterone is important not only for sexual potency and muscle strength but also for normal mental aggressiveness in animals and humans of both sexes. Adults who are treated for testosterone deficiency not uncommonly report that they feel more competent at handling stressful problems and are mentally more assertive, more forceful, and more aggressive within days after receiving replacement hormone treatment.

Estrogen Deficiency Can Cause Sleep Disturbance, Irritability and Depression

Estrogen hormone deficiency in women can cause somatopsychic disturbances including sleep disturbance, unprovoked irritability and depression. Estrogen-deficient women suffer from abnormal regulation of their brain LH/FSH hormone system. When due to estrogen deficiency, estrogen replacement treatment alone can eliminate feelings of depression and irritability, promote the return of normal sleep patterns, and enhance the ability to focus mentally.

Glucocorticoid Hormones in Excess Can Cause Psychosis

Somatopsychic disturbance can also be a consequence of exposure to high levels of certain chemicals. For example, high blood levels of the hormone, cortisol, or any of the similarly acting glucocorticoid hormones, whether high because of the ingestion of too many pills in an overzealous effort to reduce pain or stiffness from arthritis, or high because of excessive hormone release from an adrenal gland tumor, can cause dramatic mental changes including overt psychosis with hallucinations and delusions. Affected individuals usually return to their previous biochemical and mental state within three to four weeks after reducing hormone levels to normal.

Abnormal Levels of Thyroid Hormone Can Cause Psychosis

Finally, low blood levels of thyroid hormone may cause a psychotic state with hallucinations and delusions which is known as "myxedema madness." Paradoxically, high blood levels of thyroid hormone also can cause psychosis. After the restoration of normal thyroid hormone levels, affected individuals return to their previous mental state.

Thus, medical research has established that abnormal body chemistry affects brain chemistry and can result in important changes in mental function.

Unlike the examples just offered in which chemical abnormality can be measured in the blood, the disturbance in ADD originates within the brain and involves neurotransmitter and synaptic functions which cannot yet be measured precisely.

While it may be superficially appealing to those with minimal knowledge of neurobiology, it is outdated, inaccurate and destructive to continue to explain the ADD syndrome by invoking arguments that ADD is simply the consequence of a lack of manners, moral turpitude, emotional stress, laziness or, even, a desire to act out because of a love for attention. These characteristics may exist in a given ADD person, as well as an individual who does not have ADD, but they do not explain the etiology of ADD, nor do they accurately describe the neurological dysfunctions found in ADD.

ADD IS A NEUROLOGICAL DISORDER, NOT A MENTAL ILLNESS

ADD should be identified as a neurological disorder because today there are very important treatment reasons to differentiate between mental illness and neurological disorder. Health professionals who believe that ADD is a mental or psychiatric disorder all too often rely on psychotherapy as the only treatment modality. Identifying ADD as a neurological disorder directs attention to the problem of brain chemistry dysfunction, a problem that should be treated with medication when it is possible to do so.

Understanding ADD as a neurological disorder is also important to ensure that physicians prescribe medication at the start of treatment, that medication is always a part of the treatment protocol, and that the many dysfunctional learned behaviors that are the psychological consequence of living for years with medically untreated ADD are recognized as separate from the diagnostic neurological criteria.

Since ADD medication only corrects neurological dysfunctions, the adverse psychological sequelae that commonly occur in untreated ADD individuals may, of course, require additional treatment approaches if they do not disappear quickly after medication treatment is started.

The results of a historical and courageous 1937 study by Dr. Charles Bradley dramatically demonstrated that cognitive, emotive and behavioral aspects of ADD could be rapidly corrected solely with the use of medication. Dr. Bradley reported the effect of medication treatment on 30 children with learning disability and nonconforming behavior [12]. In response to the stimulant medication, benzedrine (amphetamine), given for one week, 14 children "responded in a spectacular fashion" with respect to school accomplishment as reported by different teachers. Fifteen of the 30 children became "distinctly subdued in their emotional responses. Clinically in all cases this was an improvement from the social viewpoint. In many it was accompanied by a sense of well-being; but superficially the appearance was that of a child whose mood swings had become diminished. In this group were some children who had expressed their irritability in group activities by noisy, aggressive, domineering behavior. Such children under the influence of the drug became more placid and easy-going. Coincidentally, they seemed to become more interested in their surroundings."

The only reasonable conclusion about the origin of ADD after such conclusive findings was that ADD must be caused by brain dysfunction rather than permanent brain damage or psychological dysfunction.

Although our understanding of the ADD syndrome is less than complete, it is now possible to eliminate confusion and bring clarity to the process of diagnosing and treating ADD. Enough information about ADD is presently known to make this disorder understandable as a neurological disorder and, as such, the approach to its treatment a rational process. Hence, it is no longer reasonable for health professionals or educators not to recognize the vital role of medication in ADD treatment.

In fact, when treatment with medication is avoided or delayed, the consequences of neurological dysfunction are more severe and the cost to the individual, their family, society and the healthcare system is greatly magnified.

Because of frustration and lack of understanding, parents are often blamed by professionals for the behavior of their ADD children. This kind of accusation incriminates parents as the total or major cause of the difficulties that their children are having and is rarely true. ADD children have inherited dysfunctions which, in many cases, contribute in a very significant way to why they are persistently unsuccessful in school, rejected by their more successful classmates, friendly with peers who also lack academic and social direction, and have low self-esteem, poor self-confidence, and repeated urges to escape from the expectations and the perceived criticism of their families and society.

Unfortunately, popular thinking tends to be more reflective of past ideas then open to new scientific research, and many parents of ADD children live with guilt they do not deserve.

It is not rare for me to see a parent talk about an ADD child while tears are running down both cheeks and agony is reflected in a grimace because the parent has a devastating sense of false blame for his or her child's dysfunctional behavior. At the same time, it is amazing just how much love, kindness, caring, teaching, sharing, helping, understanding, and forgiveness ... how many second chances ... and how much food, clothing and housing parents often provide to their ADD children for so little thanks in return.

These parental efforts are not a total waste of time and effort. Parenting is important! It is a critical factor in the upbringing of all children, not just ADD children. But to receive the full benefits of parenting, children must be focused and receptive, not mentally scattered, impulsive, irritable and chronically angry. Untreated ADD children are simply less able to benefit in the expected manner from quality parenting and other positive experiences. Parenting has an important but limited effectiveness with these children.

Of course, parents should always try to be effective, avoid negative reinforcement or punishment, and not heap shame and depreciation on their ADD children who already have low self-esteem and feel negative. Their limited success at parenting, however, must never be interpreted to mean that their behavior as parents has caused the ADD problems of their children or the vast array of failures which their children have experienced.

References

1. **Stevenson, J**., *Evidence for a Genetic Etiology in Hyperactivity in Children.* Behavior Genetics, 1992. **22**(3): p. 337-344.
2. **Faraone, S.V., PhD**, *et al.*, *A Family-Genetic Study of Girls With DSM-III Attention Deficit Disorder.* American Journal of Psychiatry, 1991. **148**(1): p. 112-117.
3. **Lillie-Blanton, M., DrPH, J.C. Anthony PhD, and C.R. Schuster PhD**, *Probing the Meaning of Racial/Ethnic Group Comparisons in Crack Cocaine Smoking.* Journal of the American Medical Association, 1993. **269**(8): p. 993-997.
4. **Biederman, J., MD**, *et al.*, *Family-Genetic and Psychosocial Risk Factors in DSM-III Attention Deficit Disorder.* Journal of the American Academy of Child and Adolescent Psychiatry, 1990. **29**(4): p. 526-533.
5. **Goodman, R. and J. Stevenson,** *A Twin Study of Hyperactivity -- II. The Aetiological Role of Genes, Family Relationships and perinatal Adversity.* Journal of Child Psychology and Psychiatry, 1989. **30**(5): p. 691-709.
6. **Cadoret, R.J. and M.A. Stewart,** *An Adoption Study of Attention Deficit/Hyperactivity/Aggression and Their Relationship to Adult Antisocial Personality.* Comprehensive Psychiatry, 1991. **32**: p. 73-82.
7. American Psychiatric Association Committee on Nomenclature and Statistics, *Diagnostic and Statistical Manual of Mental Disorders,* . 1987, American Psychiatric Association: Washington, DC. p. 80.
8. **Zametkin, A.J., MD**, *et al.*, *Cerebral Glucose Metabolism in Adults with Hyperactivity of Childhood Onset.* The New England Journal of Medicine, 1990. **323**(20): p. 1361-1366.
9. **Zametkin, A.J., MD**, *et al.*, *Brain Metabolism in Teenagers With Attention-Deficit Hyperactivity Disorder.* Archives of General Psychiatry, 1993. **50**(May): p. 330-340.

10. **Martin, J.B., S. Reichlin, and G.M. Brown**, *Clinical Neuroendocrinology*, in *Contemporary Neurology Series,* F. Plum and F.H. McDowell, Editor. 1977, F. A. Davis Company: Philadelphia. p. 38-41.

11. **Martin, J.B., S. Reichlin, and G.M. Brown**, *Clinical Neuroendocrinology*, in *Contemporary Neurology Series,* F. Plum and F.H. McDowell, Editor. 1977, F. A. Davis Company: Philadelphia. p. 247-249.

12. **Bradley, C., MD**, *The Behavior of Children Receiving Benzedrine.* American Journal of Psychiatry, 1937. **94**: p. 577-585.

5

The Clinical Picture of Attention Deficit Disorder Neurology in Children

The Ten Areas of Neurological Dysfunction of the ADD Syndrome

1. Inattentiveness, * especially Academic Underachieving
2. Hyperactivity and Fidgetiness *
3. Impulsivity *
4. Falling Asleep With Difficulty
5. Coming Awake Slowly
6. Frequent Irritability and/or Easy Frustration
7. Episodic Explosiveness, Rage or Tantrums
8. Negative Thoughts and Feelings With or Without Focus
9. Primary Nocturnal Enuresis (bedwetting)
10. Dyslexia (Verbal and Spatial)

* Minimal diagnostic criteria according to the *DSM-IV*

Diagnosing ADD in Children

The diagnostic criteria for ADD consists of a spectrum of ten neurological dysfunctions. Commonly, ADD children, because of their developmental age, will have at least seven and sometimes all ten ADD neurological dysfunctions at the time of diagnosis. Although after childhood has passed, ADD individuals are rarely still troubled by the full spectrum of ADD dysfunctions, most can recall having had and outgrown dysfunctions that had been present when they were younger.

In practice, it is not wise to base the diagnosis of ADD in children on the requirement of a minimum number of dysfunctions. Such a simple rating system will too often exclude ADD children who should be diagnosed and treated. In fact, even if only a few neurological dysfunctions are clearly evident, especially tantrums, hyperactivity, impulsivity or bedwetting, the diagnosis of ADD is very probable. In the absence of a more reasonable diagnosis or likely cause for the problems at hand, a trial of ADD medication may be justified.

Age has an important effect on when ADD neurological dysfunctions become evident. ADD neurology is obvious in some ADD children when they are very young and in others only when they are older. On the other hand, even two year old preschool ADD children can be obviously hyperactive, impulsive, disorganized and episodically violent in the absence of inordinate environmental stress. When such children represent a danger to themselves or others, as certainly can be the case if tantrums are violent or impulsiveness is severe, medication treatment is indicated even at this young age.

It is only possible for a child to have the full spectrum of ADD neurological dysfunctions after the age of four. Bedwetting should not be diagnosed before the age of five, and children usually have to face the challenges that formal schooling presents by this age. ADD children with academic inattentiveness, spatial dyslexia expressed as writing reversals, impulsivity in the classroom, difficulty coming awake in the morning, and persistent bedwetting stand out dramatically. The most common diagnostic mistake made by adults at this time is to ignore these clues. Even teachers and physicians may incorrectly try to relieve parental anxiety by saying that these undesirable behaviors are "normal" for the age and likely to pass with time. It is true that bedwetting usually disappears and spatial dyslexia diminishes with maturity, but the other dysfunctions of ADD persist and usually worsen.

Some ADD children do not show obvious ADD dysfunction until the expected start of puberty, that is, the age of eight to twelve. When evaluating the behavior of these children, parents and even professionals may struggle trying to decide whether what appears to be dysfunctional behavior is abnormal or not. They often believe that a number of behavioral problems can be expected to occur at this stage of childhood development. But, deterioration of school performance, unexplained irritability, episodic explosiveness, difficulty coming awake in the morning, falling asleep slowly at night, and unexplained negativity, for example, should heighten suspicion that ADD is the causative factor, not puberty or adolescence.

In addition to the fact that the time of appearance of most ADD neurological dysfunctions is variable, recognizing the presence of ADD in children is often confounded by the ADD terminology in current use. This terminology is confusing, vague, and imprecise to many parents, teachers and even health professionals. For too many people, the terms do not "make sense," "apply to", or "properly describe" the behavior of the children who clearly have ADD.

For example, hyperactivity is an extreme word which, to many adults, conjures up the vision of a child who is almost impossible to live with because of constant, always on-the-go behavior that never seems to stop. Many parents, in particular, are certain that their "very active," fidgety children should not be considered hyperactive even though they may be unable to behave properly at school, in religious meetings or in other social settings.

Another ADD term, inattentiveness, is so broad in meaning that many parents find it not applicable to their children who are often attentive when learning to play a sport, master the use of tools, read books on topics of interest, or play computer games.

Impulsivity is also a confusing ADD term. The impulsive behavior of ADD children often seems to parents more like healthy, creative, spontaneous activity than neurological dysfunction in need of correction. Because of their age and limited communication skills, it is usually difficult for adults to appreciate that it is mental disorganization caused by the rush of thoughts, or mental hyperactivity, which underlies impulsive behavior in children.

In addition, ADD children with tantrums rarely act with the destructiveness that ADD adults with rage do. Hence, the term, episodic explosiveness, often seems much too strong for what their children in fact do.

Many very young ADD children are not slow to come awake in the morning, a valuable clue to the diagnosis of ADD. Instead, they are incredibly disorganized just after waking in the morning. They have trouble getting dressed, washed, and to breakfast even though they appear to be wide awake. This clue has the same significance as waking slowly.

Some ADD children do not go to sleep easily at night, but parents may attribute this to over-excitement from the events of the day.

Finally, ADD children typically do not talk about negative thoughts and feelings and are not discovered to be negative, at least in part, because of their limited language capability.

For many parents, current ADD terminology is so imprecise or vague that it does not help them distinguish between behavior that is a variant of normal and the dysfunctional behaviors of the ADD syndrome.

Let's now move on to examine *in detail* how the behavior, cognitive function and emotions of children are affected by ADD neurology.

INATTENTIVENESS AND ACADEMIC UNDERACHIEVING

Case Study

Mother has come to accept that her son, Alex, is a slow learner. He is six years old and still not able to write numbers and letters. She is disappointed but not surprised by Alex's apparent mental slowness because she, herself, had not performed well academically in school.

Alex has a very short attention span. After about two or three minutes of trying to focus on learning numbers and letters, he becomes frustrated, his mind wanders, his eyes scan the ceiling looking for something more interesting, and he then gazes on whatever is outside the nearest window. To escape from the classroom, Alex usually asks to go to the bathroom.

ADD children are not inattentive all of the time and in all situations. In fact, inattentiveness due to ADD refers most commonly and dramatically to difficulty focusing on academic pursuits. Practically, this translates into repeated difficulty paying attention in school for more than brief periods of time, staying on task in the classroom, and completing and turning in homework assignments. The invariable consequence for the child is academic underachieving although not necessarily failing or poor grades.

If a firm diagnosis of ADD is to be made, it is important to identify the existence of focusing deficits whether they are mild or severe. ADD children with this neurological dysfunction, however, may not be easily recognized as such for a variety of reasons.

First, some children are able to hide their learning difficulty by making great efforts to pay attention and focus. When motivation is high, difficulty staying on task and problems completing and turning in homework assignments may be noticed by parents and teachers only after observing that a child is exerting much more effort than peers to do the same academic work or, having advanced into higher grade levels, is finally overwhelmed by the demands and complexity of the assigned work.

Second, some children are discovered to have ADD only because they underachieve erratically. For example, school performance may be excellent one day or one month and poor another. They may achieve highly on competitive, challenging standardized tests and even be identified as "gifted" students yet perform poorly when doing daily classroom assignments or taking weekly tests that happen to be boring to them.

Third, while inconsistent academic performance is characteristic of ADD neurology, many adults are unaware of this and are fooled into thinking that psychological factors alone, such as lack of motivation and laziness, are the cause of whatever learning difficulties there may be.

Fourth, parents may be unaware of ADD mental focusing problems in their children if they have not been actively involved in helping their children with school work or if they have low academic expectations for their children.

Fifth, in some instances, parents and teachers know that a child is underachieving, do not consider the possible role of ADD, and assume that the child is simply a "slow developer." While delayed development is a reality on occasion, all too often this unsubstantiated belief is wrong. Unfortunately, when this error is made, a long period of time may pass during which parents and teachers do little more than hope that academic underachieving will disappear with maturity. In some instances, it is only after a child experiences severe academic failure for an extended period of time that hope finally fades and a search for the cause of the underachieving is again undertaken.

Children who have difficulty with mental focusing often feel "bored." Many enliven their day and feel awake and "alive" by being disruptive. The psychiatric name for this kind of conduct is oppositional behavior, terminology which unfortunately implies that the cause is predominately willful and not driven by ADD neurology. In my opinion, it is typically more correct and clearly more useful to interpret disruptive classroom behavior as dysfunctional psychological behavior by children who have difficulty focusing on mental tasks. When understood in this way, treatment is more likely to be appropriately directed at correcting the inattentiveness of ADD rather than on punishment for the acting-out behavior.

Children with ADD can be of superior, normal or low intelligence. This point cannot be stressed too strongly. Performance in school more often than not reflects the severity of ADD neurological dysfunctions, degree of interest in a particular academic subject, personality and charm of the teacher, and, in some instances, time of day the class is held rather than innate intelligence. ADD children usually do not function as well in the afternoon, when a cycle of tiredness is common, as they do during the morning hours. Also, they are more likely to perform well academically and behaviorally when stimulated, taught using active-learning techniques, or in one-to-one learning situations. Correction of inattentiveness with medication does not elevate intelligence but does allow children to use whatever natural intelligence they have in a consistent and more effective manner.

In general, children with limited intelligence are more likely to have difficulty achieving, earning passing school grades, and staying in the mainstream of education than are the intellectually gifted ones. Their learning disability is more evident and usually more quickly recognized when they compete with students who may or may not have ADD but are intellectually more competent. They are, therefore, more likely to be identified by teachers and parents as having a problem such as ADD. It is for this reason that the ADD syndrome has been mistakenly considered to be associated with low intelligence.

Again, it should be emphasized that children with ADD neurology range from being mentally limited to gifted. I have successfully treated ADD children with the mental retardation of Down's Syndrome and individuals who are college professors.

It must be hoped that parents along with educators, school nurses, therapists and physicians will become more aware that ADD can be a primary cause of learning disability in children. When this happens, the possibility of ADD as a root cause of academic underachieving will be more appreciated, the clues that lead to the diagnosis of ADD in children more actively pursued, the diagnosis made more frequently, and treatment with proper medication started appropriately early. In extreme cases, medication treatment should be started when children are as young as two years old.

Hyperactivity and Fidgetiness

Case Study

I am sure every one knows at least one little kid like Dennis. Dennis is always racing around the house, jumping on the chairs and the kitchen counters, pushing, teasing, goading and fighting with his brother and sister.

In school, Dennis is always getting out of his seat. He goes from the pencil sharpener to the wastebasket, to the teacher's desk --- back and forth --- back and forth. He pokes his classroom neighbors, pushes when standing in line, and jumps up and down for no obvious reason at all.

His brother, Michael, almost never calls attention to himself by his behavior. When frustrated, irritated, annoyed, lonely, or uncomfortable, he merely taps the index finger of his right hand on his knee or, sometimes, on the arm of a chair. At other times, he can be seen twiddling one index finger around the other. While holding a book and reading, Michael might be observed to be fidgety but not grossly hyperactive. While reading, his fidgety feet are likely to be on the rung of the chair he is sitting in, oscillating and sending vibrations to other parts of the room.

Mom and Dad always suspected that Dennis was hyperactive, but not Michael. Until Michael's performance at school dropped off, they never realized that being hyperactive and being fidgety are both strong indicators of ADD.

Hyperactivity and fidgetiness are terms which describe intermittent body movements that are not appropriate for the circumstances, often are not goal oriented, and frequently are scattered, random and repetitive. These two terms differ only quantitatively or by degree of intensity, not qualitatively. Excessive movement is most prominent when ADD children feel bored, tired or emotionally uncomfortable. Whether labeled as hyperactivity with gross motor movements or as fidgetiness with less intense movement, they belong to the same ADD category of neurological dysfunction. Both are strong clues to the diagnosis of ADD.

The word, hyperactivity, is usually reserved for the kind of intense and excessive physical activity that is seen in children who literally run around the house, the yard, the park, the beach, the shopping mall, and other places in almost constant motion. They get up and roam about in the classroom even after being asked to stay seated, run up and down the aisles at religious meetings, and constantly dart about the walkways at the amusement park, running when walking or sitting is more appropriate. Hyperactive children, when not asleep or resting, are incessantly involved in high-energy activities such as jumping, chasing, and climbing.

ADD girls may not be recognized because, as a group, they are less likely than boys to be hyperactive. At the same time, boys may not be diagnosed if their hyperactivity is interpreted by their parents as just "high energy" behavior. Parents often enjoy high energy children. Boys are supposed to run, play hard, be aggressive and act forcefully, are they not? Some parents are exceedingly tolerant and think of their children as simply "energetic kids" who are like romping, playful puppy dogs, although most adults find hyperactive children very irritating and annoying. In some instances, parents who are told that their children are behaving in a hyperactive manner may fail to accept this diagnosis. "No, he's not *hyperactive*, he's just an *active* kid." Not infrequently, parents respond this way even after they have been asked to seek professional help for their children because the school sees them as disruptive and out of control. Sometimes hyperactivity and fidgetiness are denied when it is very difficult for parents to face that there is something wrong with their children.

Hyperactive children tend to handle and manipulate a variety of objects, even objects that they have been told to leave alone. They may move items about a room with great speed and endurance or touch and move things that they rarely stop to examine, understand or appreciate. They are likely to move a book but not look at its contents or carry a teddy bear from one location to another but not play with it. Hyperactivity is often thought of by adults as merely "very active" behavior because children are typically not expected to have goal-oriented behaviors to the degree that adults are.

Those with excessive verbal skills are likely to talk nonstop, sometimes loudly, joke around repeatedly, and laugh a lot especially in settings where these behaviors are restricted. Nonstop talkers may or may not move about a lot as well.

Hyperactive children are dysfunctional because, too often, they either do not or cannot behave in ways that are usually demanded of children in social environments. They commonly have difficulty developing social relationships. Their incessant, rapid racing about frequently disturbs and disrupts the activities of others who feel apprehensive in their presence and fear physical injury or the destruction of valued possessions from their exuberant movement. Even when on the playground, they may fidget about, fail to pay attention to the game they are involved in, and be less effective at sports [1].

Hyperactivity usually is not a highly dangerous behavior. However, it not infrequently leads to damaging accidents when children run into things or fall, items are toppled or broken, and people are bumped or knocked over. As a consequence, hyperactive children may experience disapproval, anger, and rejection from peers as well as punishment from adults.

The term fidgetiness, like hyperactivity, consists of inappropriate, extraneous, discordant body movements. Common examples include squirming about in a chair when staying quietly seated is important, tapping with a pencil while the teacher is trying to talk to the class, rhythmically shaking the feet or legs, wiggling and twisting without obvious stimulation such as music, and doing a lot of touching of people and things that should not be touched.

Fidgety children are equally as likely to have ADD as those who are more overtly hyperactive, and they do not necessarily have a milder form of ADD or fewer ADD neurological dysfunctions.

Although clearly a clue to the diagnosis of ADD, the movements of hyperactivity and fidgetiness feel natural rather than dysfunctional or abnormal to the ADD children themselves unless, that is, their behavior is repeatedly called to their attention and they are criticized or punished for it. When ADD children become adults, they may not recall having been hyperactive or fidgety unless they were chastised for it in childhood.

Both hyperactivity and fidgetiness are more common and pronounced in boys than in girls. Because of this, pediatricians have erroneously reported that the diagnosis of ADD is four to seven times more likely to occur in males than females. In fact, ADD occurs with equal frequency in both sexes.

Hyperactivity can be expressed not only as fidgetiness but also as motor tics in some ADD children. Motor tics are involuntary movements that range from sudden, rapid, brief, jerking motions to muscle movements that are slower and more like stretching than jerking. Blinking, grimacing, horizontal head movements, sticking the tongue out, licking lips, raising eyebrows, repeatedly glancing up, and jerking motions of the arms or legs are some of the many ways motor tics are expressed. They are ritualistic and repetitious.

Vocal tics, which characterize Tourette's syndrome, are just a type of motor tic. Vocal tics may be expressed as throat clearing, grunting, snorting, squeaking, sniffing, coughing, humming, barking, spitting or virtually any repetitious vocal noise that does not represent a recognizable word. Recognizable words said quietly, as if under the breath, and, more disturbing, the blurting out of loud, explosive, obnoxious, even indecent expressions that attract considerable adult attention can be another way that vocal tics are manifest.

Like the movements of hyperactivity and fidgetiness, tics are episodic, inappropriate and not goal-directed. They occur in response to boredom, tiredness and emotional discomfort and can be readily provoked by asking embarrassing, stressful questions or otherwise creating an uncomfortable environment. Individuals with tics have the same spectrum of ADD neurological dysfunctions as other ADD individuals.

Hyperactivity, fidgetiness and tics all rapidly diminish and often totally disappear after proper ADD medication treatment.

Impulsivity

Case Study

Barbara's mother was surprised when she was asked by the school to talk with her daughter's sixth grade teacher.

"Is Barbara in trouble?" mother wanted to know. "Not really," the teacher responded, "but there is something you should hear about."

"Two days ago, while waiting with two other children to ask a question, Barbara was told that she would be second to talk."

"A half a minute passed," the teacher went on, "and I was dealing with the first question when suddenly I was kicked, yes, kicked in the shin by your little Barbara."

"I've been waiting a long time to ask my question," Barbara insisted. "Isn't it my turn yet?"

Impulsivity describes a mind that is rapidly moving from one thought to another without normal pauses for reflection and reconsideration. The impulsive child has difficulty keeping mentally organized and effective. Sometimes, thoughts are acted upon but without consideration for the consequences. In some instances, fleeting thoughts drop out of consciousness and cannot be readily recalled.

The typical behavior of an impulsive child is shifting from one task to another, being easily distracted from an activity by verbal interruptions or intervening tasks, often not completing a series of tasks that have been started, not finishing thoughts being expressed, moving rapidly from one subject to another without apparent logic, blurting out thoughts of the moment whether they are appropriate or not, and prolonged indecisiveness about what to do or not do next.

For example, an impulsive child, when asked to wait in a line for more than moments, can be expected to walk away abruptly or, perhaps, push toward the front of the line but not wait patiently in place.

In the classroom, impulsive children commonly blurt out answers without remembering that it is another person's turn to respond to a question or from fear that they will not be able to hold the answer in their conscious mind for very long. Not infrequently, they say whatever happens to be running through their mind at the moment, even the angry and insulting thoughts that may come to them, especially if they feel that they are "being kept waiting a long time" and not being allowed to talk during the few moments that their mind is focused on what they are currently thinking about.

Impulsive behavior is a handicap. Modern western society values personal behaviors such as self-control and patience. Even though parents may be tolerant of impulsive behavior in their children, the school usually is not. Children who blurt out answers and often talk out of turn may be severely penalized both academically by teachers and socially by peers. They are sometimes even excluded from school activities and shunned.

Impulsivity can be dangerous. It is the impulsive child who is likely not to think about being cautious, dive into the shallow end of the swimming pool, run after a ball in the street without first looking for oncoming cars, and grab toys from another child who may then fight back.

Too often, impulsivity is erroneously interpreted as a lack of manners or maturity without considering that the impulsive actions may be the expression of a neurological disorder.

Impulsive behavior diminishes or disappears almost immediately after treatment with proper ADD medication.

Falling Asleep Slowly

Case Study

It always seems that John never wants to go to bed at a reasonable hour. He is almost seven. His parents are sure that he will fail to grow properly and be tired in the morning if he does not get ten hours of sleep the night before.

In addition to worrying about John's health, Mom and Dad would like a few moments of peace and quiet of their own, a little privacy, some time to read and talk ... so there are really two reasons why they want John in bed and asleep at a reasonable time of the night.

John does go to bed when Dad insists. But shortly thereafter, the door opens and a little voice says, "I don't want to go to bed yet!"

Usually mother now insists, "You must try to sleep." She then suggests that John read a book for a while, turn on the radio, or listen to music on the tape machine he got for Christmas.

When this fails, Mom and Dad finally turn to the old routine they had learned to use when traveling around the world in the service of an oil company. In voices that might put anyone to sleep, they sing an Indonesia lullaby.

When through, Mom and Dad tiptoe out of the bedroom and look at each other. There is hope on their faces. Lots of kisses have been planted on John's cheek. John appears to be sleep? The room is quiet.

Ten minutes later, John is up again. He hasn't fallen asleep. He wants to stay up for a while longer.

Trouble falling asleep is another valuable clue to the diagnosis of ADD which is present in about 79% of ADD children under the age of 13.

How long should it take to fall asleep at night? Five minutes? Twenty minutes? Hours? There is no fixed answer for every child on every night. But, children with ADD typically spend long, unpleasant, irritating, frustrating periods of time in bed rolling the thoughts and events of the day through their minds before drifting off to sleep.

Parents often do not know if their children are having difficulty falling asleep. They usually do not sleep in the same room as their children nor pay attention to whether or not they are asleep unless they create unwanted noise, commotion and disturbance.

Especially if parents fail to ask, they may be completely unaware that their children are having a difficult time going to sleep. Even if they do learn that such a problem exists, many parents assume that their children are normal, do not have a "problem," and just have difficulty "letting go" or "winding down" from an active day.

In reality, most ADD children take at least 30-45 minutes and sometimes one to three hours to fall asleep most nights. This is especially likely on days when they have not had intense physical activity. Because the effort to sleep is frustrating and irritating, they often develop rituals in an effort to deal with the problem. For example, many children listen to music on the radio or their tape player, read, count things in their head, or use self-hypnotic approaches such as talking to themselves about "relaxing" and "going to sleep." Even if they do not fall asleep more easily, the time spent lying in bed trying to fall asleep may seem to pass more quickly.

Not all children who have difficulty falling asleep perceive this as a problem in need of a solution. Children, more than adults, are likely to accept what happens to them as normal because it is "who they are." Many are resigned to falling asleep slowly and simply wait out the time it takes to drift off, not complaining and not expecting that their mind should function differently. They do not regard falling asleep slowly as a "problem" especially if others in the family also take a long time to fall asleep.

When trying to quantitate how long it takes for a child to fall asleep, keep in mind that children may be unreliable about their measurement of time because they live so much in the "here and now." They have not yet learned to pay attention to time as adults have. For determining whether or not a child has difficulty falling asleep, the actual length of time stated is less important than whether the child is frustrated, irritated, annoyed or troubled by whatever length of time is mentioned.

The complaint by a child of "having to go to bed" is a good indicator that a problem falling asleep exists. When children asked about this say, for example, "I hate going to bed," they are usually providing an important clue to the fact that going-to-sleep is a problem. Demands by children to stay up late should be further explored because they may reflect their inability to fall asleep easily at a reasonable hour. Even though the answer may not be reliable, professionals should always ask a child if falling asleep is slow, troublesome, hard, difficult, or a long process. A positive answer must be respected and explored.

In general, but especially when children are involved, questions of opinion should be couched in neutral language to the maximum extent possible to avoid the effects of suggestion. For example, the following leading-type question, "Is falling asleep difficult for you?," should be reframed and less suggestive of the answer. A better question would be, "How long is it after you get into bed at night that you fall asleep?" Put this way, the question does not implant the notion that falling asleep may be an abnormally slow process.

ADD children not infrequently deny that they have a problem going to sleep because they do not wanting to admit that they are not in control of themselves. They avoid the issue by simply staying up very late and going to bed only after they are so tired that falling asleep is easy in spite of their ADD neurology.

Important as the observations of parents can be, when a child reports difficulty falling asleep and the parents deny the accuracy of the child's response, it is possible that the parents are in error. When this occurs, parents should be asked to look more carefully at the facts on which they base their understanding. For example, have they made the assumption that their children are asleep merely because the bedroom is quiet and there is no obvious movement? How often do they go into the bedroom to observe their children after the lights are out?

Difficulty falling asleep because of ADD neurology should not be confused with trouble falling asleep because, for one reason or another, a child is not tired that night. Forcing children to try to sleep when they are not tired must not be classified as "difficulty falling asleep." All children are less likely to feel tired if an evening is full of excitement and interest because a friend is visiting, there is an opportunity to play with new gifts, or a high-action movie is being shown.

ADD children do not have difficulty falling asleep every night any more than the opposite is true, that is, that children without ADD fall asleep easily every night. Falling asleep with difficult is likely to be an ADD dysfunction if it is a problem without an obvious cause which is present most nights.

Treatment with antidepressant medications, and only rarely with stimulant drugs, corrects this dysfunction.

Coming-Awake-Slowly

Case Study

It is Dad's job in the morning to wake up Alice so that she can get ready for school. At the age of six, neither Dad nor Mom want to rattle Alice awake with an alarm clock. So, Dad always opens the bedroom door and gently calls to her, "Alice, Alice, it's time to get up."

It always takes one return visit to the bedroom before Alice jumps out of bed. To Dad and Mom, Alice seems to wake up without difficulty.

But, after getting out of bed, her morning struggle begins. She is typically grumpy. Worse, she is disorganized. What color dress to wear? Which pair of shoes to wear? What to do first?

Left to her own doing, she is mentally paralyzed, unable to decide what to wear or even when to come down to breakfast. Without prodding, she is always late for school.

Most parents are not aware that coming awake slowly in the morning is a strong clue to ADD neurological dysfunction. Many hope it is merely a developmental problem that their children will outgrow. In fact, 90% of ADD children under the age of thirteen are hard to arouse, disorganized, moody and/or difficult to be with in the morning.

In extreme instances, it can take a pail of cold water dumped over the sleeping head, loud screams, scary threats, or a coordinated assault during which the blankets are yanked off and cold air is allowed to chill the sluggish, motionless body of the groggy, half-asleep ADD child to promote wakefulness and get some movement going.

When asked, children often deny having difficulty waking up even though their parents are very much aware of the problem. Of course, many children are not sure how they should feel when they wake up in the morning.

How ADD children wake up often varies with age. A very young child with ADD not infrequently gets out of bed without great effort and appears to wake easily. The eyes open up without a significant delay. While apparently awake, however, the mind is often clouded and the mood is negative. The child is typically disorganized, grumpy, moody, not cheery, ill-humored and quarrelsome. Without constant reminders, encouragement, and prodding from family members, ADD children are consistently late coming to the breakfast table, finishing their meal, getting to the bus, and arriving at school. Parents often struggle to keep them away from the other siblings in the morning to minimize arguments and nasty verbal exchanges.

As children approach their teen years, even those who used to pop out of bed easily are now usually persistently sleepy in the morning. This change takes place in ADD girls by the age of eight and in ADD boys by the age of twelve. It is unlikely that puberty plays a causative role in this behavior because difficulty waking in the morning can be a problem for ADD children when they are very young, well before the time of puberty.

The most reliable approach to evaluating how young children wake up and function in the morning is to ask the parents to describe what happens at morning wake-up time and how functional their children are after getting out of bed. How many times must the child be asked to wake up before he or she gets out of bed? Can the child select his or her clothes for the day and get dressed in a reasonable length of time? Does the child get lost in the bathroom only to emerge if there is constant encouragement and sometimes direct assistance?

Because waking can be easy on mornings that promise excitement, many parents not only believe that resistance to waking, getting dressed, and heading off to school is psychological in nature but that the behavior reflects a problem of character and motivation. Perhaps their children are lazy or simply do not want to go to school because they do not like their teachers, are having separation problems, or desire to play rather than study. Worse, parents sometimes come to think of their ADD children as stubborn, obstinate, and thankless for choosing not to wake up and for bringing problems on themselves and their families.

There is good reason why this aspect of ADD looks like a psychological disorder to many parents. Many ADD children who have extreme difficulty coming awake and being organized on school mornings jump out of bed on weekend mornings without any prodding because they are excited to see cartoons on television, go to Disneyland, play with a new bicycle, go skiing, or get into some other appealing, high-adventure, high-interest activity. ADD children, like ADD adults, respond with lots of interest and energy to high-energy stimuli. Unfortunately, most mornings, especially school mornings, do not promise high adventure activities.

Misunderstanding how psychological and environmental factors influence and alter the expression of (I did not say cause) ADD neurological dysfunction can lead parents to feel frustrated, angry, and negative. They may then act in punitive ways that almost always serve only to damage the parent-child relationship and rarely have a long-lasting beneficial effect on dysfunctional ADD behaviors.

When one or both parents also have ADD and suffer from waking slowly, they commonly think of this behavior as a family trait. They either do not want to believe or have difficulty accepting that it is an abnormality in their ADD children.

Since coming awake slowly as well as being grouchy and disorganized in the morning occurs on a consistent basis in most ADD children, this neurological dysfunction is a strong clue to the diagnosis of the ADD syndrome.

It is also one of the first dysfunctions to disappear when ADD children are treated with antidepressant, not stimulant, medication.

Frequent Irritability and/or Easy Frustration

Case Study

Sierra is easily frustrated. Mother does not think of her as irritable.

Tell her that she cannot have ice cream because supper is just a few minutes away --- ask Sierra to let her friend have another turn with her toy --- deny Sierra almost any immediate gratification.

She is likely to throw herself to the floor, pout and sob. She does not take denial easily.

Parents sometimes experience their young children as "irritable," that is, almost constantly upset without obvious reason. Most describe them as "easily frustrated," repeatedly overreacting to specific negative experiences. To some parents, their children are both irritable and easily frustrated much of the time. Either dysfunction, however, is a strong clue to the diagnosis of ADD.

Irritable and/or easily frustrated ADD children pout, act withdrawn, seem sad, and sometimes make noisy and loud demands for gratification when their wants are not immediately met. They can be amazingly challenging to parents who deal with these behaviors on a continuing basis. When neither discipline nor punishment is effective, parental anger and frustration is almost inevitable.

On the other hand, parents not infrequently feel guilty and inadequate when asked about how they discipline their cranky, demanding children. They hate to admit that reasonable parenting methods have not been effective and that they are tired, exasperated and even overwhelmed by their struggle to reign in their irritable, easily-frustrated, demanding children.

Most parents do not realize that this type of behavior is par for the course in ADD children. They are usually amazed when the persistent irritability and easy frustration of their children disappear almost like magic after ADD medication treatment is started.

Should medication treatment alone not correct an irritable and demanding child, it is important to look for causes other than ADD. For instance, some parents are ambivalent or inconsistent about discipline and fail to demand that their children show virtually any self-restraint. These parents inadvertently encourage and reinforce acting-out behavior in their children, and these families end up with many complex problems for which family therapy and other forms of psychological help are very much indicated.

Episodic Explosiveness, Rage or Tantrums

Case Study

Mary Jane was brought to my medical office by her adoptive parents when she was just seven years old. She had dark hair, pretty brown eyes and the ability to be very quiet. She cautiously waited to see what I might do or demand of her during my medical examination.

Her school had already refused to allow her to return to the classroom. She failed the first grade the year before and was doing no better repeating the first grade this year. Academic failure, however, was not the reason for her visit to my office. Nor was it the major concern of the school or her parents.

Mary Jane was repeatedly violent! On the playground, without provocation, she punched other girls and boys, bit some with her lovely white teeth, and episodically kicked and screamed at classmates. Although her explosive behavior lasted only minutes at a time, she persistently disrupted playground activities and frequently drove the playground supervisor into a frenzy. "Mary Jane," the principal finally said, "had to go!"

Mary Jane turned her home into a madhouse after dinner each night. She could not play with siblings without eventually kicking or hitting them. She went to bed when asked, could not fall asleep, and typically returned to the living room where she resumed her disruptive and violent behaviors until forced back into bed. Her parents wondered if something had happened to her before the adoption that could explain why she had such violent behavior.

When I examined Mary Jane, she was quiet. She stayed physically close to her father as if seeking protection against what I might do .... sizing up the unfamiliar setting of my medical office.

It did not take more than twenty minutes for her to realize that I was not going to harm her or be punitive. She begin to fidget, talk incessantly, touch whatever was within her reach, and resist being restrained by verbal commands from Mom and Dad.

Mary Jane was trying not to explode, and I was hoping that I could get through with her examination before she did.

"Rage" is not a term parents often use to describe episodic explosiveness in young children with ADD. They are more likely to choose "temper tantrums" or just plain "tantrums."

What are tantrums? They are sporadic, episodic emotional outbursts. Tantrums evolve over a few seconds to a few minutes, usually triggered by relatively minor events including comments, requests, denials and frustrations. Initially, anger feelings grow in intensity and ultimately, if unchecked, result in violent verbal and/or physical explosions.

Tantrums even in young children can be amazingly destructive of property and harmful to others. ADD children can break toys, knock holes in house walls, smash windows, and throw things as well as kick, hit and bite others. Tantrums are clearly examples of dysfunctional behavior. They may have a temporary, short-term benefit in terms of giving ADD children some immediate control of a situation, but there is little or no long-term benefit to the child from this type of behavior and often substantial negative consequences. Tantrums fail to contribute toward the constructive resolution of problems and typically lead others to direct negative energy toward an ADD individual who is usually in dire need of love and acceptance.

The ability of ADD children to show restraint when in the middle of a tantrum varies with the intensity of the provocation and the severity of their particular neurological dysfunction. The intensity of tantrums commonly is less when the parenting skills of the parents are substantial.

Episodic tantrums are a behavior of 75% of ADD girls and 85% of ADD boy under the age of thirteen. They are a very strong clue to the diagnosis of ADD. Hyperactive boys are slightly more likely to have tantrums than non-hyperactive ADD boys.

Most of the ADD children who do not have episodic tantrums channel their explosive energy into less physically destructive activities such as crying. A few are simply able to "hold back" from being physically violent but would be explosive if they felt safe doing so. Their explosiveness sometimes becomes overt later in their adulthood when parental supervision is absent.

Women, more than men, report that their father "would not allow" them to be violent, scream, hit walls or strike other people even though they had wanted to do so on many occasions. Parenting had created limits beyond which behavior was "unacceptable" in the family. "I did not do it, no matter how much I wanted to do it, and sometimes I simply cried if my feelings of anger became too intense to deal with any other way," an ADD woman recently told me.

Tantrum behavior is different from "psychotic" or "crazy" behavior. ADD children, however, are sometimes treated with antipsychotic medication in an attempt to suppress their ability to be enraged. This is an inappropriate and unfortunate use of tranquilizing medicine. While it may reduce the intensity and frequency of tantrums, tranquilizers do not correct any of the other neurological dysfunctions of the ADD syndrome, and they almost always severely compromise cognitive function. Moreover, one or another of the antidepressant medicines can almost always be found which controls explosiveness but does not have important negative consequences on cognitive function.

Kay's story, written by her father and not edited, describes a young child who has both a learning disability and tantrums. Her father was well aware that these problems were destructive of family relationships, and he was extremely pleased when she dramatically improved after starting antidepressant medication.

STORY

When Kay was in first grade, we went to England for a year, so she was enrolled in a small English private school near Bristol. Unfortunately, her classmates had been learning to read for a year already, so she was very lost in the reading classes. Her teacher, Mrs. Higgins, gave her special attention when she could and Kay made some progress, but it was hard. When she came back to California, Kay again found herself behind in reading because in England they had used the "look and see" method for teaching reading and in California they used the "phonics" method. Her classmates were once again a year ahead of her! Throughout second grade she worked very hard at her reading and had special tutoring, but still she had terrible problems. Her spelling was awful and her reading was mainly inspired guesses.

Eventually, we took her to a local dyslexia center for testing and it was found that Kay had medium dyslexia. She was immediately enrolled in special reading tutoring twice a week for dyslexics.

When the dyslexia was diagnosed, we were concerned that she would feel bad about it so we tried very hard to make her feel that it was OK - just another problem to be dealt with and certainly nothing to be ashamed about. We played games of making lists of the things that dyslexics are good at and we made sure that she knew that a lot of very famous, creative people had dyslexia. Albert Einstein, Thomas Edison, etc. Our fears were unfounded when the next week at school she suggested that the word "dyslexia" should be a bonus spelling word for the class and when she was asked by one of the other students what dyslexia was she defined it as "when you're good at math and bad at reading." However, on another occasion we discovered that she had said that she had a learning problem, but it was OK because she had the same problem as Frankenstein!!!

The special reading tutoring at the Dyslexia Center helped a lot, but life was still very tough. Even though she did reading with her parents every night, it was still so hard and spelling was a nightmare. Typically she would get four out of twenty on her spelling tests. She would resist her reading and spelling practice and fly off in incredible tantrums, hiding under her bed and crying for an hour or more. She hated going to school and often refused to get dressed in the morning. Once, in the middle of a large shopping center, she decided that she wanted a new cage for her hamster and when told that she couldn't have it she hid at the back of the store and refused to budge. The only solution was to carry her out of the shopping center screaming. Fortunately, her father played racquetball each week with the author of this book and, while resting between games, would tell the latest Kay stories. We discussed the possibility of Kay having Attention Deficit Disorder and the use of medication. Since Kay was very good at some activities, particularly art projects like beadwork, and could maintain tremendous concentration for long periods of time on these projects, we were not convinced that she had any fundamental attention problems, and the thought of long term medication for the mind was very frightening. Eventually, however, things got so bad that we decided to try an experiment for three months to see what the results would be. My racquetball partner posed the key question that we could not answer: "What if it's true that a simple well-understood medication taken once a day would make a dramatic difference to her ability to function in life. Would you ever forgive yourself if you didn't find out until twenty years later." A hard question!

In February 1993 we started a course of Norpramin (brand desipramine), starting at 25 mg per day and increasing the dosage by 25 mg a day. Immediately we had a serious problem --- she couldn't swallow the pills! It wasn't that she was being obstinate, she just couldn't get them down. They would stick in her mouth or fall out into the water glass! We tried everything! We ground them up and baked them in pancakes and waffles, we mixed them in peanut butter and sugar and yogurt. Everything that we did to disguise the taste failed --- the medication tasted awful and Kay wouldn't take it. At this point we were ready to give up. We had traded a problem that happened a couple of times a week for a problem every morning! Surprisingly, it was Kay's older sister who encouraged us to keep going. She had always treated Kay as a bratty little sister, but at some level she realized that she was sick, not bratty, and that they could do much better together. Finally, in desperation, we tried the age old technique for motivating kids - pure unadulterated bribery! Kay had never been allowed candy, and she was offered one roll of Lifesavers for every pill that she got down! The first morning of the new program she got up half an hour early and, with lots of encouragement from her mother, got two pills down in thirty minutes. The next morning it was twenty five minutes, then twenty. It stuck at fifteen minutes for about a week and then one morning Kay figured out a technique that would work for her. She would stand in front of her father with her arms out, put one pill and some water in her mouth and then lean way back with her father supporting her so that her body was about forty five degrees to the floor. In this position, she would throw her head back as far as it would go and swallow. Since her throat was now vertical and gravity was on her side, the pill went down every time! Using this technique, she could swallow two pills in about twenty seconds!

At the following week's racquetball session I told the author of this book what worked for Kay and he now teaches this technique to other kids as the "Kay technique!" Once the problem with taking the medication had been solved, we upped the dosage to 200 mg per day.

We had expected the medication to somehow have a miraculous effect on Kay's learning problems. Probably because we were so desperate for some change in our lives. This didn't happen. Kay still found reading and spelling very difficult. However, after a week or two we started noticing that the tantrums had almost disappeared! At first we thought that it was purely coincidental but as time went on it became clear. Kay's ability to handle conflicts had somehow increased dramatically. She was able to take "no" for an answer and, even though she occasionally got upset, she was able to work through it in a couple of minutes instead of going down the downhill spiral of a screaming match that would last for an hour. I also started noticing that she was much more focused when doing her spelling and reading. It was still very hard for her, but previously she would climb all over my office when doing homework and now she didn't.

Slowly, her homework improved. Her reading was still a terrible struggle, but at least there was steady progress, and her scores on her spelling tests went from around 4 out of 20 to about 16 out of 20. There was great celebration one week when she got 20 out of 20 right! The Norpramin hadn't eliminated her dyslexia, but it had allowed her to concentrate on learning the skills necessary to overcome it!

The other big surprise was that Kay's older sister started treating her a lot better! With the medication she realized that her sister had a medical problem and wasn't just being bratty. This was helped by Kay's new ability to not react as violently.

However, occasionally the tantrum behavior would reappear. We noticed that it always happened at the end of the day and we concluded that if Kay hadn't eaten properly she could fall back into the problem behavior. This was illustrated beautifully one day after we had been out canoeing with a friend of hers. On the way home she suddenly went irrational, demanding that her friend tie her shoelace for her because her hands were busy tying the other shoelace! Previously, I would have given her a lecture on how this sort of behavior was unacceptable, but this time I rushed to McDonald's and got some french fries inside her! It was like turning a light switch off - once she ate her bizarre behavior stopped immediately! I learned a lot from this experience. If the problem is a chemical imbalance of the brain, no amount of lecturing will fix it!!! A few weeks later, Kay went away to camp and I was amazed when she asked me to tell the camp nurse about "the problem that she has when she doesn't eat properly." She had acknowledged her problem behavior and was taking responsibility for it!

Kay has now been on the Norpramin for six months and life at home is a lot smoother than it used to be. In fact, in writing this I realize how much I have forgotten about how very hard everyday things used to be. The dyslexia hasn't changed, and reading and spelling are still very difficult, but Kay has a great attitude and I am confident that, together, we'll be successful in overcoming her problems.

* * * *

More often than not, parents do not realize that childhood tantrums, like academic underachieving and impulsivity, are ADD dysfunctions. Tantrums may even be thought of as normal responses to the stress of the world or the expected behavior of a "difficult" child.

Tantrum behavior may be so embarrassing to parents that they will not talk about it even with the child's personal physician unless encouraged to do so.

Treatment of the ADD syndrome with proper medication almost always reduces and usually eliminates tantrums, but resolution is slower for tantrums than for other ADD dysfunctions because there is an important amount of learned behavior and secondary gain involved in this super-controlling way of dealing with frustration and anger. New behaviors need to be learned and substituted for old ones, a process that may take weeks or months to complete. Medication is always of value, however, because the intensity and frequency of tantrums diminishes immediately with the start of treatment. In almost all cases, tantrum behavior is virtually gone by the end of a year of medication treatment.

Persistent Negative Thoughts and Feelings

Case Study

Five year old Rebecca is almost never asked to come out and play by the kids in her neighborhood.

At supper, she rarely talks of having had a fun time no matter what she did for play that day.

Mother is especially disturbed when Rebecca sits with a sewing needle and picks at her skin or scratches sores until they bleed. She never cries even when blood is dripping from a sore.

A mental alarm button did go off in mother when Rebecca said she wanted to "die." Mother tried to find a reason for what Rebecca said, asked her what she meant by the word, die, and encouraged her to think about what might bring her happiness ... Rebecca is unable to offer an explanation for why she is feeling negative.

Mother is sure that Rebecca is depressed even though the family unit is stable and both mother and father pay a lot of attention to her.

When a five year old child tells her mother that she wants to "die," it is not entirely clear exactly what she means. Could she be imagining suicide? Possibly yes, but not very likely! Suicide is not a common event in this age group. Clearly, however, such a statement by a child should tell adults that the child is feeling and thinking in an unhappy, negative way.

Like hunger and easy frustration, persistent negative thoughts and feelings have a unique, specific brain chemistry. One day in the future, there will be a laboratory test available to measure this chemistry. For the time being, however, persistent negativity can only be recognized clinically by getting to know the child and the family. It is expressed in the posture and movement of the face and body. Verbally, negative children are self-depreciating, angry, belittling and unappreciative when talking about situations and circumstances that others have positive feelings about.

Most children experience only brief negativity in response to environmental factors or short-term illness. They tend to move rapidly from one event in life to another, not easily remembering what went on before, and not spending a lot of time anticipating the future. Because they usually do not dwell on the past or worry about the future, they are less capable of remembering, accumulating and holding on to negativity over time when compared to teenagers and adults. But children do not live entirely in the present. To some degree, therefore, they can hold on to negative thoughts and feelings.

ADD children, because of their ADD brain chemistry, feel negative more of the time and more intensely than they would if they did not have Attention Deficit Disorder neurology. Environmental factors can contribute to their negativity but, if present, are an additional causal influence. When ADD children hold on to a lot of negative thoughts and feelings, they are likely to be described as depressed rather than merely negative. Chronically depressed children frequently cry, and they have difficulty falling asleep, staying asleep, and waking in the morning. They are tired and fatigued a lot of the time and make statements of guilt and self-reproach. Some have a tendency to self-mutilation and suicide.

Being children, they are not likely to talk about feeling "negative" or "depressed." Rather, they are likely to use substitute words and phrases such as "not interested," "bored," "feel disliked by others," and "feel ugly." These expressions may seem too mild for parents to bother taking seriously, but they should be heard, understood as possibly due to ADD, and treated if ADD is present.

When persistently and intensely negative and depressed, ADD children are prone to say that "nobody at school likes me," or complain that they "want to die," "hate everybody," or wish they were "dead." This kind of talk should alert parents to explore with care whether or not their children have any specific complaint that they should immediately address or any plans to harm themselves or others. Counseling along with the use of proper ADD medication is usually indicated and is likely to be very helpful.

Unfortunately, mild to moderate negativity can be a very difficult dysfunction to recognize in ADD children because it is not physically obvious as are hyperactivity, coming-awake-slowly and bedwetting. At the same time, parents may have trouble recognizing negativity in their ADD children if they believe that negative behaviors such as whining, crying, and clinging are unpleasant but acceptable and expected behaviors for a child. Parents also may even consider persistent negativity to be merely a temporary response to stress without understanding that it may be indicative of ADD neurology.

Children who are only negative and do not have any other dysfunctions of the ADD syndrome probably do not have ADD, should not be given ADD medication, and are likely to benefit from extra personal care and attention from parents, psychotherapy, and possibly modification of the environment.

Primary Nocturnal Enuresis (Bedwetting)

Case Study

Mom answered for Pete. "Yes," she said, "he wets his bed almost every night." Pete had told his mother that he did not want this subject talked about in front of others, not even the doctor.

Pete is eleven years old, an age when friends sometimes spend the night at the home of other friends and when many children go to summer camp. Pete is afraid to stay away from home overnight because of his bedwetting, fearing that he will be discovered and labeled as "a baby" by insensitive classmates.

The night alarm system did not work for Pete. Mom and Dad knew about DDAVP medication and did not even want to try it. It is a medicine that they felt was scary to use. Punishment was not even entertained, and, of course, was of no value since Pete was already feeling punished by his social isolation.

Initially, Pete resisted coming to my office for treatment of his ADD. He insisted that his ADD problems were not important until he learned that bedwetting is one of those problems. He was willing to try medicine for his ADD if it also stopped his bedwetting.

It was only a week after medication treatment was started when he returned to the doctor for reevaluation. Not only had the bedwetting stopped, but Mother had loaded him with three cans of soda pop one night before bedtime to see what would happen.

What did happen? When Pete's bladder became full, instead of wetting the bed he woke up, went to the toilet, then came back to bed and returned to sleep.

Primary nocturnal enuresis (bedwetting) is a fancy medical name for an ADD neurologic dysfunction that describes individuals five years old and older who urinate in bed while sleeping. Bedwetting is not a conscious, voluntary act. It is not a psychological process because the child is asleep at the time of the event. It is only after they wake up that these children become aware that their bedding is wet. Some remember that they had dreamed about urinating, but most do not.

In the absence of physical abnormality or disease of the urinary tract, bedwetting is a very strong clue to the diagnosis of the ADD syndrome. In fact, in my experience it does not occur in children who do not have ADD neurology. Fifty percent of ADD children have a history of being bedwetters.

This high incidence of bedwetting in ADD children shows that ADD neurology is common in our society. If, as my experience shows, primary nocturnal enuresis (bedwetting) occurs only in children with ADD and if "approximately 10 percent of children between 4 and 14 years of age" from a nonselective population in this country are bedwetters, then about 20% of the general population of children (and by extrapolation, adults) should have ADD neurology [2].

Some studies conducted abroad report an incidence of nocturnal enuresis in children that is higher than that reported for children in the United States. For example, approximately 17% of Irish children and 52% of "black" students presumably without sickle cell disease (a common cause of kidney disease in that population) who were going to a government school in Kingston, Jamaica were found to be bedwetters [3,4]. This data would suggest that the incidence of ADD in certain other countries might be even higher than that found in children in the United States.

A recent study of 167 twelve year old children with an ADD-like disorder from Groningen, The Netherlands, reported that the incidence of primary nocturnal enuresis or bedwetting was 15% in males and 25% in females. These individuals had "minor neurological dysfunction" characterized by a "need for special education," poor academic performance that was reflected in an "inappropriate grade for age and/or lower test results," and behavior that was described as "hyperactive" [5]. Whether all of these children had ADD is unclear, but it can at least be said that this report is consistent with my experience that enuresis is common in children with ADD-like dysfunctions.

Primary nocturnal enuresis is transmitted from parents to children in a way suggestive of a familial pattern and, like ADD, transmission may be genetically determined because "concordance for the disorder is greater in monozygotic than in dizygotic twins" [6]. Translated into simple English, the genes of monozygotic twins are identical while the genes of dizygotic twins differ. Accordingly, primary nocturnal enuresis is more likely to be present in the two monozygotic twins than in the two dizygotic twins when genetic factors are important.

Bedwetting stays stopped, except occasionally for breakthrough enuresis associated with illness or unusual stress, as long as medication treatment is continued. Should medication be discontinued, bedwetting immediately returns, unless of course, the child by chance has spontaneously outgrown the problem. When medication is restarted, bedwetting again disappears.

There is a popular belief even among many professionals that bedwetting happens to children who sleep "too soundly." This concept is without validation and makes little sense when it is realized that children who have a history of enuresis and are in treatment with ADD medication often sleep more deeply, more soundly, and more restfully than before treatment yet do not bedwet.

Scolding, punishment and attempts to embarrass children are not useful approaches to the treatment of bedwetting. Moreover, they are harmful since they cause pain, embarrassment and the further loss of self-esteem in children who are already suffering and have no conscious control over their enuretic behavior.

Alarms and other devices that wake children from sleep as a reminder to use a toilet are reported by parents to be of help in some cases.

DDAVP, a synthetic analogue of a natural human antidiuretic hormone that affects water conservation in the kidney, can stop bedwetting but does so by drastically reducing the ability of the kidney to make urine, a potentially harmful action. Because this medication does not effect any dysfunctions of the ADD syndrome other than bedwetting and has an extreme physiological action on kidney function, DDAVP should, in my opinion, be a drug of last choice if used at all.

The antidepressant medications are effective ADD treatment in about 80% of children, have virtually no side-effects in this age group (although all medications have potential adverse effects), stop bedwetting in about 90% of those so treated, and are, for these reasons, my first choice of drug when treating young ADD people with enuresis.

Dyslexia

Case Study

"Don't worry," Mrs. Invert was told by her son's teacher, "Seymour is just six and he will outgrow his problem of writing letters in reverse. He simply has a developmental problem. Seymour needs a few more years of growth and his dyslexia will disappear."

Mrs. Invert unfortunately believed the dyslexia story and felt relieved.

But she was surprised when the teacher continued, "What you do need to be concerned about is Seymour's short attention span and violent outbursts."

Dyslexia literally means difficulty reading and integrating written information. The term is reserved for individuals in whom there is no discernible organic or important environmental cause for their reading problem.

Children with dyslexia also have an impairment of their ability to interpret spatial relationships, and, from time to time, many "accidentally" garble the sound of words and reverse the meaning of what they are trying to say. Dyslexia is a complex neurophysiological dysfunction that is very real even if puzzling and poorly understood [7].

Equally perplexing is the fact that dyslexia is very commonly associated with the ADD syndrome. Spatial and/or verbal dyslexia is evident in 71% of ADD children under the age of thirteen.

The following are examples of spatial dyslexia:

1. Writing letters and numbers in reverse (p -- q) (b -- d) (3 -- E)
2. Jumbling the sequence of letters in a word ("hte" vs. "the") or the numbers sequence in a telephone number (354 for 453).
3. Right-left confusion.

The following are examples of verbal dyslexia:

1. Verbal reverses such as asking questions or making statements which represent the reverse of what was intended or meant. For example, "I want to invite *me* to *your* birthday party" instead of "I want to invite you to my birthday party."
2. Verbal mislabeling such as asking for salt when sugar is meant.
3. Verbal jumbling or garbling of words or sounds. For example, instead of "I want to fly the *kite very high*," the jumble might be a mixture of "kite" and "high" that would result in "I want to fly the *'hite'*." *Bedwetting* might become *wet-bedding*.

Children with clinically significant dyslexia have it to such a degree that teachers, parents or others "often" or "frequently" call attention to the problem, not just "rarely," "once a year," or "almost never." It can be a problem that comes and goes from time to time in the same child, and dyslexia may be much more of a problem for one ADD child than another. Do children without ADD have similar problems with spatial and verbal dyslexia? Rarely, they have mild left/right confusion, but they virtually never reverse the sequence of numbers or letters.

Most ADD children with dyslexia read well enough to advance through the school system and not be identified as having dyslexia even by their teachers. Part of the reason they escape being recognized is that there is a general lack of agreement about how severe a reading difficulty must be to warrant the diagnosis [8]. In many instances, however, ADD children with dyslexia are not diagnosed because they have a very strong desire to succeed and are able to endure the pain and struggle associated with reading, difficult as it may be.

Parents commonly fail to pay serious attention to spatial and/or verbal reversals in their children. Not only are they often misled into believing that dyslexia is only a "developmental" problem that will pass with time, most parents do not know that dyslexia is commonly associated with the ADD syndrome. Also, many parents of dyslexic children have dyslexia and are likely to consider spatial and/or verbal reversals in their children as behavior which is just as "normal" as their own. Verbal dyslexia is often considered little more than a "slip of the tongue," a "simple mistake," a mistake that is made when the "mind is going too fast," or a problem only when the child is "tired," not an abnormality due to a specific brain chemical imbalance.

Because it is usually one of several ADD dysfunctions, the presence of dyslexia should alert professionals to look for the other nine clues to the ADD syndrome. In my experience, dyslexia does not exist as an isolated dysfunction in the absence of ADD, but this impression needs to be further investigated.

Treatment of the ADD syndrome with medication does, in many instances, eliminate or significantly reduce dyslexic behavior, but the benefit of medication treatment for any given individual is unpredictable. Because of this, it is reasonable to believe that dyslexia does not always represent the same brain chemistry abnormality in each individual. Accordingly, researchers need to continue searching for additional medications which will be effective in ADD children who do not now respond to presently available ADD medications. However, the fact that the ADD medications now in use do not always correct dyslexia in ADD children should not be taken to mean that dyslexia is not a dysfunction of the ADD syndrome.

Attention Deficit Disorder in Very Young Children

To what extent can ADD neurological dysfunctions be recognized and the diagnosis of the ADD syndrome made during fetal life, in the perinatal period, and in preschool children?

Diagnosing ADD in Fetal Life is Not Yet Possible

Some day, when the chromosomal abnormality of ADD is known and genetic testing can be performed, the diagnosis of ADD will be possible even *in utero*. For the present, ADD neurology can be diagnosed only on the basis of specific clinical findings which cannot be observed in fetal life.

There is no scientific evidence to document that an ADD fetus kicks and punches harder or more often than a non-ADD fetus. Nor is it presently more than unsubstantiated speculation that kicking, thrashing about, and being restless *in utero* are related to the phenomenon of hyperactivity.

Assertions that factors such as maternal age at the time of pregnancy, maternal health status, fetal trauma during birth [9], and smoking cigarettes during pregnancy are a cause of ADD neurology in offspring also have not been substantiated.

Illicit drug use and alcoholism in parents, while very common behaviors in adults with ADD, are only clues to the possibility but not the cause of ADD in their offspring. Cocaine and alcohol may cause fetal abnormality but not ADD neurology.

Because ADD is inherited, the diagnosis can be suspected in a developing fetus if one or both parents are known to have ADD neurology, but thus far there is no way to document this suspicion until the individual reaches childhood.

Since ADD is genetically determined and its occurrence in children is governed by the laws of inheritance, genetic counseling is of value. Knowledge about ADD neurology in the parents can be used to predict the likelihood of ADD neurology in their children. When parents are aware that ADD neurology can be passed on to their children, they are more likely to recognize ADD dysfunctions should they develop.

In addition, knowledge of ADD genetics can serve to prevent parents from being misdirected and misled into believing that environmental factors are the cause of ADD in their children or that ADD can be avoided in future pregnancies by one action or another. ADD is neither caused by the environment nor induced by environmental factors in susceptible individuals. Simply, ADD is present in children with the ADD gene and absent in those without the gene.

To the detriment of all, not understanding that ADD neurology is genetically transmitted can lead parents to lay mistaken blame for why their children have ADD on hospitals, doctors, and others involved with their healthcare during the pregnancy or at the time of delivery.

Diagnosing ADD in the Infants is no More Accurate Than Genetic Counseling

During their first couple of years of life, there is no scientific support for claims that ADD children are more colicky, cry more, or are less cuddly than children without ADD, logical as such claims may seem. Parents with babies that turn out to have ADD sometimes describe their infants as having been quiet, good eaters, sound sleepers, easy to wake, and often smiling while others describe the opposite.

The absence of recognizable clinical manifestations of ADD during the fetal period and early infant years must never be interpreted to mean that the child of an ADD parent will not eventually show signs of ADD neurology.

On the other hand, even if the child is difficult for a parent to manage, medication treatment of newborns and infants should be withheld. Practically, it is extremely difficult to be sure if observed behavior represents ADD neurological dysfunction or not in children less than about two years of age. To use medication treatment in this circumstance has more danger than potential benefit. Remember, the correction of neurological dysfunction is, as yet, the only basis for assessing treatment effectiveness.

ADD Can Be Recognized in Preschool Children

Preschool children with ADD, even some as young as two years of age, can sometimes be diagnosed and treated with medication. While bedwetting, inattention and impulsivity are not reasonable guideposts at this age, hyperactivity and episodic explosiveness can be. If preschool hyperactive children are violent and a danger to themselves and others and they certainly can be at this age, treatment with ADD medication should be considered. The sooner that medical treatment is started and neurological dysfunctions corrected, the less time will elapse for an ADD child to accumulate negative experiences and live with learning deficits and emotional dysfunctions which can lead to the development of secondary, maladaptive psychological behaviors.

Case Study

Maria was two and a half years old when she was diagnosed to have ADD and treated with medication. The diagnosis had been suspected since before birth because mother, father and the two older children were diagnosed to have ADD and successfully medicated. Maria had only a small chance of not having ADD.

Mother started to feel the strain of living with Maria almost as soon as her little girl could walk. In fact, by the age of two and a half she almost never walked. She ran! She ran around the dining room table, between the furniture in the living room, from one room to another, up and down the isles of the supermarket, around the examining table in the doctor's office, and up and down the playground.

Maria also hit other children, screamed when frustrated, and was not responsive at all to the behavioral restraints that her mother tried to impose on her. Even at this young age, Maria was shunned by other children because of her aggressive ways.

On antidepressant medication, Maria kept the bubbly, giggly, charming parts of her personality, but she became focused, was peaceful with other children, and stayed interested in projects for long periods of time. She became a delight to be with!

Some preschool children attract attention because they behave in ways that severely and adversely disrupt their nursery school classes and the harmony of their home environment. Even at this young age, ADD children can be repeatedly violent, easily frustrated, impulsive, hyperactive, talk compulsively and have tantrums. These ADD children can be diagnosed with considerable certainty and will benefit from medication treatment even though certain important clues to the diagnosis of ADD are not discernible or are difficult to be sure of in children under five years of age.

The diagnostic clues to ADD that are not available at this age include primary nocturnal enuresis (bedwetting) which can be defined as a dysfunction only if the child is at least five years old. Dyslexia is not evident until a child starts to read and write. Negativity is often difficult to recognize in preschool age children, and crying is probably more likely due to colic or other physical problem than to ADD neurology. Impulsivity can be easily mistaken at this age for spontaneity. Very young children may not be sleepy in the morning and may not go to sleep early in the evening if they take daytime naps. Thus, preschool children, unless they have obvious hyperactivity and frequent tantrums, usually cannot be diagnosed with certainty as having ADD at this early age.

Roadblocks to the Medication Treatment of ADD in Children

ADD cannot be treated if it is not recognized. Knowing the ten neurological dysfunctions of ADD is essential to understanding who has the syndrome. But, by itself, this is not always enough to guarantee that a diagnosis of ADD can be made. There are realities in the home, at school, and with respect to lack of clinical awareness on the part of health professionals which hinder the recognition of ADD behavior and inhibit the acceptance by parents of their ADD medication for the treatment of ADD children.

Too often, parents do not entertain the possibility of ADD or consider medication treatment because they are simply less concerned than they should be about poor academic performance in their children. "As long as my child gets along with the teachers and the other students in grade school, he should be left alone to achieve as he can."

In other instances, ADD is missed and medication treatment is not considered when parents and teachers assume that the underlying reason for academic underachieving is disruptive school behavior because a child is suffering from delayed socialization.

However, even when ADD is recognized and learning disabilities are evident, many parents and teachers will recommend that children have psychotherapy. Often, they are hesitant to advise that children take medication for their underlying ADD syndrome. Even many physicians recommend only psychotherapy for children with ADD, feeling that medication, which only they are licensed to prescribe, is not needed.

Some adults are uncomfortable with the idea of children taking medication for the purpose of correcting academic underachieving because of prejudice against the use of prescription drugs, fear that drugs will have an adverse affects on the growth and development of their children, or concern about the possibility of medication toxicity.

One of the ways that prejudice against the use of medication for the treatment of ADD may be expressed is illustrated in the following unsolicited letter about George. Because of the wisdom of his mother, he began taking antidepressant medication for his ADD one month prior to the start of a new school year when he was twelve years old. The letter was written by the reading specialist teacher who had been helping George academically the entire previous school year without much success. She made the assumption that George was not taking medication for ADD but had received additional psychological or special parenting help:

Dear Mr. and Mrs. Brown:

You must consider this a letter of congratulations to yourselves. I find a high correlation between good, well-organized students and a good home.

On his own this year, George has worked out a good system of organizing his school work so as to present a well-organized access to materials needed in his classes. He always has paper, pens, pencils and homework easily accessible and can make a good start to do well.

Again, I commend you and congratulate you for you excellent efforts as parents.

Sincerely,

George continued to take ADD medication and do well in school. His parents, of course, were delighted, but they knew of nothing that they had done to warrant such a letter of congratulations except to identify George as having ADD and make sure that he took his ADD medication.

Most children do amazingly well academically after medication treatment. An example of the rapid improvement in school performance that can occur is a story about Jacob which was written by his mother:

Story

For most children, the process of beginning school is exciting, stimulating, and inspiring. My son's schooling began with frustration, humiliation, and indignity. His kindergarten year was characterized by his relegation to the "time out" chair. First grade brought his assignment to the "early bird" reading group (always reserved for the "slower" students), and trips to the reading resource teacher for additional help. By second grade, caring but uninformed teachers recommended counseling to "enhance his self esteem." Third grade brought a recommendation for special education. Fortunately, by then, I had begun the search for an answer to how best to help my son.

My search brought me to a testing laboratory. Tests indicated a learning disability, and an above average classification on the WISC-R intelligence test. Teachers at this laboratory were able to assist Jacob in his reading growth, yet Jacob's resistance to and frustration with school continued and my search for answers resumed.

I had heard a local medical specialist describe the profile of the ADD child on several occasions, but never connected that profile with Jacob. Then, one evening this same specialist commented on the genetic aspects of ADD and went on to describe the ADD adult. That profile was a flawless description of Jacob's father. Finally, I looked more carefully at the symptoms of ADD, both in the DSM-III-R and in other literature. I was convinced that treatment for ADD should at least be attempted with my son.

Jacob began taking Norpramin in October of 1985. His special education testing had just begun, and his third grade teacher had already begun a behavioral program with Jacob. The results of his taking his medication were dramatic. His teacher commented on the improvement in Jacob's ability to "operate" within the classroom. His testing revealed similar results in intelligence scores to testing done earlier in an outside testing laboratory, but his performance on the Bender Gestalt Test improved significantly (from the 79th percentile to the 95th percentile) following the introduction of his medication.

While none of his schooling has been easy during the ensuing eight years, I am clear his development has been greatly enhanced by the medication he has been taking. He has experienced considerable success in school, and is proud of his demonstrated ability to achieve in the face of substantial odds. His willingness to put in the additional time and energy to accomplish his goals speaks to his belief in himself and his ability to focus and sustain attention.

* * * *

Not correcting ADD neurological dysfunctions with medication often perpetuates poor academic performance and leads to increasing educational deficiencies in children over a long period of time, even years. Also, there usually is the progressive, evolutionary development of a variety of psychological dysfunctions and social problems if medication treatment is delayed. Sadly, when parents finally realize and accept that medication treatment is needed, the children are older and many have become so dysfunctional that they refuse to take the medication that is offered even though they may have been expelled from school, in trouble with the law, or otherwise functioning poorly in society.

Unmedicated children not infrequently turn away from completing even their required studies and deteriorate to the point of becoming identified and socially secure with a peer group which is similarly indisposed to academic achievement. They may even hang around with other children who are using alcohol or illicit drugs to escape from the frustration and pain of their social and scholastic reality.

Drug treatment of ADD can be expensive and not without medical complications. Parents who are willing to give ADD medication to their children need and are entitled to be informed of the value, safety, possible side-effects and possible adverse reactions of any medication that is prescribed. Physicians must also address the issue of what constitutes proper medical reevaluation of children receiving medication including the need for electrocardiographic testing and blood level monitoring which are of value when certain medications are used. Parents must be made to understand the need for follow-up visits to monitor medication efficacy and safety.

REFERENCES

1. **Pelham, W.E., Jr**., *et al.*, *Methylphenidate and Baseball Playing in ADHD Children: Who's On First?* Journal of Consulting and Clinical Psychology, 1990. **58**(1): p. 130-133.
2. **Adams, R., MD and M. Victor MD**, *Chapter 27. Normal Development and Deviations in Development of the Nervous System,* in *Principles of Neurology*. 1985, McGraw-Hill Book Company: New York. p. 446.
3. **Devlin, J.B**., *Prevalence and Risk Factors for childhood Nocturnal Enuresis.* Irish Medical Journal, 1991. **84**: p. 118-120.
4. **Readett, D.R.J., MRCP, T. Bamigbade, and G.R. Serjeant MD**, *Nocturnal Enuresis in Normal Jamaican Children. Implications for Therapy.* West Indian Medical Journal, 1991. **40**: p. 181-184.
5. **Lunsing, R.J.**, *et al.*, *Nocturnal Enuresis and Minor Neurological Dysfunction at 12 Years: A Follow-up Study.* Developmental Medicine and Child Neurology, 1991. **33**: p. 439-445.
6. American Psychiatric Association Committee on Nomenclature and Statistics, *Functional Enuresis,* in *Diagnostic and Statistical Manual of Mental Disorders*. 1980, American Psychiatric Association: Washington, D.C. p. 80.
7. **Vellutino, F.R**., *Dyslexia,* in *Scientific American*. 1987, p. 34-41.
8. **Sawyer, D.J.W**., *Dyslexia: Introduction to the Special Series.* Journal of Learning Disabilities, 1992. **25**(1): p. 38-39.
9. **Chandola, C.A**., *et al.*, *Pre- and Perinatal Factors and the Risk of Subsequent Referral for Hyperactivity.* Journal of Child Psychology and Psychiatry, 1992. **33**(6): p. 1077-1090.

6

The Clinical Picture of Attention Deficit Disorder Neurology in Teenagers

The Ten Areas of Neurological Dysfunction of the ADD Syndrome

1. Inattentiveness, * especially Academic Underachieving
2. Hyperactivity and Fidgetiness *
3. Impulsivity *
4. Falling Asleep With Difficulty
5. Coming Awake Slowly
6. Frequent Irritability and/or Easy Frustration
7. Episodic Explosiveness, Rage or Tantrums
8. Negative Thoughts and Feelings With or Without Focus
9. Primary Nocturnal Enuresis (bedwetting)
10. Dyslexia (Verbal and Spatial)

* Minimal diagnostic criteria according to the *DSM-IV*

ADD Teenage Behavior is not "Normal" for the Developmental Age

Most teenagers do things, at least occasionally, that appear to be "crazy." But are they really crazy? Usually not! Are they dysfunctional? Not necessarily! Are they experimenting with life? Probably yes!

It is important that ADD dysfunctional behavior not be confused with the expected behaviors of teenagers who are experiencing tremendous physical and mental growth, stress from social and cultural expectations, as well as intellectual and personal challenges that normally occur at this stage of human development. Testing-the-water behaviors are desirable and healthy ventures of young people going through adolescence. No teenager should be considered dysfunctional because of an occasional misstep, bizarre remark, misjudgment, error, or outlandish act.

Only persistent behaviors that have predictably negative and harmful repercussions on the doer and others should be considered dysfunctional. Teenagers with ADD neurology live on the edge, constantly striving to control their cognitive and emotive behaviors while at the same time creating extreme situations which cause psychological problems and social rejection. Their on-the-edge living pattern should be considered dysfunctional if it leads to repeatedly negative consequences.

Conflict and Confusion about the Issue of Self-Control

Those who live with teenagers probably have heard comments such as, "Who is in-charge here? Of course, I am! I do just what I want to do when I want to do it, just like other teenagers."

So goes the battle cry of many adolescents with or without ADD neurology. The strong desire to be normal, like everyone else, and in control of one's destiny not infrequently overrides many other important considerations. Even when the diagnosis is obvious, ADD teenagers often will not admit to anyone else, and sometimes not even to themselves, that they are imperfect or often out of control, let alone accept that there is something "wrong" with their brain.

They rarely are able to acknowledge that their ADD diagnosis is a medical "gift," that is, the diagnosis of a serious problem that is readily corrected with medication. To do so is painful because it implies that they cannot take effective charge of their lives or make behavioral changes through personal effort simply by trying to do so. In fact, many ADD teenagers reinforce the feeling that they are in control of themselves by seeking out and associating with peers who are tolerant of their behaviors out of friendship or because they also have ADD. Sometimes, teenagers insist that their dysfunctions are normal behaviors because "everyone I know" has the same kind of problems.

Occasionally, parents inadvertently reinforce the denial of ADD by their teenagers. Caught up in trying to be maximally sympathetic and understanding, parents can fall into the trap of not challenging the judgment of their teenagers who are refusing to believe that they have ADD. At least initially, some parents may even believe that the

ADD dysfunctional behaviors of their children are learned behaviors in need of psychological, not medical, treatment. Unfortunately, the failure to recognize the role of ADD neurology as a cause of dysfunction precludes the use of potentially very helpful ADD treatment medication.

Many teenagers are too old to be easily intimidated by adults, and they are often skilled at rebelling against their parents and school authorities. Teenagers with ADD are, therefore, especially capable of getting into deep trouble both personally and socially for long periods of time. When disaster ultimately strikes, it is usually intense and damaging.

School failures contribute to intense self-criticism and low self-esteem along with dislike and rejection of academic learning. If not treated with effective medication, ADD teenagers often try to escape from the pain of ordinary living through high-adventure activities which generate enthusiasm and positive feelings yet typically lead to worsening of their academic performance, suspension from school, and sometimes involvement in criminal activities.

Acceptance by teenagers and their parents of the diagnosis of ADD neurology too often does not happen until there is severe criticism or censure from outside the family. Exclusion from school, arrest, or being fired from a job may be the necessary first events which awaken awareness that important ADD-related cognitive and emotional problems exist.

At some point in time, regardless of what their initial understanding may have been, most parents do come to realize that something out of the ordinary is wrong and that it is important to act more firmly toward encouraging their teenagers to stop academically underachieving and correct social failures.

The initial efforts of caring parents to help their teenagers are likely to be gentle approaches such as merely providing "reminders" that they hope will stimulate a keener sense of responsibility toward homework, improved academic performance at school, and a heightened awareness of the need to conform and adapt to organizational rules and ordinary restrictions.

Should these gentle approaches fail, and without proper medication treatment they usually do, many parents become more assertive, sometimes issuing frank warnings of impending future disaster with respect to college admission, job opportunities, and financial success. If the teenager is incorrigible, parent frustration often escalates and some take even more drastic steps including restrictions such as grounding, loss of a monthly allowance, restricted use of the family automobile, and even physical beatings.

Warnings, threats, and punishments, however, rarely bring about enduring change in the social behavior and academic performance of ADD teenagers. Worse, this sort of parenting usually generates heightened feelings of anger, resistance, and rebelliousness in teenagers.

Without medication treatment, Attention Deficit Disorder in teenagers can lead to disaster. Why, then, is it so hard for teenagers to take a pill or two and deal with their ADD dysfunctional behavior? Let's look at this issue from the teenager's point of view.

Is it not true that teenagers are expected to use psychological strength and willpower to cope with their sexual urges, their strong need for social acceptance, and their intense desire for independence? Just listen and you will hear teenagers say, "Logically, why should I use pills to help me control my impulsivity, academic underachieving, irritability, explosiveness and negativity of ADD but not use pills to control my other stresses in life?"

Looked at in this way, it is easy to understand why many teenagers might reject pill treatment for the stresses that are a consequence to their ADD neurology. Unfortunately, rejecting medication and, as sometimes happens, turning to psychological treatment instead, is not an ideal therapeutic approach because it is minimally effective at best and often not effective at all.

To limit the denial process and gain cooperation, health professionals, in particular, should try to win the cooperation of teenagers and that of their parents. Teenagers must be full partners in the diagnostic and treatment process. To do this, health professionals must not only diagnose ADD when present but also communicate to teenagers and their parents the basis for the diagnosis, describe the cognitive and emotive changes that are and are not expected from medication, and clarify that "personality," likes, and values do not change with the proper use of medication.

Medication Treatment Should Start as Early in Life as is Possible

The earlier that medication treatment is started, the better. Early treatment helps ensure that there will be adequate academic success and minimal damage from the strain of overwork, failure to develop essential basic knowledge and learning skills, repeated criticism, academic failures and self-depreciation which ultimately lead to low self-esteem, rejection of school activities, and loss of interest in academic learning.

Most teenage students without ADD have to struggle when they compete academically against others in school, and those with ADD usually struggle extra hard. Medication treatment should not be withheld from teenagers who clearly have ADD just because they have passing school grades. If they are underachieving, given their innate cognitive ability, adding to the academic strain by not providing medication simply imposes an extra, unnecessary burden on ADD teenagers.

If left untreated, the academic future of a teenager with ADD can be compromised forever. As stress mounts, ADD teenagers too often simply reject academic pursuits and turn to nonacademic activities that are easier and more fun for them despite negative academic consequences. These alternative behaviors typically are forms of release, attention-getting and avoidance taken by those who want to escape from the boredom and criticism that follows from their unsuccessful and difficult experiences trying to cope with academic demands. Unfortunately, they not infrequently include self-destructive behaviors ranging from being disruptive in the classroom, failing to participate in classroom activities and behaving in negative and annoying ways at home to the use of street drugs, excessive alcohol and to involvement in violent criminal activity.

Detailed Description of Teenage ADD Dysfunctions

The diagnosis of ADD in teenagers is based on an evaluation of the same ten areas of neurological dysfunction that define the syndrome in individuals of other ages. While the areas are the same, the clinical presentation of ADD in teenagers is unique enough to be discussed separately from ADD in children and adults.

Inattentiveness and Academic Underachieving

Case Study

As far as Jacob is concerned, it is no longer a question of finishing reading assignments. He now refuses to even start them. The mere thought of doing any homework is repugnant.

"No sooner do I pick up a book to read, then I want to go to sleep. If I do read anything, it simply does not 'stick' or register on my brain."

"Why should I continue wasting time and feeling inadequate, stupid and incompetent? I am able to learn by just listening to the teacher, and that is how I am going to deal with my schooling!"

"I must admit, however, that I am puzzled because on some days, and without reason," he went on, "I read like a whiz and it all sinks in. Also, if I read what I enjoy reading, I have no problem with comprehension."

"What's wrong with me. Why am I dumb part of the time but not all of the time?"

The ADD syndrome does occur in teenagers of above normal, normal or below average intelligence. This point is worth emphasizing again!

Teenagers with limited academic ability are most likely to have difficulty achieving in school and are, therefore, more likely to be identified as having a learning disability and ADD. It is for this reason that ADD is sometimes believed to be a problem only of those with medium to low intelligence.

ADD neurological dysfunction always causes some degree of inattentiveness which interferes with the ability of students to achieve at their maximum. In spite of this, gifted teenage students do not necessarily receive low grades. In fact, they can be very successful if they are highly motivated and make a vigorous effort to study hard and compete. Given their level of natural intelligence, many gifted ADD teenagers are first recognized as underachievers not because of poor school grades but because they spend excessive amounts of time completing academic assignments.

It is not in the best interest of ADD teenagers who are underachieving to withhold medication treatment until grades finally deteriorate severely. Most teenage students without ADD struggle as they compete academically against others in school, and those with ADD struggle more.

Not all teenagers with ADD are identified as having a learning disability and ADD. By one maneuver or another, to protect their ego, a significant number are not identified, not treated and many actually abandon academic pursuits to escape from being detected and diagnosed. This is a tragic waste of our human resources.

As dropouts, they typically offer a variety of reasons for abandoning formal education, but almost all describe their experience at school as "boring." Some have additional explanations for why they quit formal education such as the need to deal with the demands of being married, rearing children, or to repay debts. Others immerse themselves in and profess to prefer careers in sports, offering this as an excuse for their poor academic performance.

Educators and parents often misinterpret the cause of school failures and inappropriate behavior in ADD teenagers as due to a lack of "motivation." Sometimes, with the mistaken belief that the student is not being rewarded enough to perform better academically, parents will offer prizes such as a bicycle, automobile, trip to Europe, ski camp in Australia, clothes, or extra spending money in the hope that the offer will be an incentive for improvement. Rewards of this nature may provide enough stimulus for temporary improvement to happen but are rarely effective over the long-term. Unfortunately, even the suggestion that ADD teenagers lack motivation only adds to their feelings of inadequacy, failure and rejection.

Convincing evidence that most ADD students are dealing with neurologically-based inattentiveness and difficulty focusing rather than lack of motivation is that their ability to focus on academic material and their performance in the classroom improves dramatically within days after starting the proper dose of an effective ADD medication. With medication, these ADD teenagers become able to complete their homework on their own and improve their academic performance even in the absence of parental supervision, bribes or rewards. This improvement reverses rapidly when medication is discontinued. The value of medication is so dramatic that it is difficult to support the idea that ADD teenagers have a predominantly psychological problem and poor motivation rather than a biological, dysfunctional cognitive problem due to ADD brain chemistry.

Starting medication treatment early is valuable for preventing or, if necessary, reversing the development of adverse psychosocial and academic consequences that are common to ADD teenagers.

Hyperactivity and Fidgetiness

Case Study

Nancy used to be a virtual "Dennis the Menace." The grade school teachers would struggle desperately to help her not talk, sit still, and stay seated ... all too often without success. Nancy visited the principal's office frequently. She was clearly hyperactive.

Nancy is now fourteen and still not treated with medication. She is only fidgety, able to stay seated in the classroom, but, when feeling emotionally stressed and bored, her legs shake, she fiddles with the ends of her long hair, and she talks to classmates when she is supposed to be quiet.

Her parents still believe that she is doing poorly with her studies because she is a typical teenage girl who has a lot of distracting social interests. They are not sure what Attention Deficit Disorder is, think it might be a made-up disorder by doctors trying to make extra money, or just a fancy excuse for kids not doing well in school. They are certainly not convinced that their daughter has this ADD thing.

A few ADD teenagers are almost as physically active and on-the-go as the severely hyperactive child who jumps off kitchen counters and races from one room to another without specific reason to do so. They talk a lot, are constantly restless, sit down and stand up frequently, shift from one leg to the other when standing for even short periods of time, and nervously pace around their room, house, the yard, school auditorium and the like.

In most instances, though, the-run-around, jump-up-and-down hyperactivity of childhood is not present in adolescence. In its place are movements of a less gross nature which are more accurately described by the term, fidgetiness. This kind of behavior is sometimes mistaken for the movements of agitated, fitful or "nervous" individuals. Like hyperactive behavior, however, fidgetiness also is inappropriate, extraneous, and discordant body movement that has no goal-oriented purpose.

Fidgetiness is hyperactivity in a less intense form. In some teenagers, it is expressed less as body motions and more as excessive, inappropriate talking in the school classroom, at religious meetings, or in a theater while others are trying to listen to the movie. It is as important a clue to the diagnosis of ADD as is hyperactivity.

Some teenagers with considerable social skills successfully hide their fidgety behavior. When feeling the need to move a lot, they might escape detection by announcing, "I can't sit here any longer and talk with you. I need to get up and move around a bit. Can I buy anyone something at the store?" Others, with less social skill, are more obvious and appear impulsive, careless, intolerant, irritable, impatient, impetuous or unfocused. Their need to keep moving and talking is beyond what is normally allowed by common etiquette and politeness. To attribute these fidgety behaviors mistakenly to a lack of social training is to misunderstand ADD neurology.

Some ADD teenagers express their hyperactivity or fidgetiness mainly as motor and/or verbal tics. Tics, in ADD teenagers, are defined the same way they are for children. Motor tics are repetitive, involuntary movements that range from sudden, rapid, brief, jerking motions to muscle movements that are slower and more like stretching than jerking. Eye blinking, facial grimacing, horizontal head movements, sticking the tongue out, licking lips, raising eyebrows, repeated glancing up, and jerking motions of the arms or legs are some of the many ways motor tics are expressed.

Vocal tics, which characterize Tourette's syndrome, are a type of motor tic. Common expressions of vocal tics are throat clearing, grunting, snorting, squeaking, sniffing, coughing, humming, barking, spitting or virtually any repetitious vocal noise that does not represent a recognizable word. Vocal tics can be recognizable words said quietly, as if under the breath, but they also can be loud, explosive, obnoxious, even indecent expressions that attract considerable adult attention.

Like the movements of hyperactivity and fidgetiness, tics are episodic, inappropriate and not goal-directed behaviors. They occur in response to boredom, tiredness and emotional discomfort and can be readily provoked by asking embarrassing, stressful questions or otherwise creating an uncomfortable environment. Individuals with tics have the same spectrum of other ADD neurological dysfunctions as hyperactive teenagers without tics.

Hyperactivity, fidgetiness and tics all rapidly diminish and often totally disappear after proper ADD medication treatment.

IMPULSIVITY

Case Study

"Randy, you brought the wrong furnace filter home from the store," his father shouted from the basement. "Would you please go back and get the right one?"

Dad was not angry. He understood the problem.

Randy always has about ten thoughts running through his head at one time. It is always easy to forget any one thought when others can move into his consciousness so easily.

Randy ran out of the house and to the store without his notes that described the dimensions of the replacement furnace filter needed. At the store, he was too scattered to call home for the dimensions and too impatient to pause and realize how long it would take to drive to and from the store again if he did pick the wrong filter.

Impulsively, he just grabbed a filter that looked like the right size and raced home.

By teenage years, a veneer of control and a modicum of social skill can obscure the blatant acts of impulsivity commonly seen in young children such as blurting out answers in class or difficulty awaiting one's turn in social situations. ADD teenagers have difficulty waiting their turn, such as in a ski-lift line, but they are likely to cover over their impulsivity by posturing as avid skiers who deserve not to have to wait in line. In other settings such as waiting in line for movies, plays or football games, they are likely to search out friends at the head of the line to move ahead and avoid the boredom of a long wait.

They may deal with their impulsivity and impatience by acting *blasé* and self-assured. For example, rather than take the time to be sure that what they are buying is what they need or should be buying, impulsive teenagers might buy whatever remotely looks similar to what they want. Their impulsive, hyperactive minds shift from one thought to another and one task to another without much pause for reevaluation and contemplation. They want to get out of the store as quickly as possible and move on. As a result, impulsive teenagers are likely to race through the purchasing process by acting as if they are sure about what they are doing to avoid even the minimal frustration often felt by ordinary, almost expected shopping service delays.

Because they are more socialized and sophisticated than children, impulsive teenagers often make an effort to cover over their impulsive actions by trying to make them look like reasonable responses to boredom, disinterest, the need for comic relief, adventure, or being in a hurry because of other demands on their time.

But, their ability to manage time effectively and to program activities is deficient because impulsive ADD teenagers are likely to be diverted much too easily by interrupting thoughts and emotional impulses. An impulsive teenager might try to justify his or her absence from school one day by explaining, "While walking to school, I suddenly got an urge to go to the beach." The impulsivity of a teenager can lead to deep trouble especially if he or she is less able than others to pause and reflect appropriately on behavior and remember that this particular absence, for example, would constitute a third truancy and have severe consequences if discovered.

Impulsive behavior diminishes dramatically when the ADD teenager takes proper ADD medication.

Falling Asleep with Difficulty

Case Study

"No way! If I went to bed at 9 o'clock, I would just lie there for two or three hours still awake. No, not every night, but almost every night."

"So, I wait until it's really late and I'm really tired. Then, falling asleep is not hard. I don't care if Mom complains that I am not getting enough sleep or I need to go to bed earlier to get up in time for the school bus. I cannot seem to get up easily no matter when I go to bed."

"I hate just lying there not able to turn off the day and fall asleep!"

Falling asleep with difficulty is a problem for about 75% of ADD teenagers. "Difficulty" is a subjective term, and it certainly includes an element of discomfort. It is usually possible to quantitate, to some degree, just how "difficult" difficult is because most teenagers can estimate with reasonable accuracy the time it takes them to go from lying down in bed to actually being asleep.

Three types of scenarios are common.

In one, the teenager becomes tired, yawns, has great difficulty continuing to study or do other tasks, feels overwhelmed with sleepiness, and decides that it is time to go to sleep. Lying down, sleep comes rapidly, but within moments, the individual wakes up without obvious cause, feels wide awake, and is full of one thought after another. These thoughts are not necessarily distressing nor exciting, but they do not stop flowing. Commonly, sleep does not return for at least thirty minutes and sometimes not for two to four hours.

In a second and more distressing scenario, the ADD teenager feels tired and unable to continue with tasks, lies down to sleep, but cannot fall asleep even for a brief moment. The mind typically does a "flip," acts as if it were rebelling, and does not "turn off." These teenagers sometimes learn to never try sleeping without first reading or listening to a talk show on the radio or music from a tape recorder. Some use self-hypnotic approaches and other relaxation techniques to fall asleep. In most instances, these approaches help time to pass more easily but do not induce sleep immediately.

A third nighttime scenario common to ADD teenagers who have difficulty falling asleep is simply to ignore early urges to go to bed, stay up late doing projects of one sort or another, and wait until extreme fatigue virtually ensures that sleep will come on rapidly after lying down. These individuals sometimes stay up until 3-4 AM to the consternation of their parents who try to wake them at 6 or 7 AM to go to school, work or other activities.

Is falling asleep difficult every night? No, not every night! Even for ADD individuals, falling asleep can at times be easy for no obvious reason. In addition, intense physical exercise prior to bedtime, including sexual activity, often allows sleep to come easily.

The desire to be "normal" and feel in charge of their body functions can be so great that some ADD teenagers deny difficulty falling asleep. For others, falling asleep is not a "problem" because they accept the slowness of the process. "I fall asleep when I want to," is a response especially from those teenagers who have learned to stay up until tiredness overwhelms them. It is the need to stay up until exhausted that distinguishes these teenagers from those without ADD who typically become tired at a reasonable evening hour, lie down when tired, and simply go to sleep.

When the ADD syndrome is properly treated with medication, falling asleep becomes dramatically more easy and complaints about the problem disappear.

Coming Awake Slowly

Case Study

Marshall thinks it began when he was about eleven. He cannot remember having trouble waking in the morning before that age.

Now, at sixteen he can hardly recall ever waking easily, and usually not waking before ten or eleven o'clock in the morning .... on school days, that is.

Of course, three weeks ago, when the airplane for Disneyland left early in the morning, Marshall had no trouble waking and was up and ready. But that was once, three weeks ago.

On school days, it is father's job to try to get him out of bed and off to school. On these mornings, the alarm clock goes off, but the snooze button allows him to dose in between at least three buzzing episodes.

Typically, with twenty minutes to go before the start of classes, Marshall rolls out of bed, stands, drags himself to the bathroom, showers, and finally shows up downstairs awake and ready for breakfast. His eyes are finally wide open, and he is set for the race against time to get to school without being late again.

Approximately 92% of ADD teenagers, regardless of sex, come awake slowly. The issue of concern is not whether or not a teenager leaps out of bed quickly. It is whether or not a teenager easily and quickly goes from being asleep to being awake. Waking slowly may start early in life, "ever since mother can remember," which usually means since the age of three or four. If not, it almost certainly becomes evident not later than ten in girls and twelve in boys.

Lots of teenagers think and say that they are "just fine" in the morning because they eventually do get out of bed, but they wake slowly. Most need prodding by their parents or siblings to feel awake and even to get out of bed. An unusual presentation of this problem is the teenager who wakes and gets up easily but does not feel good emotionally. Both coming awake slowly and/or feeling grouchy most mornings are indicative of ADD neurology.

A careful clinical distinction should be made between, "How easily do you get out of *bed* in the morning?" to which the answer often is, "Without a problem," and "Do you feel *awake* when you first open your eyes in the morning?" "Well, certainly not *right away* but within five to fifteen minutes," is a typical answer from an ADD teenager. The truth may be more like fifteen to thirty minutes if the parents are consulted.

If the teenager says, "Most mornings, I wake up after washing my face," or, "Most of the time, I *really wake up* ten to thirty minutes after being out of bed," then the process of coming awake in the morning should be considered a dysfunction. Teenagers who grow up with parents or siblings who also come awake slowly are not likely to be aware that people without ADD generally come awake easily and without special encouragement.

The severity of waking slowly is variable from individual to individual. There are some ADD teenagers who wake so slowly and feel so drowsy that they cannot function adequately during the first half of the school day. Some of these teenagers end up in "home study" programs because they generally cannot be aroused enough in the morning even to get to school. Typically, they miss morning appointments with the doctor, the parole officer and others as well as show up late for work and have difficulty holding jobs.

Because environmental influences affect the expression of this dysfunction, parents often believe that their teenagers do not "want" to wake up and that their difficulty is a consequence of "psychological dysfunction." Parents remember well the mornings when, to their amazement, their teenagers woke up easily and felt bright because they wanted to watch television, play with a new dirt bike, drive their new automobile, greet a special friend who just dropped by, get on the ski slope, or race to the kitchen to put out a fire that mother accidentally started. They usually wake easily if their expectations are that the morning will bring them an activity of high-interest or high-pleasure.

Because coming awake slowly can be influenced by environmental and psychological factors, some parents and even many health professionals attribute morning tiredness and coming awake slowly to laziness, irresponsibility, depression and other "psychological" causes. This conclusion often leads to punishment, scolding, lecturing and finally to treatment with psychotherapy. But, trouble waking up on ordinary days is a common neurological dysfunction of ADD and requires correction with medication. With the correct dose of the proper medication, this dysfunction can disappear within twenty-four hours confirming that it is a neurobiological abnormality rather than a character problem or psychological disturbance.

Occasionally, parents will believe that their teenagers wake slowly because of an inadequate amount of sleep. They often point to what they perceive as their own need for sleep or mistakenly think that there is a specific and fixed amount of sleep an individual "should" get to feel rested every day. Trying to be helpful, parents often encourage their teenagers to go to sleep early in the evening, and some even try to establish a bedtime hour.

As teenage independence becomes more firmly established, parents recognize the need to be less dictatorial. Accordingly, they often turn to cajoling, encouraging, reminding and urging their teenagers to go to bed early. Logical as these remedies may seem to parents, they are ineffective. The lack of sleep theory has little scientific basis and does not explain why most ADD teenagers wake easily when there is an exciting reason to do so, regardless of how little sleep they have had.

A small percentage of ADD teenagers have no trouble waking in the morning and functioning. When questioned carefully, they often are "driven" or highly motivated to get up and get going. When asked about why they wake up easily, they are likely to respond, "I *have to* get up." This "have to" commonly refers to a feeling of great need to get to their school classes or start their paper route job on time. Whatever the reason for the underlying reason for the "have to," and it is usually not obvious, they certainly come awake quickly much like ADD adults with workaholic personalities who also come awake quickly in the morning.

Waking slowly is a strong clue to the diagnosis of the ADD syndrome in teenagers.

Frequent Irritability and/or Easy Frustration

Case Study

"I think that I'm pretty calm and relaxed. I am sure my friends would say the same about me," Mike insisted with considerable seriousness when asked whether or not he thought he was unusually, inexplicably and chronically "irritable."

"Most things don't bother me. I don't let them bother me," he continued.

"Well," his ADD doctor asked, "What happens when another car cuts in front of your car on the highway?"

Mike at first grimaced, then a sheepish smile became evident. "In that instance," he said, "I always think about driving my pickup truck right up the tailpipe of the person who could do a thing like that! For some reason, that kind of driving really bugs me."

Irritability is an imprecise term, but teenagers are sophisticated enough to know what it is. In the jargon of ADD terminology, "irritable" is the opposite of "mellow." Of course, mellow must never be confused with or used to mean "sedated." Teenagers often think of themselves as irritable and "easily bugged," "crabby," "bitchy," or "high strung." A few would say that they are "easily frustrated" more than "irritable."

Some teenagers are quick to talk about the fact that they often feel irritable and annoyed by "little things." But whether or not they easily talk about these feelings, they dislike and depreciate themselves for being irritable without good cause. If they could, they would choose not to be irritable. Without medication, the best that ADD individuals can do is to make a conscious effort to suppress feeling irritable and hope that, with time, such feelings will occur less often and less intensely.

It is more common for adolescent women than men to be aware and speak out about recurrent irritability. Regardless of gender, however, most teenagers do not comfortably admit to being frequently irritable and do not like being labeled as such by others, including physicians. Even just inquiring about this matter often feels like an accusation of misbehavior to most teenagers, not just the search for medical information that it is.

If sympathetically asked, however, only a few teenagers vigorously deny being irritable a lot of the time. What brings out irritability? Certain situations are common causes. Driving on crowded highways; being asked to complete chores that they are expected to do by themselves such as clean their bedroom, take out the garbage, pick up tools they have been using on a project; being asked to finish homework that is due. They are also often annoyed by the behavior of a sister or brother, the cat playing on the bed, and by the ordinary "what have you been doing today" questions from the parents.

Many ADD teenagers say, "I only feel bugged when around my family," but they are usually less mellow than they like even when around others outside of their family, especially those with whom they are emotionally close such as girlfriends and boyfriends. The degree of annoyance can be so intense that ADD teenagers may complain that their entire day was spoiled. Interactions with others are often so negative that what should have been fun experiences turn out to be unpleasant events.

Many ADD teenagers make a great effort to find psychological solutions to their irritability feelings. Aside from simple denial, they expend considerable effort using positive thinking techniques to try to "let go" of annoyances. Others seek drugs such as alcohol, marihuana, cocaine, tranquilizers or sedatives. Many neutralize their irritability by participating in high adventures such as motorcycle racing, driving cars fast, being involved in promiscuous sex, and participating in adventurous gang activitics. These behaviors can be quite dangerous. Proper ADD medication dramatically diminishes the intensity and frequency of this problem right from the start of treatment.

While treatment with proper ADD medication is usually dramatically helpful, some teenagers need extra help to break out from behavior patterns that have become part of their lifestyle. To find new, replacement activities that are healthy, some teenagers need to change schools, find new friends and receive psychotherapy. The starting treatment, however, should be medication.

Even early after the start of medication treatment, friends and family members very often sense a dramatic change and commonly remark on "how well," "how nice" or "how happy" the ADD teenager "looks," "seems" or "is acting."

Episodic Explosiveness or Rage

Case Study

"I was being a good girl ... washing the dishes for my aunt. This was my way of thanking her for the work she did to make me a lovely meal."

My cousin was being a "pill." He refused to help, and he would not leave me alone. I was trying hard to not break any of the dishes or glasses I was washing."

"Yes, I did scream at him twice to leave me alone and not bug me. He just laughed. I then grew more angry and picked up a steak knife. Without much thought, I threw it at him."

"Oh!" the doctor listening to this story said, "what a frightening experience that must have been."

"Well, that's not the worst of it," she went on, "I really became upset when the knife actually stuck in him! It was then that made up my mind to never throw a knife at a person again."

83% of ADD teenagers are episodically explosive. Moreover, they are old enough and big enough to be able to have important negative impact on others and do a lot of damage.

Episodic explosiveness, more commonly called "rage," is fundamentally the same as tantrums in children. It is probably synonymous with the psychiatric term, "emotional outbursts," and is more than just being frustrated and irritable.

Episodic explosiveness, or rage, refers to intermittent feelings of intense anger that not infrequently result in physical actions which exceed the usual limit of acceptable behavior for useful family interactions and societal norms. Characteristically, anger progresses over a just a few seconds or minutes to become extreme in intensity.

Rage in the ADD teenager is almost always triggered by relatively minor events, comments, questions, demands or frustrations. For example, something as trivial as a parent making the third request that their teenager pick up the dirty clothes on the floor or finish homework before the television set is turned on is often enough to provoke a rage reaction. In addition to being triggered by interactions with family members, explosive behavior in ADD teenagers can be precipitated by small mistakes while sewing, working on art or carpentry projects, fixing a flat automobile tire, or being held up in traffic as well as by noticing the first scratch on the paint of a new car.

By contrast, much more monumental events such as a fire at home or serious automobile accident involving personal injury rarely if ever are lead to episodic rage. In fact, one of the strengths of ADD neurology is that events and threats of this magnitude are commonly handled courageously as challenges to be met. ADD teenagers generally handle catastrophic events better than people without ADD neurology.

Teenagers can be big and strong. Consequently, their rage can result in considerable damage including holes kicked in doors and walls, broken windows, precious objects thrown and smashed, people physically beaten as well as verbal attacks with episodes of screaming and yelling. Episodic rage almost never serves in a constructive way to resolve the circumstances or issues that precipitated the explosiveness.

Teenage boys are more likely to exhibit episodic explosiveness than teenage girls. One explanation for this difference is that boys in our society are expected to be aggressive while similar behavior in girls is not "lady-like." Girls are not supposed to express strong emotions in physically violent ways, and family dictates and practices often successfully inhibit ADD girls from physically hitting people, breaking property or being verbally abusive. Unable or unwilling to strike out physically, some girls release rage by crying hysterically.

Most physicians recognize that rage is not the same as "psychotic" or "crazy" behavior, but occasionally physicians treat these ADD teenagers with antipsychotic medications. This approach almost never has lasting benefit. Antipsychotic medications are not proper treatment for ADD neurological dysfunctions. Moreover, they cause sedation and severely compromise cognitive function in the ADD individual even if they reduce the intensity and frequency of overt physical violence. The proper use of antidepressant and stimulant medications is always preferred treatment because these medications reduce or eliminate rage without compromising cognitive function.

Episodic explosiveness or rage behavior can occur on a daily basis especially in young children but is more likely to occur a few times a week or only a few times a month in teenagers. The intensity of the anger and ensuing violence varies from episode to episode. Both the provocativeness of the stimuli and the degree of ADD neurological dysfunction influence the severity of each episode of rage. But, other factors such as sickness and hunger also can increase the likelihood and severity of rage in ADD teenagers.

Fortunately, many teenagers are aware, in retrospect, that the cause of explosive reactions almost never explains or justifies the intensity of their responses. Most can moderate the intensity of their rage to some degree. They have enough insight to know that their explosiveness can assume extreme proportions and have very negative and harmful consequences on themselves, their environment and others if allowed to be fully expressed.

Some ADD teenagers with insight are able at times to "walk away" from provoking stimuli before they become enraged. They may have to leave the house, go to their room, or whatever, to remove themselves from additional or continued provocations. A few have found creative solutions. One teenager reported having a special tree in the backyard at which he throws knives when enraged; he continues throwing as long as the rage feelings persist. Another teenager reported that he smashes the metal body of his pickup truck with a sledge hammer until he emotionally recovers, avoiding, of course, striking the windows.

It is realistic to fear that severe harm, permanent damage, and death can result from teenage ADD rage attacks. One ADD teenage boy told the following story. He was at a Saturday night party. His older brother was with him and was verbally insulted by another party-goer. The teenager left the party, went home, found a gun, came back to the party, then shot and killed the person who had insulted his brother. Murder can clearly be one of the consequences of ADD rage.

Even when no serious damage or harm has yet happened, the relationships of ADD teenagers with, for example, their parents, teachers, spouses and friends can be compromised because others fear them. It is not uncommon to hear that a girlfriend chose to break off a romance after she was screamed at, forcibly grabbed, or watched her angry boyfriend kick a hole in the bedroom wall.

Episodic explosiveness is virtually unique to those with ADD neurology and, not surprisingly, diminishes and often disappears after ADD medication treatment. Rarely, uncommon disorders such as hyperthyroidism and certain brain tumors may cause similar explosive behavior. In the absence of another medical cause, episodic explosive behavior is a strong clue to the diagnosis of ADD and should stimulate the search for other ADD neurological dysfunctions.

Unlike most of the other neurological dysfunctions of ADD which correct immediately, rage quickly diminishes in intensity and frequency but disappears only over days, weeks or months of proper medication treatment. Resolution of ADD-related rage following medication treatment takes longer to correct than the other neurological dysfunctions of ADD because there is an important amount of learned behavior involved in how ADD individuals handle anger. Rage is an inappropriate response to anger which has to be unlearned and new behaviors substituted for the old ones. The mental process of giving up old and learning new behaviors, in general, takes a substantial amount of time in all individuals whether or not they have ADD.

The extreme susceptibility to be enraged and act explosively is dramatically moderated by ADD medication much as the threshold for pain is reduced by analgesic medicines. Rage is more likely to occur in teenagers whose parents are explosive.

NEGATIVE THOUGHTS AND FEELINGS

Case Study

"I'm never going to go to another party," Sierra was mumbling while at breakfast the next morning.

"I hardly talked to anyone, no one was nice to me, the other girls acted as if they didn't like me, and even the skit wasn't funny."

I have a hard time having fun any more. Things are not going well for me. And, the more I feel this way, the more things go wrong in my life."

"If life doesn't have some fun in it soon, I'm going to get depressed."

When the neurological dysfunction, negativity, is a prominent complaint in teenagers with ADD, it is a potentially ominous situation because of the possibility of subsequent depression and suicide.

Negativity makes ADD teenagers especially prone to feeling pessimistic. It is difficult to quantitate, however, because it does not have a reasonably measurable and specific expression like other ADD neurological dysfunctions such as hyperactivity, sleep disturbance, episodic explosiveness, enuresis and dyslexia do.

Negativity can be mild or severe in nature. Its intensity in a given individual varies from time to time. Like other ADD neurological dysfunctions, its intense is influenced by intercurrent illness and environmental factors.

When mild, negativity is short-lived like hunger. It can last for minutes or hours then disappear for variable periods of time. Clinically, teenagers with mild negativity look like they are not having fun. They report going to parties where no one seemed interested in them, no one was fun to talk or dance with, and they did not experience anything especially nice happening even though many others had the opposite reaction. They talk about going to an amusement park and getting splashed with cold water but none of the cute and funny events that also happened. They might go to the cinema but are likely to find the movie dull even though their friends fully enjoyed it.

When severe, teenagers who feel negative will hold on to and have difficulty forgetting or "letting go" of unpleasant experiences for long periods of time. They may even hold grudges and vendettas for days, and in some cases months and years.

When negative feelings and thoughts accumulate and persist without periods of relief, teenagers are likely to become blue, hopeless, disparing and clinically "depressed." Clinical depression is a consequence of something, in this instance ADD neurological dysfunction, and, as such, is a second-order phenomenon. Depression is a more severe and painful psychological state than negativity because it includes both negativity and an important loss of psychological strength and will power. Depression can lead to suicide, an important cause of death in teenagers.

Negative thoughts and feelings have a neurobiological basis in the same way that irritability and hunger do. The neurobiology of negativity in ADD teenagers can be induced by environmental factors, of course, such as living with repeatedly drunk and abusive parents. But, ADD teenagers can experience negativity even in the absence of contributing environmental influences because of the nature of their brain chemistry. For individuals with negativity due mainly to ADD, ADD medication treatment is always indicated.

Because depression *per se* is a reactive phenomenon, when it becomes apparent and significant in teenagers with ADD two treatment approaches indicated. Both should proceed in parallel. Insight and supportive psychotherapy should be started to protect the individual from harm. And, proper medication should be prescribed immediately to correct the ADD neurological dysfunction that is at the root of the underlying, persistent negativity.

When negativity is directed mainly inward, ADD teenagers feel unattractive, not liked, bored, stupid, and uninterested in their environment. When negativity feelings are projected outward against other people, the ADD teenager feels anger, disappointment and may harbor feelings of revenge.

ADD teenagers with negativity also may experience so-called "awful spells." These are periods lasting minutes to hours when life seems "bleak" and during which negative feelings and thoughts have no specific focus on an event or a person. It is a time period that some ADD teenagers describe as living in a "dark, black hole." "Awful spells" often dissipate when interrupted by environmental events such as a ringing telephone or another person entering the scene, any external occurrence that demands a change in the mental focus of the individual involved.

For those with severe negativity and depression, psychotherapy is usually of immediate value but may not be needed after a few weeks or months. Medication treatment for the underlying ADD neurology should continue permanently.

PRIMARY NOCTURNAL ENURESIS

Case Study

It is hard to be seventeen and wake up lying on wet sheets four days out of seven each week. God help you socially if others outside of your family should know that you were a bedwetter.

Ralph did not want to talk about his bedwetting. He slept in his own room, and he could not even imagine sleeping with others outside the family who might discover his problem. The prospect of going to summer camp or having an overnight with friends or relatives was too embarrassing to even consider.

He felt different, abnormal and isolated from the kids around him while he protected carefully what he came to consider his family secret. His albatross included shame, embarrassment and a reason for avoiding normal socializing.

Primary nocturnal enuresis refers to bedwetting while a person is sleeping. It is a term that should not be used to describe a teenager who is unwilling to leave the warmth of bed to go to the toilet, or who wets the bed out of spite.

It is generally accepted that bedwetters must be at least five years old and have no discernible organic abnormality to account for the problem. Even sporadic bedwetting is abnormal for a child who is five or older, but the DSM-IV recommends that, for a very secure diagnosis of primary nocturnal enuresis, there should be an occurrence at least once a month.

In my experience, primary nocturnal enuresis is unique to people with ADD neurology. Accordingly, while not yet adequately appreciated, bedwetting in a five year old child should immediately tell the parents, doctor and others that this child has ADD neurology. This does not mean that treatment must begin immediately, but it should alert the parents and others to begin the search for other neurological clues to ADD in the child.

My experience is that primary nocturnal enuresis is one of the ten neurological dysfunctions of the ADD syndrome. Studies in the scientific literature also show a correlation between enuresis and other dysfunctions common to individuals with the

ADD syndrome including temper tantrum or episodic explosiveness [3-6]. In my own study, teenagers with enuresis characteristically have difficulty with coming awake in the morning, going to sleep at night, and dyslexia.

There is a familial pattern to the transmission of bedwetting and evidence for genetic inheritance much as my research experience shows that there is for the ADD syndrome [7]. Enuresis is equally as common in hyperactive ADD males (47%) and ADD females (37%) as it is in ADD males without a history of hyperactivity (47%). Non-hyperactive females have a 22% incidence of enuresis which is not inconsequential, but it is significantly lower than the incidence in females with a history of hyperactivity and in males whether or not they are hyperactive (P=0.002).

One of the best ways to convince bedwetting ADD teenagers to accept medication treatment for ADD is to let them know that one of the expected benefits will be that bedwetting will stop immediately. Even if the family is tolerant and understanding, most teenagers with enuresis live in virtual terror that peers will discover that they are bedwetters and that they will then be teased and called "immature," "a baby," a "freak," or just made to feel "different." They carefully choose activities that will allow them to keep their "secret" and thus many often appear reclusive, withdrawn, standoffish, aloof, or snobbish to their peers. Even if untreated, enuresis almost always spontaneously stops by the age of 18. It rarely continues into adulthood [1].

In teenagers, bedwetting disappears in about 80-90% of those receiving tricyclic antidepressant medication as treatment of their ADD syndrome [2]. Terminating enuresis is medication specific, however. Not every kind of ADD medicine effectively stops bedwetting. A tricyclic antidepressant will stop bedwetting if it can be taken in adequate dosage and even if it is taken along with another type of ADD medication which does not stop bedwetting such as the stimulants, trazodone and Prozac.

When tricyclic medication is withdrawn for any reason, bedwetting reoccurs. Medication is not a cure, but it is a very effective treatment for enuresis while the neurological dysfunction persists.

The popular belief that enuresis is due to teenagers sleeping so soundly that they are unaware of the need to go to the toilet makes little sense. Teenagers treated with tricyclic antidepressants usually sleep more soundly, deeper and more restfully than before treatment and stop bedwetting.

It is important to be sensitive to the psychological stress that a teenager with bedwetting feels. Heaping scorn on such an individual is never helpful since enuresis is not a disturbance that is under conscious control.

Treatment with alarms and other devices which wake the individual from sleep as a reminder to use the toilet are reported to be of help in some cases, but these devices fail to treat the ADD syndrome in general and create dependence on a device that severely restricts the flexibility and mobility of the teenager.

The use of DDAVP, a synthetic analogue of a natural human antidiuretic hormone that affects water conservation in the kidney, also should be discouraged, in my opinion, because this medicine treats none of the other neurological dysfunctions of the ADD syndrome and has an extreme action on kidney function.

Because most physicians and psychologists never ask a teenager during their history taking if bedwetting is a problem, they miss an important clue to the diagnosis of ADD. The fact that almost all teenagers eventually outgrow their enuresis does not diminish the value of a history of bedwetting as a diagnostic clue to the ADD syndrome.

Dyslexia (Verbal and Spatial)

Case Study

Rebecca used to reverse her b's and d's, p's and q's, and E's and 3's when she first learned to write.

Now she is older and does not make that kind of mistake anymore.

As a teenager, she started to reverse the meaning of some of her spoken phrases and sentences and sometimes used words that meant the opposite of what she was intending to say.

She once created a birthday invitation for her mother that read, "I want to invite me to your birthday party." Her mother has recently been concerned because Rebecca too often uses the wrong name for an object she knows well. Just the other day at the dinner table, she asked for salt but meant pepper.

The most dramatic and comic slip-of-the-tongue mistakes involve garbling words, for example, 'gumblebee' for bumblebee."

Rebecca insists that she makes these mistakes when her mind "is going too fast" or she is "tired."

Dyslexia is a neurological dysfunction in which there is difficulty storing and coding new information as well as cross-referencing and retrieving coded information already stored in memory [8].

Clinically, dyslexia in teenagers specifically means difficulty reading, although there is little agreement among professionals about how much difficulty there must be to justify the diagnosis [9].

Also included within the definition of dyslexia is impairment in the ability to interpret and/or reproduce spatial and verbal relationships. For example, it is common for teenagers with dyslexia to have a problem sequencing (not not remembering) telephone numbers. They also often have left-right discrimination difficulty. When told to turn left, they are likely to turn right. Not uncommonly, there is a tendency to speak using words that reverse the meaning of what is intended and to create word-mixes that are a gibberish synthesis of two words. Bedwetting might be reversed to "wet-bedding." Bumblebee might garbled into "gumblebee." Teenagers who wrote letters of the alphabet in mirror-image reversals when younger usually no long do this as teenagers. But, either by history or current behavior, about 60% of teenagers with ADD have significant dyslexia problems.

Mistakenly, parents and teachers often think of dyslexia as a temporary problem that is part of "normal" childhood development. In fact, it is often assumed by parents and many professionals that teenagers have outgrown being dyslexic when they stop writing letters or numbers in mirror-image reversals even if they still have a problem with number sequencing, left-right discrimination or verbal reversals.

Not only is dyslexia often not identified as an important neurological handicap, it is missed as an important clue to the diagnosis of ADD. In fact, it is commonly categorized as little more than a slip of the mind that usually is funny or worth laughing at. Parents, in particular, are likely to minimize the importance of dyslexia because it does not disrupt the function of the home or family interactions.

Teenage reading difficulty is sometimes not attributed to neurological dysfunction at all but to a lack of interest in reading. This impression is understandable when dyslexic teenagers complain that reading is "boring" yet not difficult to do. The issue is even more confusing when ADD teenagers with dyslexia have difficulty reading only school-related or academic material but not stories of keen interest such as are found in sports magazines, detective books, computer manuals or tales of love.

It is truly an academic crisis when dyslexic teenagers abandon reading entirely. Some stay in school and learn only by relying on the oral presentation of material in the classroom. Others learn by having family members or friends read out loud to them. Many simply fail and leave school permanently.

Medication treatment of ADD can, in some teenagers, virtually totally correct their reading difficulty, but there are some who show little improvement from medication even though their other ADD neurological dysfunctions dramatically lessen. At this point, we still need to rely on hope that new medications will be discovered for treating the ADD syndrome which will effectively correct dyslexia in those whose dyslexia does not responding to current ADD medications.

Teenagers with dyslexia which does not adequately respond to medication treatment should be evaluated by dyslexia specialists.

References

1. **Rittig, S.**, *et al., Adult Enuresis. The Role of Vasopressin and Atrial Natriuretic Peptide.* Scandinavian Journal of Urology & Nephrology Supplementum, 1989. **125**: p. 79-86.
2. **Bhatia, M.S.**, *et al., Enuresis: An Analysis of 82 Cases.* Indian Journal of Medical Sciences, 1990. **44**: p. 337-342.
3. **Anders, T.F. and E.D. Freeman**, ed. *Enuresis.* Basic Handbook of Child Psychiatry, ed. J.D. Noshpitz. Vol. 2. 1979, New York. p. 546-555.
4. **Kanner, L.**, ed. *Enuresis.* Child Psychiatry, ed. L. Kanner. 1971, Charles C. Thomas: Illinois. p. 439-453.
5. **Desouza, A., D.C. Parekh, and D.R. Doongaji**, *Enuresis Nocturnal Analysis of 63 Cases.* Indian Journal of Pediatrics, 1963. **1**: p. 2-8.
6. **Pierce, C.M.**, ed. *Enuresis.* Comprehensive Textbook of Psychiatry, ed. A.R. Kaplan and B.J. Sadock. 1985, Williams & Wilkins Co.: Baltimore. p. 1842-1847.
7. American Psychiatric Association Committee on Nomenclature and Statistics, *Functional Enuresis,* in *Diagnostic and Statistical Manual of Mental Disorders.* 1980, American Psychiatric Association: Washington, D.C. p. 80.
8. **Vellutino, F.R.**, *Dyslexia,* in *Scientific American.* 1987, p. 34-41.
9. **Sawyer, D.J.W.**, *Dyslexia: Introduction to the Special Series.* Journal of Learning Disabilities, 1992. **25**(1): p. 38-39.

7

The Clinical Picture of Attention Deficit Disorder Neurology in Adults

The Ten Areas of Neurological Dysfunction of the ADD Syndrome

1. Inattentiveness, * especially Academic Underachieving
2. Hyperactivity and Fidgetiness *
3. Impulsivity *
4. Falling Asleep With Difficulty
5. Coming Awake Slowly
6. Frequent Irritability and/or Easy Frustration
7. Episodic Explosiveness, Rage or Tantrums
8. Negative Thoughts and Feelings With or Without Focus
9. Primary Nocturnal Enuresis (bedwetting)
10. Dyslexia (Verbal and Spatial)

* Minimal diagnostic criteria according to the *DSM-IV*

Adult ADD is a Recognized Disorder

In 1980, the American Psychiatric Association created the diagnostic category, ADD-RT, for adults with a history of hyperactivity in childhood and persistent inattention and impulsivity in adulthood. By doing so, the American Psychiatric Association confirmed that Attention Deficit Disorder is not just a childhood problem, as had been generally thought, but also a possible cause of dysfunctional behavior in adults.

More than two decades of scientific studies now document the existence of ADD-RT or, as it is commonly called today, Adult ADD. These studies show that hyperactivity [1-8], impulsivity [9-13], and learning disability [2, 7, 11-16], hallmarks of ADD neurology, are observable in many adults with a history of hyperactivity in childhood.

Recently, positron-emission tomography (PET) scan measurements have documented that the brain metabolism of hyperactive adults is different from that of non-hyperactive adults. This laboratory test helps to confirm that the brain of people with hyperactivity is chemically different from that of those without hyperactivity [3].

ADD Often has a Cloudy Clinical Presentation in Adults

The diagnosis of ADD in adults should be based on the same ten neurological dysfunctions that define ADD in children and teenagers. Unlike young people, however, adults rarely have only ADD neurological complaints and their ADD clinical presentation is less straight forward.

By the time they reach adulthood, many of those with ADD neurology are also coping with dysfunctional psychological behaviors which reflect their sometimes desperate efforts to cope with untreated ADD neurology since childhood. Because most Adult ADD people were never diagnosed with ADD in childhood, they usually do not recognize behaviors which are due to their ADD neurology. Instead, they interpret whatever personal and social coping problems they now experience as obviously psychological in origin. The possibility that they have Adult Attention Deficit Disorder is not likely to have even entered their minds.

Moreover, by the time adults feel a need to seek help, their psychological disturbances are often so severe that they dominate the clinical presentation and the ADD neurological dysfunctions hardly feel like "problems" at all by comparison. Even health professionals usually do not identify underlying ADD neurology as an important causative clinical factor in adults who present with intense psychological distress. For example, the ADD adult is likely to be diagnosed as having depression, antisocial behavior, an anxiety disorder, panic syndrome, agoraphobia, socioeconomic maladjustment, addiction to illicit drugs, criminality, intermittent violence, oppositional behavior, conduct disorder or alcoholism with no effort to look for ADD neurology.

The psychological impact of growing up with untreated ADD can be enormous, and the time needed for mental healing even with the help of ADD medication treatment can be long. Illustrating this point is the following letter written by a patient describing how he relied on psychotherapy for many years before becoming aware that many of his problems were related to ADD neurological dysfunction. Medication did dramatically diminish or eliminate his ADD neurological dysfunctions and help him deal more effectively with personal problems that he had previously considered psychological in origin.

But, his psychological problems did not totally vanish with medication treatment. They continued to interfere with his everyday life although in a less intense and disabling manner. To help him cope, he continued to turn to psychotherapy from time to time. As you read the following "testimonial," try to distinguish between the ADD neurological dysfunctions described and his dysfunctional thoughts and actions which are psychological or learned in nature.

Letter

"My testimonial about ADD may enlighten the skeptic who is deliberating about beginning treatment for ADD. My approach to this decision was carefully planned and well informed.

After nearly one year of treatment, I consider myself a convinced skeptic, though it took a lot of hard work and a leap of faith for me to become convinced. The hard work involved my effort to combine psychotherapeutic and pharmaceutical treatments in order to change some detrimental behaviors.

The leap of faith occurred when I admitted to myself that what I had tried to do in the past to remedy problematic behaviors had not worked. In the last twenty years I have tried many ideas and programs, like goal setting, to improve my focus, managing stress, and demonstrating a positive attitude. Yet no approach has been effective in managing my behavior *under stressful conditions.*

Nine months ago, I was enlighten to learn that my behaviors may be explained by ADD. Treatment for ADD has benefited my interest in achieving two paramount goals in my life: maintaining my peak productivity and experiencing self-love and inner peace.

These goals have eluded me for many years. Since childhood, I have demonstrated behavioral tendencies that were problematic to my parents and my teachers. My energy would escalate to the point where I would not be able to focus. My quick temper would heighten to the point where I would become explosive. My moods would swing with my perceptions beyond happiness to elation, and beyond discouragement to despondence.

These behavioral tendencies have profoundly impacted my life. Though in my childhood I was aware of my hyperactivity, volatility, and moodiness, it was not until my twenties that I became aware of how these tendencies were influencing my direction.

It took some major losses in my twenties to help me realize that these behavioral tendencies were detrimentally influencing my attitude, my perceptions, and my self-esteem. My hyper intensity prevented me from maintaining the focus and self-confidence necessary to accomplish my professional goals. My quick temper undermined my belief in my ability to cope with stressful situations. My mood swings kept me from consistently demonstrating a positive self-image and a commitment to people and ideas I cared about.

Readings in popular self-help books taught me that I could control these detrimental behaviors by my power of choice. So in my twenties and thirties, I chose to channel negative energy into passionate and creative endeavors. I employed the high standards and expectations that were inculcated in me by my parents to push systems and people to grow and improve. My friends and colleagues have perceived my intensity to be an enormous ally, enabling me to both lead and manage many great successes.

I have fostered a love for learning and fitness in the minds of many children. I have completed marathons. I have won sales contests. I have attained academic degrees at excellent schools. I have won the affection of beautiful women. I have raised and nurtured two wonderful children. I have earned a lot of money. I have risen to the peak of my profession in three different careers.

However, my friends and colleagues did not see the other side of these successes. My choice to channel intensity actually increased my tendency to demonstrate destructive behaviors. Behind my intensity lay much personal dissatisfaction and self-degradation. I often felt like an undernourished lion lived inside me somewhere, growling to be fed accomplishments. This lion distracted me from a singular focus. It deprived me of opportunities to feel love and pleasure. It undermined my desire to commit. This lion seemed to provoke me to a level of hyperactivity that caused volatility and moodiness.

Going into my thirties, I found myself feeling burnt out, distracted from my real hopes and desires in life, incredibly impatient, and more dependent upon external stimulants to sustain my interests and high energy.

A nasty divorce prompted me to seek psychotherapeutic help. The divorce clearly illustrated the impact of my destructive behaviors and forced me into survival mode. I began working with a renown psychiatrist expecting that I could dissipate the detrimental effects of my intensity by understanding their root cause. I believed that my problematic behaviors were rooted in my dysfunctional relationship with my parents and my tendency to link achievements with self-worth, and caring with responsibility.

Yet this psychiatrist's intervention strategy has not been so focused on understanding my past issues as it has on maintaining awareness of my present habits of mind. We have worked on my ability to recognize where my attention gravitates, and how my attention directs my behaviors and attitudes. I have learned that by controlling where I place my attention, I can control my tendencies toward hyperactivity, volatility and moodiness.

For example, while working on a project, my attention may gravitate toward a habit of mind, the obsession for perfection that was inculcated in me by my mother. This habit of mind will typically drive me to a level of intensity that can either be constructive or destructive depending upon my original intent when I began working on the project. So I may embrace the intensity and demonstrate increased enthusiasm and commitment in the project, or I may resent the intensity and demonstrate anger and discouragement about having to work harder or longer on the project that I originally intended. When I become aware that this habit of mind is driving me, I can make decisions that more truthfully represent my best interests.

I have learned to manage intensity by maintaining awareness about its effects on my energy. Regularly, I practice tracing my energy to where my attention lies. I do exercises that enable me to breathe, relax and become aware of my intensity so that I can focus on my habits of mind. Alternatively, I have learned that the lion inside me influences me most when I have not made conscious decisions about where to place my attention.

It is so subtle a distinction that motivates my actions, between my true intent and my habits of mind, that I find it necessary to maintain a line of self-talk to ensure I am thinking and behaving in ways that benefit my best interests and well being.

This intervention strategy has been successful to a point. I have also learned that my habits of mind are so strong and subconsciously driven that I am not always able to notice where my attention focuses. There are times when I have to work very hard to recognize that some perception about myself is negatively influencing my actions. For example, my tendency to idealize often interferes with my perception of what I can and cannot change.

Under stressful circumstances, I find myself most subservient to such habits of mind as idealizing. I can still react explosively to anything that gets in the way of my image of the ideal. For example, working to meet a deadline, I can escalate my activity to such intensity that the slightest obstacle will 'tick' me off: I'll kick the lawn mower that won't start, or swear at clippers that aren't sharp enough to cut efficiently. When I'm committed to be somewhere on time, I'll vent on some faceless car that appears to be holding up traffic, or self-righteously berate "management" for the line I have to stand in.

My inability to control my intensity during instances of high stress has frustrated me. At these times, it feels like the lion inside me is out of control. I become volatile and unpredictable. When the stress stretches over many days or weeks, I won't be able to focus on one task. I become jumpy and restless. I won't sleep well. I'll be up one day and down the next.

These are times when my treatment for ADD has been most helpful. It has evened out my intensity, enabling me to be more consistent in my behaviors and attitudes. I feel less driven and more in control of my decisions. I am also better able to manage my employees using coaching rather than driving techniques to motivate their most productive efforts.

More importantly, the treatment of ADD has enabled me to employ the way of thinking that I have learned through psychotherapy. I am better able to mediate in the midst of stress about where my attention lies. I am able to quiet the lion that feeds on my intensity.

When I deliberated about beginning ADD treatment, I asked my psychiatrist to indicate to me any behavioral changes he observed. On several occasions since, he has noted that I appear more calm even in the midst of discussing some difficult issues with him. He has also indicated that my responses to some stressful situations I've described has improved. This feedback makes me feel confident that I am on my way toward achieving my goals in life. I am getting feedback that I am consistently performing at peak productivity and I am more often experiencing self-love and inner peace."

* * * *

Perhaps the most obvious message from this letter is that when psychological dysfunctions do not diminish after weeks or months of psychotherapy, the co-presence of ADD neurological dysfunction must be suspected.

What are some of the psychological dysfunctions (often called mental disorders) that health professionals usually treat only with psychotherapy but which, in fact, should raise strong suspicion that ADD neurology is a contributing factor and ADD medication is needed?

Agoraphobia	Dystonia Musculorum
Alcoholism	Deformans
Anorexia Nervosa	Episodic Explosive Syndrome
Bulimia	Hyperventilation Syndrome
Chronic Pain Syndrome	Reactive Hypoglycemia
Chronic Fatigue Syndrome	Hysteria
Compulsive Eating	Panic Syndrome
Compulsive Gambling	Sexual Promiscuity
Depression	Suicidal Ideation
Drug Dependence	Tourette's Syndrome
	Workaholic Behavior

In people with serious, persistent psychological dysfunction, both neurological and psychological problems are likely to coexist. A program for diagnosing and treating ADD adults should include (1) a proper medical evaluation, (2) assessment of the kinds of dysfunctions present and their severity, and (3) carefully designed psychotherapeutic interventions if indicated and acceptable to the adult.

Treatment should always include medication for correcting ADD neurological dysfunctions that are present. And, when necessary, ADD adults should be referred for individual and/or group psychotherapy to eliminate dysfunctional, learned behaviors, facilitate the development of needed new behaviors, and reinforce of existing healthy behaviors.

To ensure that ADD adults can cooperate effectively with physicians, they need to be thoroughly familiar with which of the ten areas of neurological dysfunction of ADD they are dealing. With such knowledge, adults are more able to cooperate with their own treatment program and understand what medication is supposed to do and not do. As a corollary, health professions will be maximally effective only if they, too, have this knowledge of their patients.

The following detailed descriptions of how the ten major neurological dysfunctions of ADD present in adults can be understood by both professionals and nonprofessionals. Because ADD is only a clinical syndrome, the clinical findings should be no more confusing than those of the common cold or chickenpox.

Academic Underachieving and Inattentiveness

Case Study

Larry was born with a lot of brain power! He appeared to have no problem getting good grades in secondary school, just a hard time getting along socially with his family and peers.

Later, during his college days, he found that his parents and sister critical and unaccepting of him . . . including the subjects he chose to study and the personal friends he chummed with. In spite of his emotional turmoil, he earned all A's and graduated summa cum laude.

He saw very little of his family when he was in graduate school but noticed that he now often had troublesome interactions with classmates and his professors. Academic performance continued to be outstanding.

Larry felt that he needed to make changes in how he related to other people and felt about himself. He decided to seek the help of a psychoanalyst to feel more comfortable with himself and others and to reduce his unexplained anger and negativity toward others. Psychoanalysis was personally interesting and demanding but minimally helpful for achieving the behavioral and mental changes he desired.

His first job after graduation was teaching at a major university. Classes sometimes started at eight in the morning, a time when Larry had difficulty feeling awake and interested in teaching. His negativity affected his attitude toward his students whom he felt were intellectually less inadequate academic progress and their slow than he wanted.

In spite of psychoanalysis, Larry was not able to be organized enough to buy a computer and get started writing the books he had outlined in his head. Life was frustrating and irritating, and important tasks were not being completed. Could his failure to follow through with projects reflect "inattentiveness?" Was it possible that he was "underachieving" in spite of his considerable innate intelligence?

At the suggestion of a friend, Larry decided to explore the possibility that he had Attention Deficit Disorder. Could ADD could be the underlying cause both of his emotional difficulties and his current academic inattentiveness?

Treatment with ADD medication answered the question. Larry was amazed! Just after starting medication, he purchased a computer, learned how to use it, and began writing the books he had outlined in his head. He started to do what he said he wanted to do. He also changed emotionally. He grew more mellow and tolerant of others. He even came to accept that he needed to put more effort into relating to the members of his family, pay less attention to his own wants and desires, and be more accepting of hard-working students who were doing the best they could.

Larry continued his ADD medication and, at the end of six years, had finished his fifth book. Teaching had become a pleasure. His interaction with students and fellow teachers had become a source of joy. He was now feeling emotionally positive most of the time.

For the first time in his life, he was performing at what was probably his full academic and emotional potential.

Inattentiveness or, more specifically, academic inattentiveness and underachieving, the hallmark of ADD in children and teenagers, is generally not an obvious aspect of the clinical presentation of ADD adults. In fact, uncovering a history of academic underachievement in ADD adults is sometimes difficult because acknowledging the existence of this kind of problem heightens feelings of inadequacy and failure they may already exist. And, of course, there usually are no teachers calling home to complain of inadequate school performance because most ADD adults are no longer in school.

When asked about their past study experience, ADD adults tend to recall only the successes of their academic struggles and not the hardships. Those who were able to complete college and, in some instances, graduate school in business, law, medicine or engineering may have worked harder than others for their grades, but they reached their goal and graduated. They would clearly not have been identified as having ADD because of low grades.

Many ADD adults who had trouble academically when young often deny that they had been inattentive. Rather, they are likely to blame environmental factors for their underachieving. Some blame the school for being boring, the teachers for teaching poorly, or the books for being poorly written, badly selected and not interesting enough to read. Others say that social and financial pressures were unavoidable environmental factors which interfered with their ability to become interested in various academic pursuits and limited the time that they had to study.

Difficulty performing academically often does not stand out as an obvious problem especially in those ADD adults who ultimately chose work which requires little reading or study. One of my patients, for example, entered the heat-ducting business rather than becoming an electrical engineer to avoid an occupation that he anticipated would demand voluminous reading and study. "I took a job which did not make my head spin or require too much thinking," he once quietly told me.

In some cases, adults with ADD forgot that they underachieved academically as young people until they became involved in adult education courses at the local junior college or a company sponsored education program taken for job advancement. For many adults, it requires experiences of this kind to awaken memories of just how hard formal schooling used to be and to confirm that environmental factors were not, in fact, the major reason for their academic underachievement in the past.

A past history of academic underachievement does not necessarily mean that the same ADD adults will perform poorly in formal school situations as adults. If "turned on" or emotionally excited and feeling challenged, many ADD adults can complete assignments and tasks with almost dramatic ease. They become highly functional because what they are now doing is exciting and "not boring." When the educational process is stimulating, courses have clear and relevant goals, the benefit of study is an obvious path to a potentially lucrative future, and the subject matter is personally rewarding for whatever reason, intelligent ADD adults usually perform with unusual competence. In ADD terminology, they are responding to a high-adventure situation.

Determining if inattention or academic inattentiveness in ADD adults is a neurological dysfunction can be difficult. To do so often requires careful questioning about the academic present and past, and, in some cases, reviewing records of past school performances.

Hyperactivity and Fidgetiness

Case Study

Ralph Jones was a very successful engineer. He supervised the structural engineering that was done for several large office buildings in San Francisco.

His wife did not have ADD, and she did not know that the syndrome existed until recently. What she had known for a long time, however, was that her husband had a strange habit of rhythmically shaking one leg or another when he was bored or under stress.

She had learned that she could lightly tap his knees with her hand and the shaking would stop. She never understood why her very successful husband had this strange "habit."

Mr. Jones seemed to pay little attention to his own leg shaking, that is, until one night when he was at a dinner meeting with other engineers in an elegant restaurant at the top of a major city hotel. Oblivious to his boredom, sitting quietly with his wife, listening and watching the events of the evening, Mr. Jones was suddenly shocked into awareness of his fidgetiness.

A waitress rushed over to the tables where the engineers were gathered and tried to comfort them in the sweetest voice she had.

"I am sure you all realize that there is a minor earthquake going on right now. But, don't worry, this building is strong and safe," she said.

Her announcement was abruptly followed by the "end of the earthquake." The floor stopped shaking because Mrs. Jones had just tapped on her husband's knees and his legs stopped vibrating.

Hyperactivity and fidgetiness refer to the same ADD neurological dysfunction. Both are strong clues to the diagnosis of the ADD syndrome. These terms differ only with respect to the intensity of the body movement each describes.

While very uncommon, ADD adults can be as active as hyperactive children and manifest body movement that is of similar intensity and persistence. These "Dennis The Menace" adults are, needless to say, very dramatic to see. While they do not jump on kitchen counters or race up and down halls as hyperactive children are likely to do, they otherwise clearly look like oversize hyperactive kids in almost constant motion. Their arms often flail about. They might sit for moments, only to then stand, and then sit down again ... and repeat the process a multitude of times. They typically shuffle from one foot to another when standing, talk rapidly and incessantly, sometimes scratch various parts of their body as if they had a nervous habit, and constantly nod when listening to others talk.

Similar as it may seem to the casual observer, hyperactive behavior is not the same as that of an agitated or "nervous" person whose body movements are usually disorganized and random in nature nor of a person with palsy and tremor. Moreover, when distracted by talk or interesting events, the hyperactive behavior usually abruptly stops although often not for long. In fact, if asked to be still and not move, hyperactive adults may try to do so but usually succeed only for brief periods of time.

In most cases, ADD adults appear fidgety rather than hyperactive. The most common, obvious expression of their fidgetiness is the rhythmic shaking of the feet or legs. Leg-shaking often starts after one leg is crossed over the other or when the instep of a foot rests on the rung of a chair. The rhythmical movement is without obvious purpose or usefulness and can be so persistent and vigorous that others in the room will feel the floor vibrate.

Fidgetiness can be expressed as movement of other parts of the body than just the legs and feet. For example, finger tapping and head-nodding is also common. Unless criticized, most ADD adults are minimally conscious of being fidgety and often feel that their repetitive body movements are as "natural," self-pleasing and relaxing as are those of breathing.

Fidgetiness and overt hyperactivity are responses to stress such as troubled feelings, thinking about upsetting issues, boredom, or performance anxiety. This ADD dysfunction is commonly evident when ADD adults are in a variety of situations: a school classroom; a college lecture hall; the waiting room of a hospital; a bus station; an airport; also, during periods of test-taking and interviews, when listening to an unexciting concert or boring speakers at a meeting, and when trying to pass the time by making small-talk in a restaurant.

To help establish the diagnosis of ADD in adults who are no longer hyperactive or fidgety, it is important to know if either of these ADD characteristics had been present at an earlier age. Simply asking adults about this may not be fruitful because they generally do not remember if they had been hyperactive or fidgety when young unless they had been criticized, scolded or punished for it at the time. Many hyperactive children appear to parents and teachers as only normally "active" or "vigorous," and adults who had never been punished for being hyperactive or fidgety when young are likely to deny this ever was a problem.

Those who remember being hyperactive when young were almost always scolded by their teachers, parents or friends for excessively moving or talking in situations where they should have been calm and quiet. Difficulty sitting still and inappropriately talking is easily recognized in the classroom setting. It is often helpful, therefore, to question an adult about being in "trouble" with teachers for this when in primary or secondary school.

Occasionally, fidgety ADD adults refuse to accept that they are fidgety because they consider the term itself to be harsh for a behavior they have grown accustomed to living with. After a while, fidgetiness can feel no more "strange" or "unnatural" than eating does when one is hungry. The published criteria of Dr. Paul Wender for retrospectively establishing the diagnosis of hyperactivity in childhood using questionnaires and information from parents are excellent. Unfortunately, these criteria cannot always be satisfied in a private medical practice setting [2, 19].

Tics Including Tourette's Syndrome

ADD hyperactivity and fidgetiness may be expressed as motor tics of various parts of the body including verbal tics which are diagnostic of Tourette's syndrome.

In adults, just as in ADD children and teenagers, motor tics are involuntary movements that range from sudden, rapid, brief, jerking motions to muscle movements that are slower and more like stretching than jerking. They commonly take the form of blinking, grimacing, horizontal head movements, intermittent protrusion of the tongue, jerking motions of the arms or legs. These movements also may include repeated licking the lips, raising and lowering of the eyebrows or glancing up and out as if accessing thoughts.

Verbal tics are really a type of motor tic which has achieved a heightened degree of notoriety because of the social disruption and disturbance it usually causes. This is especially true when verbal tics include inappropriate and/or offensive language. They may also be any repetitious vocal noises that do not represent a recognizable word including throat clearing, grunting, snorting, squeaking, sniffing, coughing, humming, barking and spitting.

Like hyperactivity and fidgetiness, tics are episodic, inappropriate, ritualistic in nature, and not goal-directed. They occur in response to boredom, tiredness and emotional discomfort, and they may be activated by embarrassing and stressful questions or other uncomfortable environmental factors.

In rare circumstances, motor tics are limited to a slow, firm, sustained contraction of a single group of muscles which lasts for many minutes to hours and results in distortion of body posture. This type of tic is called dystonia musculorum deformans. The contractions cause grotesque posturing of various parts of the body although they most commonly affect the head and neck muscles.

Motor tics, verbal tics and dystonia musculorum deformans should serve as clues to the diagnosis of the ADD syndrome. Individuals with tics have a spectrum of ADD neurological dysfunctions which is similar to ADD individuals without tics.

Tics diminish in frequency and intensity over time, and sometimes disappear entirely, with proper ADD medication treatment. Because social isolation and diminished self-esteem may result, not infrequently psychotherapy is very helpful along with ADD medication treatment for those with tics.

Treatment of dystonia musculorum deformans with botulinum toxic is recommended by some medical specialists. This treatment approach can result in reduction in muscle spasms, but it does not reduce the other neurological dysfunctions of the ADD syndrome and should be a treatment of last resort if ADD neurology is present [20].

Impulsivity

Case Study

"He never listens! Even when I corner him in the bedroom where he has only me and no other distractions, even if I am crying and telling him how sad and frustrated I am,

my husband never seems to listen to me. He acts as if he does not care about how I feel," John's wife, Marilyn, sobbed to her psychotherapist.

"But you've been married over seventeen years. Has it always been like this?" the psychotherapist asked.

"There are many times when John is wonderful," Marilyn continued. "He works hard to support the family, sometimes struggling excessively to keep his business organized and efficient. He often comes home tired but at least he always comes home at night to the children and me."

"He acts likes he does not care about me only when I am upset and demand his undivided attention."

"His explanation is that his mind is so full of racing thoughts that he cannot stay on track, cannot focus on what I have to say for more than moments, and sometimes does not even hear me because he has drifted off in his thinking while trying to listen to me."

"He is very intelligent," Marilyn continued, "How can he be so mentally scattered? It is as though his mind were hyperactive. Is this what impulsivity really means?"

Impulsivity can be a disastrous ADD dysfunction, and it is often the main reason ADD adults seek medication treatment.

Impulsive adults have difficulty completing tasks that have become boring to do and are not urgent to finish. Juggling what feels like ten, a hundred, or even a thousand thoughts at almost the same moment, and not able to reflect on any one thought for very long before the mind moves on to other thoughts, impulsive adults have difficulty listening patiently to others and bringing projects to closure.

The mind of an ADD adults "races" even when there are minimal external stimuli, and a flood of new thoughts serves as distractions for present and past thoughts. They have a "listening" problem, not a problem hearing noises and sounds.

They get into trouble in three major ways. First, they have difficulty staying on task when the chore is not extremely interesting and exciting, and that often applies to listening to others talk. Second, impulsive adults may interrupt others or blurt out comments for fear that if they do not do so immediately, their mind will move on to other thoughts and they will forget what they had wanted to say. Third, with the social and economic freedom to act as they want, impulsive adults are prone to following immediate urges to feel good and escape from pain without substantial regard for the long-term consequences of their actions.

Impulsivity in some ADD adults is a key factor promoting compulsions and addictions such as drug and alcohol abuse, compulsive gambling, binge eating and bulimia. The excitement and high adventure of the moment is enticingly attractive, and the impulsive mind is too much on the go to pause and think about long-term consequences.

"Just one more beer," the alcoholic mumbles when he is already more drunk than he should be. And, what about the impulsive adult who promised to avoid cocaine "for ever more," a promise that falls apart as soon as the drug dealer shows up on the block or cocaine becomes available at the party. Notice how compulsive gamblers who, just seeing the entrance to the gambling hall, forget their resolve, enter, and stay until they lose all the money they have on their person, and sometimes more. Peek into the life of a bulimic adult who repeatedly promises to never again binge and vomit but, feeling depressed by the loneliness of the night, succumbs again to bingeing and purging. Think about your friend who just bought two more pairs of earrings she does not need and cannot afford to pay for? Reflect on why chocolate and candy are often next to the checkout line at the supermarket where many people commonly become irritable waiting for service and act impulsively.

Impulsivity is commonly a first step toward the destruction of interpersonal relationships because of the broken promises, addictions, extramarital affairs, inappropriate behaviors at work, and an inability to be patient, listen and respond even to urgent messages from others.

Almost all adults are occasionally impulsive to some degree, but ADD adults are often impulsive to an extreme degree unless treated with ADD medication.

Falling Asleep at Night with Difficulty

Case Study

(From a letter written by a patient)

"When I lie down to sleep, there is always noise. As soon as my head hits the pillow, a dog barks, an airplane flies over head, neighbors start talking in the street, or my kids turn on music. Sometimes I dose off for a brief moment, then wake up again. Most often, I lie there in bed for hours, too tired to get up and too awake to fall asleep.

"I am only thirty-seven. It feels as though I have not slept more than a wink my whole life. As soon as I drop into bed, problems start floating through my mind. Solutions to troublesome issues keep popping into my head. Instead of falling asleep, I carefully find answers which unfortunately feel worthless the following morning.

"I dread even thinking of going to bed. The very process of trying to fall asleep almost does not seem worth the effort. Staying up and doing almost anything often is more appealing. I wish my hypnotic sleep-tapes were more helpful!"

Falling asleep slowly is an almost nightly problem in 71% of adults with ADD. The term "slowly" is, of course, a relative term. Generally, slowly means that an individual will spend at least a half an hour and sometimes several hours lying in bed trying to fall asleep before actually going to sleep.

Whatever "slowly" actually turns out to mean, it indicates an uncomfortably long period of time for the person in question. Included in this troublesome sleep category are those who fall asleep rapidly but almost immediately come awake again and stay awake for long periods of time such as one to three hours before returning again to sleep for the night.

Clinically, falling asleep slowly is analogous to those other ADD dysfunctions characterized by difficulty in "letting go" of the present and moving into another state of being. ADD adults commonly "hold on" to anger and negative emotions. Most do not wake easily in the morning as if "holding on" to being asleep. Difficulty "letting go" often includes even ideas about ways of doing things, old books, old clothes and hurt feelings.

Self-treatment approaches are sometimes helpful and are usually not harmful. Eating a small late-at-night snack, having a warm drink before bed, reading or listening to music in bed, engaging in intense physical activity each day, and being sexual before trying to go to sleep are common remedies that often reduce the time it takes for ADD adults to fall asleep.

Unfortunately, a number of solutions for inducing sleep do have adverse consequences. Over-the-counter sleep-inducing remedies such as antihistamines and prescription sleeping pills often bring on sleep easily but leave individuals groggy for at least part of the following day. Alcohol and illicit drugs such as marihuana promote sleep but can easily evolve into addictions.

One of the most commonly used self-treatment approaches for adults is to stay up until fatigue is overwhelming and sleep follows quickly on retiring.

Falling asleep slowly is often missed as a clue to ADD neurology if ADD adults have become resigned to this recurrent, nocturnal battle and do not view it as a "problem." Some think it is a normal behavior for them because of "who they are" (whatever that means).

Difficulty falling asleep should not be confused with waking for long periods of time in the middle of the night, a behavior that is usually caused by severe stress from viral illness, intense worry, ambivalent feelings or unresolved emotional conflict.

Waking briefly in the during the night to go to the bathroom or to change one's sleeping position should not be equated with difficulty falling asleep. Middle-of-the-night waking may be a complaint of an ADD adult, but it is not a specific clue to ADD neurology.

ADD treatment with the proper medication greatly improves the control that ADD adults have over their ability to fall asleep at night when they feel tire and choose to retire.

Coming Awake Slowly

Case Study

Michael changed jobs four times this year alone. In each instance, the boss had to fire him because he repeated failed to show up for work on time.

It is difficult for Michael to tell others, even his former bosses, that he pounds on the snooze button, usually three or four times on the mornings that he is supposed to go to work. Coming awake has always been a slow process for Michael. Recently, he learned not to hammer away at the snooze button. Instead, he now literally rolls off the bed onto the floor and, with all the energy he can muster, forces himself awake by struggling to a standing position much like a camel, first rising onto the knees, then the elbows, and finally up into a standing position.

He is still not fully awake, but Michael is at least moving. Once in the bathroom, after dabs of cold water on his face, a shower and two cups of coffee, he is ready to leave for his new job and be there on time.

Coming awake slowly is a neurological dysfunction that affects 88% of ADD adults. It is a biological process that can be dramatically influenced by environmental factors and, hence, appears to be a consequence of laziness or lack of motivation. If the house were on fire, a child hurt and in need of immediate attention, or an intruder was threatening the spouse, waking would be immediate. Unfortunately, for many ADD adults, the average morning does not start with a dramatic challenge or offer what is considered high adventure.

Coming awake slowly is a handicap which specifically means difficulty "waking up" rather than "getting up" or getting out of bed. Most ADD adults do get out of bed in the morning. But, when they first try to open their eyes or reach for the snooze button on the alarm clock, they find it very difficult to let go of being asleep. Because of the economic reality and family demands of adult living, most ADD adults muster the energy to do something that forces them to wake up. It is not uncommon for some to stagger around half asleep for five, ten, or twenty minutes before feeling awake. Those who do not force themselves awake are generally in serious trouble economically and socially in terms of providing ordinary comforts for their families and holding their marriages together.

Some ADD adults make very intense efforts to wake up in the morning and think that this kind of struggle is simply "normal." When initially asked if they wake with difficulty, they often say no. It is always rewarding to me to hear these same adults report with great surprise and a lot of glee that ADD medication treatment made them aware of a dramatic, almost startling improvement in the speed with which they come awake and feel alert.

There is an important subgroup of ADD men and women who are exceptions and for whom waking is generally not a problem. They are "workaholics," individuals who spend most of their waking hours doing projects which are related to their jobs, chores around the house and other activities which they find especially challenging. They have a hard time sitting quietly and patiently waiting for an appointment, watching the ocean waves, or being caught in traffic.

On the other hand, they are likely to enjoy being at a picnic if they can be active in a game or other physical activity, being at home if they have projects such as modifying the automobile engine or adding a new room to the house, painting, or in some cases shopping. They are alert, energetic and interested in the world as long as they are involved in projects or work-related tasks.

Whether men or women, as long as they are wrestling with new ideas, promoting events, perfecting products, or involved in other types of adventure, they stay awake. Workaholic ADD adults act with urgency and vigor as if they are "driven" by tasks that they enjoy. They almost always wake up without difficulty.

When it is time to stop working or the challenge of the task is gone, workaholics very suddenly feel overwhelmed with fatigue, sometimes irritable, and too tired to stay awake any longer.

These ADD adults often express the "need," "excitement," and "importance" of waking and getting on with their "projects," "work," "schooling" or whatever constitutes what they believe are essential, "chosen duties" for the day. They appear to be driven by a need for personal recognition, money or fame, or so it seems. But, more importantly, having this kind of drive makes them feel good, alert and functional even in the early morning.

Workaholic women, in particular, may or may not be in the formal workplace. Many are driven intensely toward child rearing and maintaining the household, while some choose to work intensely outside the home and are virtually indistinguishable from workaholic men.

Both workaholic men and women, like other ADD individuals, usually come awake slowly on non-work, non-project days, assuming they allow themselves to have such days.

When severely debilitated from an injury or illness that leaves them for weeks or months unable to go to work or perform work-related tasks, some workaholic ADD adults develop what is called the "Chronic Fatigue Syndrome." This syndrome is not a mysterious disorder of viral origin that is untreatable, contrary to current myth. It is merely how workaholic ADD individuals experience life when they no longer feel charged during the day or "have to get up" to get "essential" projects completed.

The price they pay for learning that their work is not "essential" and that the world will go on without them if they are disabled for a while is waking slowly and feel lots of overwhelming daytime fatigue, much like what "ordinary" ADD individuals usually experience most of their lives. Because of their period of incapacity, they discover that what they had been doing was not essential for their survival in the world. They also discover that they are not horrible and ineffective people just because they do not completed a variety of "goal-oriented" deeds each day. Now, not driven, they wake slowly and feel enervated at various times of the day, dysfunctions common to almost all ADD individuals. They often seek peer support and medical help because their chronic, severe, lack of drive and energy which prevents them from returning to their previous activities including work.

ADD individuals who develop what is called the "Chronic Fatigue Syndrome" are clinically confusing to professionals because these patients insist that they were "just fine" and "without problems" prior to the onset of their chronic fatigue. In reality, however, a careful history will show that they have the same frequency of ADD neurological dysfunctions as other groups of ADD individuals except for the incidence of coming awake slowly in the morning.

Finally, there are a group of ADD adults who hold the belief that "not getting enough sleep" is the cause of their chronic morning tiredness. This cause and effect explanation is rarely true. Many adults with and without ADD sleep for long periods of time at night yet wake tired in the morning, especially if they have an illness such as a viral infection. At other times, adults with and without ADD can sleep for only a few hours and wake easily if very excited about the anticipated events of the coming day. ADD adults, like younger people with ADD, wake easily in the morning if they anticipate a high adventure activity, excitement, or a thrilling experience. The functions of falling asleep and waking are separate clues to ADD neurology and are independent of each other.

Coming awake slowly is one of the first ADD dysfunctions to be corrected with the use of proper medication. ADD adults without the so-called "Chronic Fatigue Syndrome" who come awake slowly in the morning as well as those with the syndrome become normal shortly after the start of proper medication treatment and, in my experience, are able to return to previous activities, including work.

Frequent Irritability and/or Easy Frustration

Case Study

Mr. Jim McDonald runs his own insurance agency. He is the father of two young boys and an older twelve year old girl. Business has been good and the family usually takes three vacations a year. But, traveling with his wife and the three kids is always stressful.

Whether the family travels by car or airplane, the two boys never stop fighting with each other, that is, unless they decide to pick on their sister.

Father does not hesitate to scold mother for not having more control of these situations. He also repeatedly threatens to end each vacation prematurely unless the boys stop fighting. He spends a lot of each day grumbling that the family ought to go back home and never go on vacation together again.

Father would like not to think about it, but he has as much difficulty being mellow as do the boys. Mother also is starting to believe that family travel is not worth the struggle even though she loves her family and feels they should be together on vacations.

Father is aware that he feels more peaceful when he is "left alone." The noise and commotion caused by others, even family members, is annoying, rattling and unsettling. He is aware of his tendency to be impatient, frequently irritable, and often frustrated by the very people he cares the most about, his family.

He is also aware of problems dealing with some of the people at work who also often annoy him for uncertain reasons. These people do not constantly argue with him, but they annoy him anyway. As much as he tries, he is not very successful at hiding his chronic irritability which is obvious to family members as well as most of the people he works closely with.

Adults with ADD are more likely to say that they are "irritable" rather than "easily frustrated" although some believe that both expressions accurately describe their emotional makeup. Other terms sometimes used by irritable adults to describe how they feel a lot of the time are: "shaky inside," "emotionally labile," "ill-tempered," "short-fused," "moody," "critical," "emotionally up and down," "grouchy," "crabby," "cranky," even "bitchy."

What does irritable mean? ADD adults, like young people, typically complain that "everything bothers me." They realize that even trivial stimuli, such as other people jiggling their legs, tapping with their hands, putting them on telephone hold, and the like, is very irritating and upsetting. Unfortunately, they are more likely to be irritable with people who are emotionally close to them such as their spouse, their children or associates at work than strangers.

In my experience, ADD women have more awareness of their feelings of irritable and easily frustrated than do ADD men. This may be so because women are more in touch with their feelings than men, or it may be that the consequences of feeling irritable cause more discomfort for women who have fewer socially acceptable avenues for acting-out in our society. Feeling irritable and easily frustrated is one of the major reasons why women seek treatment for their ADD neurology.

Regardless of sex, ADD adults who lack insight into their emotions are likely to blame the outside world for their irritability. Even those without pathological paranoia feel that they would be different if others did not provoke them. These individuals are reluctant to accept the diagnosis of ADD or agree to medication treatment because they believe that their environment needs to change more than they do. "If only the lawn mower hadn't broken down, I would not have become irritable." While I was examining her husband, a wife recently tried to illustrate how easily he became intensely irritable. "But honey, don't you remember trying to fix the broken lawn mower last week by pounding it with a sledge hammer?"

In our society, irritability is often considered by men as a natural and expected expression of maleness or machismo. Unpleasant and offensive as it may be, irritable acts often enhance a man's self-image of his virility and ability to be aggressive.

Fortunately, many ADD adults are able to realize that constantly feeling irritable has negative consequences. They become aware that they cannot relax even when it is appropriate to do so, at the beach, while listening to music, or when home with the family. They learn that it is they who suffer the most when they overreact to drivers who cut in front of them on the highway or become angry when a child accidentally spills food. They notice that relationships suffer when others interpret their irritable behavior as a lack of caring, affection or respect. The effect on others of irritability often becomes painfully obvious when loved ones begin to withhold affection that they think is not wanted. Children start to react to irritable adults by becoming rebellious or withdrawn. Friends may limit how much they choose to be with an adult who is extremely irritable. As the Adult ADD syndrome becomes better known, it is easier for knowledgeable, irritable, ADD adults to explore the possibility that their brain chemistry, and not just the environment, is a factor contributing to their tendency to feel excessively irritable.

Feeling irritable is a lose-lose situation. Irritable ADD adults usually do not like how they feel any more than they would if they had arthritis and chronic pain. And, because irritable feelings usually are expressed through mannerisms, that is, body language, many irritable ADD adults experience social rejection or are disliked by others even if they are careful about how they express themselves verbally.

In the absence of a modern awareness of the ADD syndrome, many ADD adults seek their own remedies for irritability. High-energy sports such as jogging, running, tennis, racquetball, soccer, basketball and even weight-lifting make it possible for ADD adults to relax and feel mellow for at least brief periods of time. Sexual activity can also have the same benefit. Unfortunately, for too many today, the "quick fix" is alcohol and/or elicit drugs, crutches which frequently turn into addictions.

Proper ADD medication is remarkably helpful in reducing the frequency and intensity of irritability and easy frustration. The result of treatment can be so dramatic that friends, family and fellow workers are likely to notice that a change has taken place. Often, they will comment, for example, on how "relaxed," "mellow," "nice" or "happy" the ADD adult has recently begun to "look," "appear," or "seem."

Episodic Explosiveness or Rage

Case Study

"Why are you here in my medical office?" I asked one patient. "I'm in trouble," he said. "My wife has a court order restraining me from seeing her and my baby girl. I miss both of them."

"They really love me and should see me. The judge said that I can visit my little girl only if I can get rid of my explosiveness."

"What did you do to allow the judge to issue a restraining order?" I asked hoping to learn more about how he behaves when explosive.

The patient tried to be honest. "I did not mean to hit my little girl so hard that she needed to be hospitalized, but she would not stop crying. I became consumed with anger. That was really a stupid thing to do!"

"The judge was especially upset, I think, because this was not the first time I struck her or my wife."

Seventy-seven percent of ADD adults experience episodically explosive behavior [10]. In the medical literature, explosiveness is also referred to as emotional dyscontrol. But, in my opinion, to label intermittent explosiveness as dyscontrol is to inappropriately minimize the intensity of the feelings and actions that adults with this problem experience and their potential for violence.

The DSM-IV recognizes that "emotional outbursts" (not clearly distinguished from episodic explosiveness descriptively) are common in ADD people. This point is often not appreciated adequately by physicians. In particular, many psychiatrists label explosive ADD individuals as suffering from either Conduct Disorder or Oppositional Defiant Disorder, both considered as separate disorders, and both often inappropriately treated with sedating or tranquilizing medications.

Episodic explosiveness, also known as periodic rage, is a common ADD dysfunction that is the adult equivalent of childhood tantrums. It is an intense form of anger that comes on rapidly, progressing to a severe but thank goodness rarely total loss of self-control. It is as if an emotional "button" had been pushed. ADD adults capable of this kind of rage can be "triggered" by internal frustration and anger, especially jealousy and feelings of inadequacy. They also can be enraged by what are in reality minor external events, demands, insults, challenges or failures. The trigger may be little more than something that the ADD person does not like, does not want to hear, or cannot easily cope with at the moment.

The anger generated is appropriately described as rage. Its intensity and associated behaviors clearly exceed the limit of acceptability for society. At its peak, episodic rage typically involves screaming, yelling, or cursing and, all too often, physical acts such as kicking walls, smashing windows, and throwing or breaking valued objects. At its worst, it can include striking and killing animals or people.

Once started, rage peaks in magnitude after seconds to several minutes. If reinforced by others, the release of verbal anger, expressions of hate, and sometimes physically violent behavior can persist for minutes to hours.

Looked at from the point of view of the ADD adult, the only important issue is the release of anger feelings. It is the "form" that the rage takes not the "substance" of what is said or done that the rage is all about. For example, specific accusations or criticisms that are verbalized rarely have a basis in reality. A husband might feel enraged at his wife for whatever, including how she folded or did not fold his laundry, and attack her with a variety of cruel, depreciating, degrading comments. Later, when his rage is gone, it is not unusual for him to be unusually affectionate and expect his wife to be responsive, ignoring what he had said earlier because even he knew it was not really true.

Most adults who become enraged realize, in retrospect, that the events that preceded the onset of rage were amazingly minor. Yet, they often feel almost helpless in preventing future rage. On the one hand, their ADD neurology makes them susceptible to loss of emotional control. On the other hand, without a lot of insight into what is happening at the moment, they succumb to triggers that set them off. Moreover, rage can be provoked by various triggers, and many ADD adults with rage are not sure what new triggers will set them off in the future.

Of course, there are some ADD adults who are aware, for example, that drinking alcohol while watching sports on television is likely to lead to an episode of rage but, sadly, are unwilling to modify or give up even this kind of lifestyle behavior.

Rage can be directed against oneself instead of others. Those who express their rage feelings inwardly not uncommonly inflict emotional and/or physical pain on themselves. Some use needles or other sharp objects to scratch and puncture themselves. Others hit, cut or burn themselves, bang walls with their fist, feet or head, or smash, and destroy their own valued possessions. The ultimate negative consequence of rage turned inward is suicide.

When rage is directed outwardly, typical behaviors include breaking family furniture and house windows, striking out at other people or animals, and driving at breakneck speeds. Violent acts can involve throwing knives, stabbing, choking, beating, slugging, and even shooting and killing other people.

As a benefit of maturity, many ADD adults become able to sense the start of a rage reaction and "walk away" before it becomes intense. Walking away can be, literally, walking out the door and pounding the ground, or it can mean "ignoring" or "not continuing to listen to" the person who is "provoking" them.

The ability to keep rage within tolerable bounds varies not only from person to person but from episode to episode. Some ADD adults always maintain enough restraint to avoid serious injury to others or property damage. Their explosiveness is usually limited to verbal acts such as shouting and screaming or physical acts which do not cause serious damage such as slamming doors, hitting pillows or stamping. A few turn inward and explode into violent crying that lasts until their explosive feelings pass. With maturity, many ADD adults learn to recognize the beginning of rage and defuse the situation by moving away from the adverse stimuli.

Even though the rage of ADD is episodic, it is often so frightening for others to anticipate that it can destroy marital, family, and work relationships. Also, episodic explosiveness can be so violent that some individuals can continue to live in an open society only under legal restraints.

There are other dangers to being episodically explosive. For example, ADD adults with a tendency to rage sometimes choose to work for the military or law enforcement where, for example, given their ADD neurology they function well because the environment is full of high adventure. On the other hand, while they may be competent at many aspects of their work, they are often required to deal with other physically violent people. Having two explosive individuals confronting each other in violent circumstances can lead to disaster. Violent events not infrequently will be magnified and lead to unnecessary brutality. Worse, if the work happens to be unusually dull for a while, ADD individuals are likely to create high adventure, dangerous situations which can endanger others. If they are in the military or law enforcement, they are often equipped with lethal weapons that can be inappropriately used.

Episodic Explosive syndrome often has such severe consequences and is so dramatic that it has attracted the attention and interest of many who are not health professionals. For example, opera buffs are known to refer to protagonists who often rage as experiencing "towering madness." In legal parlance, individuals who are have expressed intense, blind rage and harm to others have been labeled as being "temporarily insane."

Episodically explosive individuals are not a rarity. They are reported on frequently in our society. It is not uncommon for a newspaper article to document the behavior of an estranged husband who, during the process of a divorce, returns home to gun-down his wife, and throw himself and the baby off the bridge into the cold water below. There are reports of an explosive general who apologizes to his fellow officers because of his uncontrolled, abusive behavior and of a President of the United States who screams at his support staff on a routine basis. There is also the article about the mother who became so enraged that she shot and killed a shackled defendant who had been accused of sexually molesting her son. Stories of episodic explosiveness appear almost daily.

The ADD neurological dysfunction, rage, like academic underachieving, impulsivity and hyperactivity, is not related to intelligence or social standing. Those with a higher socioeconomic status, however, usually are less exposed to public scrutiny than individuals of lower socioeconomic status whose violence is more likely to spill into the streets, be in public view, and involve the police and courts. Regardless, society will benefit dramatically when the violence of episodic explosiveness is better recognized as an aspect of the ADD syndrome because it can be dramatically reduced and often virtually abolished by proper ADD medication treatment.

Those who are medicated as children and teenagers usually grow up being minimally, if at all, explosive. Starting medication in childhood is always ideal, but treating adults is also extremely helpful. Rage behavior usually diminishes in intensity immediately but does not virtually disappear for about a year or so. Presumably, there is an important amount of learned behavior involved in how ADD individuals handle anger, and learned behaviors are always slow to disappear compared to behaviors of purely biological origin which can vanish in hours. This is one more reason for stressing the value of initiating medication treatment for ADD at as early an age as is reasonable.

ADD adults with episodic explosiveness may benefit from psychotherapy which is focused on helping them learn new ways to respond to anger and frustration. Undesirable learned behaviors have to be unlearned and new behaviors substituted for the old ones. Ideally, psychotherapy should not be provided in the absence of proper ADD medication which facilitates the process of giving up old and learning new behaviors.

Medication treatment should be continued indefinitely because episodic explosiveness is likely to return if discontinued.

Negative Thoughts and Feelings

Case Study

"I am depressed a lot! My life has not gone well for many years now. I married a guy who is really boring.

Yes, he's an engineer who also flies private planes. He has been faithful to me over many years. And, he has been materially generous with me."

"But he isn't fun to be with. In fact, nothing is fun for me any more."

"The last party I went to will be the last I ever go to. The people were boring. They were not especially interested in me and hardly paid any attention to what I wanted to talk about."

"They discussed their recent trips abroad, their involvement with community projects, the books they just read .... but nothing of interest to me. They did not seem to care whether I was there or not."

To some degree, all adults, whether ADD or not, rethink negative experiences from the past and feel some anxiety about the future. Adults with ADD, however, are considerably more prone to feeling negative, holding on to negative thoughts, dwelling on past negative experiences, almost drowning in negative thoughts, and being depressed.

Most adults experience real life hardships, but ADD adults, because of their brain chemistry, have the additional handicap of being extra prone to feeling negative and magnifying negative experiences. They interpret even ordinary encounters and events in a negative light and typically are apprehensive about the future.

Their environment is often not personally rewarding even when others respond to the same environment in a positive manner. Anger, pain, frustration and feelings of revenge are more likely to develop and persist in the mind of the ADD adult as a consequence of even minor insults or events involving only moderate pain, injury, disagreement, conflict, hardship, failure, discord, discouragement, or hurt. Too often, the consequence of this persistent negativity is long, drawn out court battles over minor matters, vendettas, feuds between families, and unrelenting disagreement about the terms of a divorce.

If the burden of negativity becomes great enough and persists, ADD adults become more than merely discouraged, they lose confidence in the possibility of positive outcomes, feel hopeless, sad, and blue, becoming frankly depressed and staying depressed for long periods of time.

When depressed, they are capable of self-harm and injuring others. Self-mutilation, suicidal gestures, rejection of others, loss of the ability to express love, withdrawal from social activities, work and/or family are common problems that depressed ADD adults face. In the worst-case scenario, successful suicide is a not unexpected consequence of persistent depression, despondency, and melancholy.

Fortunately, most ADD adults are not handicapped by long-term depression. Most can still have positive experiences and let go of negativity enough to have periods of reasonable positivity. They typically describe themselves as only occasionally depressed.

Negativity, whether or not it culminates in depression, normally increases the burden of life for the ADD adult. When behavior and thinking are negative, interactions with others, for example, a boyfriend, girlfriend, parent, spouse, sibling, fellow worker, repair service person, or salesperson, often result in unpleasant and sometimes even painful interpersonal human experiences.

The negativity of ADD adults, when not obviously due to environmental stimuli, is almost certainly a consequence of neurobiological dysfunction in the same way that excessive irritability, impulsivity and episodic explosiveness are. It is also common for

ADD adults to be negative both because of their ADD neurology and the environment they experience around them.

Proper medication treatment of the ADD syndrome, with or without contributing environmental factors, does reverse the propensity toward excessive negativity in ADD adults. Medication can serve critically to improve one's attitude toward life and prevent suicide.

However, in ADD individuals whose ability to function effectively is significantly limited, treatment with both psychotherapy and medication are indicated at least initially. In time, psychotherapy is usually not needed, although medication should be continued permanently.

Primary Nocturnal Enuresis

Case Study

Several years ago, a woman telephoned in while I was the guest speaker on a call-in radio talk show.

"I am upset with your suggestion that Prozac is not specifically an antidepressant medication. Since I have been taking it, my depressed feelings have disappeared and I feel wonderful."

"Let me restate my thoughts about so-called antidepressant medication," I responded.

"Antidepressant medication is really ADD medication, and some people with ADD are not merely negative but actually depressed."

"Is it possible that you have Adult ADD with negativity, that Prozac was of benefit because it corrected your ADD dysfunctions including negativity, and that ADD was the real reason why you became depressed and stayed depressed in the first place?"

"Of course, if ADD was at the root of your depression, you must have other ADD neurological dysfunctions in addition to negativity and depression. For example," I went on to ask, "have you ever had a problem with bedwetting?"

"Well," the woman responded, "I was a bedwetter until the age of twenty-one."

Primary nocturnal enuresis (bedwetting) is extremely uncommon in adult years, but it does occur.

Of course, it is a normal behavior in infancy. Assuming that anatomical abnormality and metabolic dysfunction are absent, however, bedwetting is virtually never present in five year olds unless they have ADD neurology. Therefore, a history of bedwetting in a five year old is a very strong clue to the presence of ADD neurology whether or not the individual outgrows the problem by adulthood.

People outgrow lots of things as they mature including black hair, but it does not mean that what they outgrow does not have clinical significance. Primary nocturnal enuresis is not simply a "developmental" disorder without prognostic meaning which some children outgrow and some do not. Accordingly, adults must always be asked about a history enuresis in childhood if ADD neurology is suspected. Forty-four percent of adults remember that they were bedwetters when they were younger.

Bedwetting is an extremely important clue to the diagnosis of the ADD syndrome. It is not a psychological problem because, by definition, it occurs only while an individual is asleep. It is a neurological dysfunction, and is commonly associated with a number of the other neurological dysfunctions of ADD such as waking slowly, falling asleep with difficulty and explosiveness.

People who bedwet sometimes simultaneously dream about the act of micturition. Those who do dream sometimes dream about urinating in a variety of places. Others dream about urinating always in the same bathroom or other specific location such as a certain place in a park.

Sadly, health professionals almost never ask about bedwetting in their routine history-taking, according to my research. It is important to ask about, however, because a history of bedwetting is rarely spontaneously volunteered by ADD adults themselves. Asking about enuresis must be done with gentleness because most adults are still reluctant to recall that part of their past and can still be very embarrassed by such a question.

In fact, about six percent of ADD adults do not seem to be able to remember their past history of bedwetting when asked about it. Some recall being bedwetters only after questioned repeatedly. Be aware that it is not rare for an adult to respond at first by looking pensive, staring around the room as if still trying to understand the question, then by expressing doubt that bedwetting was ever a problem, and lastly, after the eyes have rolled up and to the right to access memories of the distant past, by admitting that there had been "mistakes" or episodes of bedwetting in the past.

"No, I do not remember ever being a bedwetter. But, perhaps I was a bedwetter as a child. I *can remember* that my father talked to me about bedwetting when I was in the seventh grade. So, I must have had the problem, or why would he have talked to me about it. Still, I cannot now remember having been a bedwetter." I have to believe that this electrical engineer was so traumatized by having being a bedwetter that he is still embarrassment and in denial about it even now.

ADD individuals sometimes deny "being a bedwetter" and reframe the bedwetting issue by denying the label, bedwetter, while acknowledging that "mistakes" were made but no more frequently than four to eight times a year, and then they were only the consequence of dreaming.

Enuresis is a familial trait which is probably transmitted genetically [21].

ADD Adults Often Live with Verbal and Spatial Dyslexia

Case Study

"No one knows that I can't read."

"I work at a job where I talk with people a lot. Sometimes, I am asked to put items that people have returned to the warehouse back into storage. I can do it because I have learned to tell where to put things by their color and shape, not by the name of the item on the return slip or the labels in the storage room. I am still working and no one yet knows of my handicap."

"All they really know about my dyslexia is that I mix up the number sequence when dialing telephone numbers, and I call the wrong number a lot of the time."

Dyslexia is similar in teenagers and adults. It is a neurological dysfunction in which there is difficulty storing and coding new information as well as cross-referencing and retrieving coded information already stored in memory. The term originally described individuals who had difficulty reading. As such, it has been a poorly-defined term because even professionals cannot agree on the degree of difficulty reading is required to justify the diagnosis [22].

ADD adults who have difficulty reading often do not have a handicap that is obvious even to friends, fellow workers, and the individual's personal physician if the individual is no longer in school and has a job that does not demand significant reading skills. Adults who have difficulty with reading typically deny their dyslexia.

To avoid embarrassment, they rarely admit that they have a reading problem or that they have "difficulty" reading. If asked why they rarely read, they often say that they don't read because they "dislike reading." Most are never identified because they can actually read well enough to work and carry on essential adult functions.

Interestingly, some dyslexic adults are very active readers. They limit the scope of their reading, however, to materials of particular interest such as love stories, detective novels, science fiction, computer manuals, comic books or periodicals. It is difficult to be sure to what extent poor mental concentration inhibits their ability to read as opposed to the specific processing problems associated with dyslexia.

Adults with dyslexia can also be identified if they presently have, or by history had, difficulty with spatial and/or verbal reversals. Sixty-five percent of ADD adults report that they have or have had such difficulties.

As adults, they usually no longer write letters backward, i.e., d -- b, but they are likely to reverse the sequence of letters in a word, i.e. "hte" for "the," reverse the organization of words in a sentence, i.e. "house tree" rather than "tree house," and/or reverse the sequence of numbers when writing down telephone numbers. Some still have or at least did have considerable confusion with respect to left-right discrimination.

In my experience, adults who do not have ADD neurology have no more than very occasional right-left confusion or very minimal, rare verbal reversals which are typically described as of minor consequence or "not really a problem." They have no history of mirror-image reversal writing.

When speaking, ADD adults with dyslexia jumble words or reverse the meaning of what they are trying to say from time to time. The word "bumblebee" might turn into "gumblebee" or "bedwetting" into "wet bedding." The statement, "I want to invite *you* to *my* birthday party," might be reversed to, "I want to invite *me* to *your* birthday party." These "slip of the tongue" statements are often a source of laughter and, unfortunately, are too often not recognized as important clues to the diagnosis of ADD neurology. Not infrequently, they are dismissed as little more than a consequence of "the mind racing too fast" or of feeling "mentally tired."

Medication treatment of ADD adults who have dyslexia sometimes corrects reversal problems and sometimes does not. As yet, there is no way to predict who will benefit from medication and who will not.

The ADD adult whose dyslexia is not corrected with ADD medication treatment should be further evaluated by dyslexia specialists who have a variety of tests that can be performs and non-medicinal aids that might be helpful.

Concluding Remarks

Diagnosing ADD Isn't Always Straight Forward

Simple awareness of the ten major ADD neurological dysfunctions is helpful but does not guarantee that these clues to the diagnosis will be recognized as such when adults are evaluated for possible ADD neurology. In practice, a number of stumbling blocks commonly interfere with the ability of health professionals to collect and accurately interpret relevant historical medical information provided by ADD adults.

In addition to a general lack of clinician awareness that ADD exists in adults, inadequate dissemination of modern scientific information about the syndrome to practicing physicians, the failure by most medical professionals to view ADD as a spectrum of neurological dysfunctions which may or may not be associated with significant psychological consequences, and absence of laboratory tests for diagnosing ADD, there are other horrendous barriers which hinder professionals from making the diagnosis ADD in adults.

Two of the most important of these hindrances are, first, the way that clinical medicine is practiced and, second, the fact that adults with ADD commonly try to hide their ADD dysfunctions from others. Sadly, diagnosing ADD is likely to be even more difficult in the future as physicians and other health professionals join managed care medical organizations and are forced to spend even less time with their patients than they now do.

Because ADD is an important cause of disability and a predisposing factor for many of the behaviorally-induced illnesses that plague society today, it is more urgent than ever that physicians and other professionals become aware of the neurological dysfunctions of ADD, skillful at gathering information from patients about these dysfunctions, and maximally able to recognize ADD dysfunctions during interviews with ADD adults.

Let's look more closely at some specific obstacles to the clinical diagnosis of ADD in adults.

Clinical Practice Barriers to the Diagnosis of Adult Attention Deficit Disorder

Many patients, whether they have ADD neurology or not, have a variety of medical issues that they would like to discuss with their physicians if time were allowed and physicians receptive. From the point of view of the practicing physician with a crowded patient schedule, however, the most pressing clinical challenge is to identify and solve only the most pressing and life-threatening medical problems as quickly as possible.

Health professionals have to keep the amount of time they spend with patients to a very minimum. Because they examine the maximum number of patients in the shortest possible time, only the most pressing and troublesome of the medical issue will be identified and dealt with. This clinical strategy has been institutionalized and is formally recorded in medical records as the "main reason," "most troublesome concern," or "chief complaint" that brought the patient to the doctor. An evaluation of the many concerns that a patient might have is not likely to happen as long as this hurried approach to medical care is common practice.

In a medical atmosphere where time is short and most patients are still too shy to demand to talk about multiple problems in the brief time allowed by their doctor, it is likely that a complex disorder such as the ADD syndrome will commonly not be diagnosed.

Other realities of practice also limit the ability of physicians to recognize and diagnose the ADD syndrome. For a given series of complaints, physicians commonly identify the one or two that they personally and professionally feel comfortable treating. By so doing, they ignore multiple other complaints which deserve attention and which, if included in the overall evaluation, would clearly suggest the diagnosis of Adult ADD.

For example, a student who is performing poorly in graduate school might be diagnosed to have a reading difficulty based on the chief complaint. If the cause of the reading problem is simply attributed to dyslexia, colored reading glasses might be prescribed but certainly not ADD medication.

In some instances, when a physician is not knowledgeable about or comfortable with the medication treatment of ADD, clues to the diagnosis are likely to be ignored to avoid the need to deal with the challenge of treatment.

Physicians also may not recognize ADD because they commonly prefer to deal with complex medical problems by quickly referring the patient to a specialist or subspecialist. It is easy to see the disadvantage to patients of this treatment approach. For example, an adult with enuresis might well be sent to a urologist who is not likely to be familiar with the ADD syndrome and whose medical evaluation would probably reveal only that bladder function is normal, certainly not a diagnosis of Adult ADD.

Similarly, referring an ADD adult patient with inexplicable, chronic muscle-tendon pain to a rheumatologist could well lead to a diagnosis with which physician is quite familiar, fibromyalgia. It is not likely that a rheumatologist would recognize that these muscle complaints are just one of the clues to the diagnose of Adult ADD. The tragedy is that there is very effective treatment for ADD and only questionably effective treatment for fibromyalgia.

Most specialists, and especially subspecialists, are not expected to ask about a patient's full range of symptoms and signs which, if sought, would point them to a diagnosis of ADD. Accordingly, inadequate history taking by primary care physicians and quick referrals to specialists almost ensures that adults with ADD neurology will not be recognized by health care professionals.

In addition, the interaction between the physician and patient is often compromised when the complaints of the ADD individual are summarily labeled by the physician as "psychiatric" in nature. Patients may even be referred to a psychiatrist in spite of their feeling that something medical, "organic" or "chemical" is wrong with them rather than something psychological or learned. They are likely to feel angry and think that they have not been properly "heard" or "listened to" about their own beliefs as to what is wrong with them if they end up with a referral to a psychiatrist.

The physician-patient relationship is further compromised when, as is not infrequently the case, patients think that psychiatrists treat only "crazy" people and they do not wish to be so identified. Certainly in some instances, they may refuse a referral to a psychiatrist to avoid what they think will lead to a social stigma. And, it is unfortunate but true that such a referral will generate a psychiatric history which can prejudice future employment opportunities, insurance coverage, and even political opportunities.

Some patients with Adult ADD will not accept a referral to a psychiatrist if they believe that the psychiatrist prefers to treat with and spend considerable time providing psychotherapy rather than manage medication regimens. Those who want and believe that they mainly need corrective medication, not psychotherapy, will distrust the psychiatrist and many will be upset and lose faith in the referring doctor.

Health professionals can further strain the faith and trust of patients when they focus only on problems that are, in fact, only the psychological consequences of ADD. When this happens, patients receive the indirect message that "there is nothing physically wrong" and that what they are troubled by is only "in their heads." Worse, not only is the neurological root cause of their psychological problems not properly identified but appropriate and corrective medication for ADD is not likely to be prescribed.

Yet another common medical practice habit that prevents physicians from diagnosing ADD is their tendency to think of each complaint offered by a patient as independent of any other. Not only is the syndrome of ADD missed, but, as a result, they are likely to come up with a hodgepodge of diagnoses because of the multitude of complaints. This kind of error also increases the likelihood that a variety of different medicines will be prescribed for each problem even though one medicine may interfere with the effectiveness of another. When specific psychological dysfunctions are treated as separate, unique problems, the recommended treatment is likely to be ineffective, or, worse, inappropriate and dangerous.

For example, difficulty falling asleep may be diagnosed as an independent problem, labeled as "insomnia," and treated with hypnotics. Drugs which promote sleep at night may worsen daytime tiredness and cognitive function as well as produce daytime anxiety, problems ADD individuals often already face. Explosive ADD adults may be given an antipsychotic medicine which inhibits rage but worsens their inattention which is typically a troublesome area for ADD individuals. Feeling irritable may be attributed to premenstrual syndrome (PMS) or stress at home and treated with a tranquilizer which reduces irritability but causes daytime sedation.

When only the psychological consequences of having ADD are identified by physicians, ADD individuals are usually inadequately treated. For example, alcoholics may be offered a medicine such as Antabuse that makes drinking alcohol dangerous but does little to remove the urge for alcohol in the way that medication for ADD is likely to do. People with bulimia who are in group therapy but without proper medication treatment continue to struggle with impulsivity and the urge to binge. Panic syndrome individuals may be prescribed tranquilizers but not medicine for their ADD neurology which is the root cause of their extreme anxiety attacks. The failure to fully and competently treat ADD individuals all too often leads to the frustrating persistence of or return to undesired psychological behaviors.

Typical Attention Deficit Disorder Cover-Ups

All hindrances to the diagnosis of ADD do not rest with healthcare professionals or how they practice medicine. ADD adults, themselves, often act in ways that hinder others who are trying to find a diagnostic label for their problems. Even when offered adequate time to talk, most patients with ADD will not spontaneously volunteer their full medical story. While shyness may be a factor, more commonly patients do not understand which of their clinical problems are relevant to why they decided to seek professional help.

For example, adults who ask for help because they wake slowly in the morning are not likely to volunteer that they had been bedwetters when they were young. They are also not likely to be aware that bedwetting is a strong clue to ADD and that waking slowly in the morning is a common complaint of ADD adults.

Sometimes, the most aware health or education professional is handicapped when trying to make a diagnosis of ADD in individuals who deny their neurological dysfunctions, overcompensate for handicaps, seek out a niche in life that allows them to succeed without being discovered, refuse to submit to medical or educational evaluations, or use illicit drugs which alter mental function and the clinical presentation of ADD neurology.

There is a strong tendency for individuals to assume that their ADD dysfunctions are not really dysfunctions but simply a reflection of "who they are," that is, people with strengths and weaknesses "just like everyone else." This way of thinking is more likely if other family members also have ADD dysfunctions, and it is consistent with the natural inclination of adults to think of themselves and their families as normal. Difficulty accepting ADD dysfunction is not a matter of intelligence or education but, in reality, is very more a consequence of the emotional make up of the individual who has strong tendencies toward denial and avoidance behaviors. An important consequence typically is that physicians and other professionals who might otherwise have been able to diagnose and treat the ADD individual are thwarted in their efforts to do so.

Many ADD individuals feel shame and think of their neurological dysfunctions as family secrets to be hidden. Their ADD dysfunctions are embarrassing to think about or discuss with others, including their physician. For some, the diagnosis of ADD by a health professional feels more like an accusation of moral turpitude than a helpful medical discovery. For example, episodic explosiveness associated with child abuse or spouse-beating, or even a history of bedwetting, may be denied to avoid the discomfort of admitting to socially unacceptable "weaknesses."

It is important for professionals to realize, therefore, that ADD people may need a substantial amount of "warm-up" or "get-comfortable" time, perhaps thirty to sixty minutes of interaction with the professional, as well as lots of encouragement, emotional support, and non-judgmental communications before being willing to accept and discuss sensitive and embarrassing personal matters.

ADD individuals have a remarkable capacity to self-label their dysfunctions as benign problems and, by this reframing approach, reduce even their own awareness of their handicaps. These individuals often describe themselves as normal but at times "different" or "peculiar." Those who have trouble falling asleep, for example, often label themselves as "night people," because they stay up late. Of course, they have to stay up late because they would not fall asleep if they went to bed any earlier than they do. Those who experience considerable early evening tiredness often describe themselves as "morning people" because that is when, by comparison, they are most awake.

There are a number of ADD individuals who know enough to suspect that they have ADD because of what they had read or because others in the family have been so diagnosed. Yet, they are not diagnosed by professionals because they choose not to discuss their problems, hide dysfunctional behavior through extreme efforts of self-control, and avoid situations and challenges that might expose their dysfunctions. Needless to say, these tactics typically require huge expenditures of personal energy on the part of the ADD adult to succeed, require substantial manipulation and control of one's environment, and not infrequently serves to isolate these individuals from other people.

In fact, there are some ADD people who are able to compensate so well that they do not attract enough negative attention to be suspected of having ADD. They strive vigorously to succeed in the world regardless of the personal struggle needed to do so. Many of these ADD adults perform remarkably well in society, and many certainly well enough even in academic settings to earn passing and sometimes excellent marks. They also may work very hard and effectively to suppress their rebellious inclinations and tendency to oppositional behavior. Commonly, they drink caffeinated liquids for added energy and choose work which is not "boring" because it is high-stress, high-adventure and highly challenging.

For some, the diagnosis of Adult ADD simply seems absurd. They are not able to accept that such a possibility could exist until there has been severe criticism or censure from outside of the family, business associates or others. Punishment including arrest or being fired from a job may be the first awakening event that forces some adults to be aware of their ADD dysfunctional behavior.

It is not rare for parents to refuse to give prescription drugs to their children for fear that they may become addicted or drug-dependent. Of course, the misuse of stimulants such as Dexedrine or Ritalin may lead to addiction, but this concern is entirely misplaced when the choice of treatment is antidepressant medication which is rarely if ever addicting. When the correct antidepressant at the right dosage is prescribed, neither cognition nor emotion, that is neither thinking nor feeling, is compromised. Even drug dependence is not a significant issue with antidepressant medication.

Proper ADD medication simply corrects dysfunctional ADD neurology and does not create a new, "medication disorder" problem. This is in contrast to the expected side-effects of major tranquilizers, for example, which commonly cause lethargy and, in time, even tardive dyskinesia. When ADD individuals have reported negative results with the use of antidepressants, the cause is almost always the wrong choice of an antidepressant or the wrong dose.

Ironically, ADD individuals who are quick to express concern about the dangers of prescription medications are often comfortable using caffeine, nicotine and alcohol even though these drugs are clearly mind-altering, addicting and harmful.

Denial of ADD is especially likely in adults who have difficulty giving up self-destructive behaviors which happen to be pleasurable and exciting to them. These ADD individuals sometimes even will take medication for control of their ADD dysfunctions yet still try to burn the candle at both ends. Hoping to have the "best" of both worlds, they continue to drink excessive quantities of alcohol, use illicit drugs, maintain their bulimic ways, or engage in other ultimately self-destructive behaviors while taking ADD medication. Their willingness to resort to temporary comfort and escapism, especially if it involves drugs, obscures almost all of the benefit that the ADD medications can offer.

Overcompensation is a defensive psychological reaction that can diminish awareness by others of inattentiveness and impulsivity in ADD adults and makes ADD neurology less obvious. Thus, some adults with ADD choose to work in a regimented and rigidly structured environment, thus profiting from the aid of external controls as they try to order their lives. Others find work situations which do not require that attention be paid to significant amounts of paperwork, extensive reading, fastidious promptness, or considerable patience.

Workaholic individuals typically have ADD neurology and are rarely recognized as such because they are so focused on achievement and accomplishment that waking in the morning and daytime fatigue are usually never problems. Also, their driven nature and economic success often is a reward for their behavior thus obscuring their ADD diagnosis.

ADD adults who select the construction industry, the military, sports, theater, and politics often find that these work environments are accepting of their neurological dysfunctions. In these settings, learning disability, academic inattentiveness, impulsivity, fidgetiness, frequent irritability and episodic explosiveness do not lead to dismissal or failure and do not necessarily interfere with or prevent overall performance success. Without medication, they may work harder to be successful than they would otherwise have had to, but they can be reasonably productive and effective.

The recurrent fatigue and irritability that are typical of most ADD individuals are not problems for those ADD adults who constantly seek out high-adventure and high-thrill activities. These activities typically "crank up" the energy flow of ADD adults although, unfortunately, they not infrequently involve socially unacceptable pursuits including criminal behavior. Too often those who transgress societal limits are labelled as criminals but not identified as people who are prone to criminality because of ADD neurology. They need but usually do not receive medical treatment which would help them control their impulsivity and inappropriate, voracious need for excitement.

There are many ADD individuals who cover-up their dysfunctions and avoid being diagnosed by finding socially acceptable self-treatment approaches which suffice for them even though there are negative consequences. Some, for example, consume large amounts of caffeinated drinks, especially coffee, to fight morning tiredness and daytime fatigue while others use alcohol to avoid irritability at the end of the day.

Some learn to "walk away" from stressful arguments and move away from provoking situations to allow their intense feelings of anger and frustration to defuse. Thus, they avoid exploding emotionally or physically and obscure recognition of their episodic explosiveness which is virtually diagnostic of ADD neurology. In addition to "walking away," ADD individuals sometimes relieve pent-up frustration and negative feelings by turning to harmless activities such as kicking metal fences, smashing their own old pickup truck with a sledgehammer, pounding pillows in the privacy of their bedroom, or weeping instead of striking out at others.

There are a variety of ways that ADD neurology can be covered up, and it is for this reason that many professionals argue that not all young people with ADD continue to have ADD neurology as adults. It is not true that what the professional fails to see does not exist.

Sadly, those with ADD who slip through the diagnostic cracks would experience improvement in the quality of their lives if they could be discovered and properly medicated.

References

1. **Wender, P.H. and F.W.** Reimherr, *Bupropion Treatment of Attention-Deficit Hyperactivity Disorder in Adults.* American Journal of Psychiatry, 1990. **147**(8): p. 1018-1020.
2. **Wender, P., MD, F.W. Reimherr MD, and D.R. Wood MD**, *Attention Deficit Disorder ('Minimal Brain Dysfunction") in Adults.* Archives of General Psychiatry, 1981. **38**: p. 449-456.
3. **Zametkin, A.J., MD,** *et al., Cerebral Glucose Metabolism in Adults with Hyperactivity of Childhood Onset.* The New England Journal of Medicine, 1990. **323**(20): p. 1361-1366.
4. **Matochik, J.A., PhD**, *et al., Effects of Acute Stimulant Medication on Cerebral Metabolism in Adults with Hyperactivity.* Neuropsychopharmacology, 1993. **8**(4): p. 377-386.
5. **Shekim, W.O., MD**, *et al., S-Adenosyl-L-Methionine (SAM) in Adults With ADHD, RS: Preliminary Results From an Open Trial.* Psychopharmacology Bulletin, 1990. **26**(2): p. 249-253.
6. **Cantwell, D.P.,** *Hyperactive Children Have Grown Up.* Archives of General Psychiatry, 1985. **42**: p. 1026-1028.

7. **Endicott, J. and Spitzer, R. L.**, *et al.*, *A Diagnostic Review: The Schedule for Affective Disorders and Schizophrenia.* Archives of General Psychiatry, 1978. **35**: p. 837-844.
8. **Gittleman, R. and S. Manuzza**, *Diagnosing ADD-H in Adolescents.* Psychopharmacology Bulletin, 1985. **21**: p. 237-242.
9. **Roy, A., MB**, *et al.*, *Pathologic Gambling.* Archives of General Psychiatry, 1988. **45**: p. 369-373.
10. **Shekim, W.O.**, *et al.*, *A Clinical and Demographic Profile of a Sample of Adults With Attention Deficit Hyperactivity Disorder, Residual State.* Comprehensive Psychiatry, 1990. **31**: p. 416-425.
11. **Mendelson, W., MD, N. Johnson MD, and M.A. Stewart MD**, *Hyperactive Children as Teenagers: A Follow-Up Study.* The Journal of Nervous and mental Disease, 1971. **153**(4): p. 273-279.
12. **Huessy, H.R., M. Metoyer, and M. Townsend**, *8-10 year follow-up of 84 children treated for behavioral disorder in rural Vermont.* Actopaedopsychiatrica, 1974. **40**(6): p. 230-235.
13. **Weiss, G., MD**, *et al.*, *Studies on the Hyperactive Child: VIII. Five-Year Follow-up.* Archives of General Psychiatry, 1971. **24**(May): p. 409-414.
14. **McGee, R., PhD**, *et al.*, *A Twelve-Year Follow-up of Preschool Hyperactive Children.* Journal of the American Academy of Child and Adolescent Psychiatry, 1991. **30**(2): p. 224-232.
15. **Fischer, M.**, *et al.*, *The Adolescent Outcome of Hyperactive Children Diagnosed by Research Criteria: II. Academic, Attentional, and Neuropsychological Status.* Journal of Consulting and Clinical Psychology, 1990. **58**(5): p. 580-588.
16. **Wender, P., MD, D.R. Wood MD, and F.W. Reimherr MD**, *Diagnostic Criteria ADD-RT.* Psychopharmacology Bulletin, 1985. **21**(2): p. 222-229.
17. **Jankovic, J., MD and M. Brin MD**, *Therapeutic Uses of Botulinum Toxin.* The New England Journal of Medicine, 1991. **324**(17): p. 1186-1194.
18. **18.**American Psychiatric Association Committee on Nomenclature and Statistics,
19. *Functional Enuresis,* in *Diagnostic and Statistical Manual of Mental Disorders*. 1987, American Psychiatric Association: Washington, DC. p. 85.
20. **Sawyer, D.J.W.**, *Dyslexia: Introduction to the Special Series.* Journal of Learning Disabilities, 1992. **25**(1): p. 38-39.

8

Medication Treatment of the ADD Syndrome

In the United States, the usual and customary medicines prescribed for the treatment of the ADD syndrome belong to one of two classes of medication.

The so-called stimulants are the older, better established and most extensively used of the two classes. Ritalin tablets and Ritalin-SR tablets (methylphenidate hydrochloride), Dexedrine tablets and Dexedrine Spansules (dextroamphetamine sulfate), Desoxyn tablets and Desoxyn Gradumets (methamphetamine), Desoxyn norephedrine (amphetamine), and Cylert Tablets and Cylert Chewable Tablets (pemoline) are the stimulants available in this country.

The so-called antidepressants include many different preparations. In my experience, ten are commonly effective in treating the neurological dysfunctions of ADD individuals. The others are rarely if ever helpful.

Other classes of medication have been reported in the scientific literature to be useful for treating ADD individuals and are occasionally prescribed by some physicians. They include tranquilizers, antipsychotic drugs, antihypertensive medication, and antiepileptic agents. At the most, these types of medications correct a few of the ten neurological dysfunctions of ADD. Unfortunately, they almost always compromise intellectual and/or emotional function in a way that goes far beyond any usefulness they may have. In my opinion, they should never be used for treating ADD neurology.

Expected Benefits of Stimulant Medications

The stimulants are usually effective in 50-70% of children and probably the same percentage of adults. They provide benefit within minutes after they are taken. Improvement in attention and lessening of hyperactivity, impulsivity, irritability or easy frustration, dyslexia, negativity and explosiveness can be expected from medicines of this category while they are active in the body. Rarely, they help promote sleep when taken just before bedtime.

Electrocardiographic monitoring is generally not indicated because stimulants do not significantly affect the electrical activity of the heart. Blood level measurements are not needed. Dexedrine does not decrease seizure threshold but Ritalin and Cylert do.

Disadvantages of Stimulant Medications

There are nine important disadvantages to the use of stimulant medications.

1. First, stimulants are not effective treatment drugs in about 30-50% of children and presumably the same percentage of adults.

2. Second, when used alone, the short-acting forms are effective for about four hours and the long-acting forms wear off in about eight hours.

3. Third, multiple drug dosing is needed during the day for prolonged effectiveness. Multiple dosing can be a very time consuming problem if a young child does not easily swallow pills. This inconvenience also can pose considerable difficulty for working parents who are away from their young children during the day and for parents whose children are in school. It is also commonly a problem for teenagers who have to remember to take their midday dose which is usually during school hours, and who may be chided in front of classmates if they ignore or forget their second dosing.

4. Fourth, stimulants almost always severely reduce appetite, especially in young children. This class of medication has been reported to stunt growth and normal development if taken on a continuous daily basis without significant periods of time off treatment.

5. Fifth, when the beneficial effects of stimulants wear off, many experience an extreme emotional and cognitive "letdown," or "drop-off," or "crash." At this time, the individual usually feels simply terrible and is explosive, very negative and hardly functional cognitively. For those who use stimulants to treat their ADD neurology, important evening hours for doing homework or other projects are often only minimally useful.

6. Sixth, stimulants almost never correct the coming-awake-slowly dysfunction of ADD and rarely correct the falling-asleep-with-difficulty dysfunction. In most instances, if taken late in the day or in an excessive dose, stimulants cause insomnia. They virtually never help children to wake organized in the morning.

7. Seventh, stimulants do not stop primary nocturnal enuresis or bedwetting, if the problem exists.

8. Eighth, stimulants may cause tics.

9. Ninth, and finally, Dexedrine and Ritalin in particular, the more commonly effective stimulants of the three, have a well-proven potential for addiction as well as abuse by child and adults. They can be used to feel normal and also to feel "high." Stimulants are controlled substances which are more difficult to dispense than are the antidepressants.

Expected Benefits of Antidepressant Medications

Treatment of ADD neurology with antidepressant medications almost always requires only a single daily dose which is effective for twenty-four hours. The only exception is alprazolam, a drug which often but not always must be taken more than once a day. It is not used often, however, because it is effective in only about one in a hundred ADD adults. Children never require midday doses of antidepressant medications. With the possible exception of alprazolam, once effective medication treatment is established, the next dose need be given only about the same time the next day because antidepressant medication is long-acting. There is no daily "drop-off," "letdown" or "crash" with the use of antidepressant medication.

Antidepressant medications correct inattentiveness, hyperactivity, impulsivity, dyslexia, irritability and easy frustration, and episodic explosiveness just as stimulants do. The tricyclic antidepressants usually stop bedwetting, if present, and dramatically eliminate the dysfunctions of coming awake slowly and falling asleep with difficulty. They offer more complete treatment of the ADD syndrome than stimulants do.

Antidepressants are not addicting and are rarely if ever abused. Excessive doses cause undesirable, negative consequences. They can be prescribed on regular prescription forms. They do not stunt the growth of children even if taken continuously. They do not cause tics.

Because there are many preparations to choose from, treatment is successful in about 95% of ADD individuals using antidepressant medicine, a combination of antidepressant medicines, or occasionally the mixture of one or more antidepressants and stimulant medicine.

Even when first started, antidepressants are effective within hours if the right medication and the correct dose is known and prescribed. Since this information is rarely known at the start of treatment, and only low doses should be used at the start of treatment, in reality therapeutic effectiveness usually takes about one week to achieve. The *PDR* admonishes that antidepressants can take up to three weeks to be effective, but this warning refers to the treatment of depression, not ADD.

Disadvantages of Antidepressant Medications

All medications can have side-effects and adverse affects. The antidepressant medications are no exception. Fortunately, when the choice of medication is tailored to the age of the ADD individual and proper monitoring performed, both persistent side-effects and adverse effects are rare or at most uncommon.

Parnate when used properly almost never has any side-effects in children or adults.

The most dramatic and well known of the adverse effects of monoamine oxidase inhibitors such as Parnate is "hypertensive crisis," that is, a severe, acute rise in blood pressure which can cause disorientation, headaches, stroke, coma and death. This adverse reaction is uncommon and can be further minimized, if not eliminated, by having patients avoid tyramine amino acid containing foods in their diet. Parnate is also contraindicated with the use of certain drugs which should be avoided if possible. Because of the nature of the warnings that must accompany its use, Parnate should be prescribed for young people only under very special clinical circumstances.

Adverse effects of monoamine oxidase inhibitor drugs are uncommon, but, of course, adverse effects from monoamine oxidase inhibitor drugs cannot be totally avoided any more than they can with any other medication, prescription or not.

The tricyclic antidepressants generally have few or no side-effects when given to young people, especially those under the age of fifteen. In this age group, orthostatic dizziness, or dizziness when getting up, is the most common side-effect, and it typically disappears with time. Dryness of the mouth because of a decreased volume and increase in the concentration of saliva is expected to a minimal or modest degree only in those who are fifteen years old or older, but not in those who are under fifteen. Tricyclic antidepressants do affect the electrical activity of the heart which should be evaluated prior to starting this type of medicine. If no significant abnormality is found, repeat electrocardiographic monitoring should be performed from time to time, especially in young people, while tricyclic medication is being taken.

As an act of conservatism, I prefer to monitor the electrocardiogram of those in my practice even though available published studies indicate that the electrical changes in the heart due to tricyclic medications are usually quite benign.

In addition, especially in the young and the elderly, the blood level of tricyclic antidepressant medication should be monitored carefully. The blood level may not be stable over the first one to three months of treatment, and high blood levels can cause grand mal epileptic seizures. Even weekly testing may be indicated in children under twelve, especially those under seven.

With respect to the antidepressants, Prozac, Paxil, Zoloft, trazodone, and alprazolam, dosing can be safely monitored clinically without blood testing. However, blood level testing is useful to establish a correlation between the desirable clinical status and the associated blood level of the medication. The blood level can also help determine, if a change in clinical status occurs, if it is related to medication use or some other difficult to determine influence such as viral illness or psychological stress.

In general, antidepressant drugs are safe and effective treatment of ADD neurology but require that the treating physician be aware of their potential side-effects and adverse effects as well as be familiar with what these medications are expected to do and not do.

WARNING: Of course, any use of prescription medication must always be with the recommendation and supervision of a licensed physician who is knowledgeable about ADD and the medications prescribed.

When using medications for nonapproved purposes, informed consent must be provided to the patient, family, and/or other people involved in guardianship or responsibility for the health of the patient.

Starting with the Right ADD Medication

There are no pretreatment clinical measurements or findings that are useful for predicting which medication, whether of the stimulant or the antidepressant class, will be effective in any given ADD individual. Finding the right medication remains a trial and error procedure. In view of this, it is wise to proceed by first eliminating drug choices for which there are contraindications or relative contraindications.

For example, do not start with the stimulant medications if the following: a child is a poor eater and further caloric restriction might retard growth; a teenager is resistant to a multiple dose medication regimen because of the demands of school or fear of social embarrassment if discovered taking medicine; an individual is using excessive alcohol; a person is likely to abuse the stimulant; or, a 24 hour a day benefit is very desirable.

Again, considering contraindications and relative contraindications, decide if there are reasons not to start with one or another of the antidepressants. For example, do not prescribe a tricyclic antidepressant for an individual with significant heart disease or with a history of seizures unless anticonvulsant medication is being taken. Avoid monoamine oxidase inhibitor medications in those with severe self-control problems such as teenagers and adults who are active bulimics.

Also, do not prescribe antidepressants which are likely to interfere with the life-style of the ADD individual. Adults who are serious singers are very unlikely to tolerate tricyclic antidepressant medications which usually cause dryness of the mouth. Similarly, public speakers, trial lawyers and politicians, for example, all of whom often talk in public settings and cannot easily stop talking to drink, commonly will not tolerate tricyclic medications. Avoid trazodone in those whose responsibilities make it important that they be easy to awake from sleep at night, for instance, a mother with a young baby, a member of the police squat team or fire fighter.

Compliance, of course, is necessary if treatment is to be effective. In general, antidepressant medications correct more of the dysfunctions of ADD than do the stimulants and therefore should be favored as the drugs of first choice.

As often as possible start with a medication that is likely to be effective. Do not start with a medication that almost certainly will be rejected because of side-effects. To do so encourages the patient to question the skill of the physician, implies that the treating physician is insensitive to the concerns and needs of the patient, and strains the doctor-patient relationship. As a treating physician, always stress that a starting medication is an educated "guess," is effective in a certain percentage of patients, and not be helpful in the others, and will be quickly changed if not the right choice in the judgment of the patient.

Remember, people with ADD neurology start out being easily frustrated, irritable, negative and impulsive, all traits that do not allow them to easily and patiently tolerate even temporary treatment failures.

Treatment Algorithm

First, think about the class of medication that is most reasonable to prescribe to a given ADD individual. Then, choose the one from that group which is most likely to be effective.

Of course, it would be ideal if there were a simple laboratory test to determine the best medication and the most effective dosage for each person with ADD neurology. This is not yet possible. Therefore, selecting the most effective drug is currently limited to knowing which medications are most likely to work and prescribing those medications first. Finding the optimum dose of the medication selected is best discovered by starting with a small initial dose and subsequently evaluating the effect of progressively larger doses.

The following treatment algorithm is derived from an analysis of the 1377 people with ADD neurology from my private medical practice.

Only two individuals required and responded to Ritalin as the sole drug when no antidepressant medication could be found that was effective enough to warrant continued use. Six individuals who benefited significantly from Prozac also needed Dexedrine and four needed Ritalin added to their treatment regimen to enhance mental focusing.

All of the other 1365 ADD individuals in the study responded successfully to either a single antidepressant medication or, in a few cases, a combination of antidepressant medications.

A NECESSARY WARNING: The comments that follow about drug usage are guidelines which may not follow *PDR* recommendations and which physicians may choose to use but only if they have considerable medical expertise managing ADD individuals. Be reminded, however, that the *PDR* has many warnings and considerable advice which is not discussed in this chapter, is of value, and should be fully understood and followed by physicians treating people with ADD. The non-physician reader should never try to use these medicines on themselves, their children, or any other person without medical advise and supervision.

Stimulant Medications

Both Ritalin and Dexedrine preparations are effective in only about 60% of individuals. Cylert is successful less often as a treatment of ADD. The ease of use of stimulants makes them ideal when there is a medical contraindication to the use of antidepressants.

If a child is younger than the age below which a stimulant medication has not been approved for use by the FDA, the parents or guardians must be told of this. For example, Dexedrine is not approved for use in children under the age of three, Ritalin and Cylert under the age of six, and most antidepressants under the age of twelve.

At the same time, parents should be made aware that the federal Food, Drug & Cosmetic (FD&C) Act "does not, however, limit the manner in which a physician may use an approved drug. Once a product has been approved for marketing, a physician may prescribe it for uses or in treatment regimens or patient populations that are not included in approved labeling [*PDR*]."

Ritalin and Dexedrine are not identical medications. Some individuals find that one or the other is beneficial but not both. Sometimes, individuals report that one stimulant will increase mental focusing in particular or specifically relieve tiredness more than the other one. Most physicians have come to prefer Ritalin because it does not carry the burden of being known by street names such as "speed," "uppers," "whites," or "crank," names which "street people" often use when referring to the amphetamines. Recently, there has been media criticism of the emphasis that has been placed on the use of Ritalin as a drug of first choice by some leaders of the ADD community in this country because of financial contributions made by the manufacturer of Ritalin to non-profit groups and perhaps others. In fact, Dexedrine is clinically effective more commonly, in my experience, than is Ritalin.

Moreover, Dexedrine Spansules are less expensive than Ritalin and has a prolonged action. By itself, it lasts about six to eight hours, but mixed with an antidepressant it can be effective for over twelve hours. Short-acting Ritalin is helpful over about a four hour. Long-acting Ritalin often has a delay of an hour or more before it starts acting in the body and then has an effective that ends about six to eight hours after it is taken. Often, short-acting and long-acting Ritalin must be mixed to get immediate and late effects from one dosing.

Using Dexedrine Spansules alone usually means twice a day dosing, but both short-acting Dexedrine and Ritalin may require three or four-time-a-day dosing for effective coverage during the waking hours.

Underdosing is a not uncommon problem. Physicians tend to prescribe stimulants cautiously, if at all, because they are perhaps overly concerned about providing an individual with large amounts of a substance that has a significant potential for abuse and addiction. Underdosing is an important cause of treatment failure.

What happens when an ADD individual is overdosed with a stimulant? Most patients in my practice reject an overdose because they feel "hiked up," "speedy," "anxious," or "not right." They are not looking for a "high. The dose of stimulants used should be adequate to eliminate undesirable ADD dysfunctions and maximally heighten wakefulness and mental focusing. To find the proper dose, it is reasonable to increasing the dose of a stimulant to above tolerance then reduce back to a comfortable dose level, using side-effects such as inability to fall asleep or feeling overly stimulated or sedated as indications of overdose.

Close monitoring of patients taking stimulants is important. There must always be vigil to ensure that abuse and addiction does not happen with the patient, to guarantee that other family members do not use and abuse what is not prescribed for them, and that efficacy is persistent and maximal.

In general, the failure of stimulants to correct all the neurological dysfunctions of ADD and the need for multiple dosing, burdens that promote noncompliance with the use of many other medications, too, are the major reasons for not considering them as first choice drugs.

Tricyclic Medications

In children and teenagers, tricyclic antidepressant medications should be the first drugs tried, in my opinion, if there are no contraindications. Again, of course, it is essential that the parents or guardians of children be made aware of whether or not a particular medication is or is not approved by the FDA for use because of age. This applies to the use of stimulants as well. The physician should document in the medical chart that the FDA issue was discussed.

Tricyclic antidepressants were the drug of choice for approximately 45% of the ADD children, teenagers and adults in my study. If only young people under the age of twenty are considered, antidepressants are the drug of choice in 82%. Of the three most effective tricyclics available, desipramine is successful in 86%, protriptyline in 11% and nortriptyline in 3% of these cases. Doxepin and amitriptyline are effective only rarely. Of those treated successfully with desipramine, 66% were children or teenagers and 34% were adults.

After the age of fourteen, some degree of mouth dryness is expected from the use of tricyclic antidepressant medications. Side-effects in adults such as dryness of the mouth, constipation and/or excessive sweating is expected, and about only 24% of all ADD adults were able to tolerate and continued to take the tricyclic antidepressants for a prolonged period of time.

For ADD individuals under the age of twenty, the starting daily dose of desipramine and nortriptyline is 25 mg and that of protriptyline is 10 mg. The dose can be increased by one pill or capsule each subsequent day, if tolerated, assuming that each is the same strength as the dose of the starting pill or capsule.

A blood level of medication should be obtained and a repeat electrocardiogram evaluated either when the optimum dose is found or at a dose no higher than 150 mg a day for desipramine and nortriptyline or 50 mg a day for protriptyline, which ever comes first. It is possible that a clinically effective dose can cause a high blood level of medication leading to seizures. It is also possible that a safe blood level can be associated with undesirable electrocardiographic changes. If the blood level is high and/or electrocardiographic changes unacceptable, the medication dose must be lowered or, if necessary, discontinued. The likelihood of seizures and electrocardiographic abnormality can be recognized only if proper clinical follow-up and laboratory monitoring takes place. In my experience, it is safe to reevaluate patients of any age five days to one week after starting tricyclic medication treatment. Subsequent laboratory and clinical follow up is weekly or every two to three weeks in very young ADD individuals and less often in adults. Such testing becomes less important after about three months of continuous treatment.

The following is a very conservative approach for treating adults over the age of twenty who do not have complaints consistent with prostatic hypertrophy. Use a starting dose of desipramine and nortriptyline of 10 mg once a day and protriptyline 5 mg once a day with daily increases at the rate of one pill or capsule each subsequent one to three days. If such treatment is prescribed for male adults with prostatic hypertrophy, dosage increase should take place only after a seven day period, not daily.

The effective dose of desipramine can be as low as 25 mg and as high as 600 mg a day. In the *PDR*, the stated "usual" adult dose is 100 to 200 mg a day. The effective dose of protriptyline can be as low as 10 mg and as high as 120 mg a day, but the stated "usual" adult dose in the *PDR* is 15 to 40 mg a day. When medicating ADD individuals, it is important to focus on finding the effective dose and not be limited by the concept of the "usual" dose. Whatever the effective dose turns out to be, of course, it must always be monitored for safety.

Blood levels of desipramine that are over 800 ng/ml must be considered possibly dangerous because they sometimes rise quickly to higher levels, while blood levels of 1000 to 1200 ng/ml not uncommonly do cause seizures. Seizures will occur at blood levels between 500 and 700 ng/ml in patients with a seizure diathesis who have not been effectively pretreated with antiepileptic medication.

Prolongation of the QTc interval above normal as measured by an electrocardiogram is, in my opinion, a mandatory reason for reducing or discontinuing treatment with a tricyclic medication. In rare instances when individuals are born with a prolonged QTc, the Long QT Syndrome, tricyclic medication should not be prescribed and the individual referred immediately for a heart evaluation by a cardiologist, unless such an evaluation has already been conducted. The appearance of an incomplete or complete right bundle branch block due to medication treatment as measured by an electrocardiogram in an individual without significant heart disease is rarely, if ever, dangerous, even though it is an abnormality. It is always wise to ensure that the heart is normal before tricyclic medication is started. If abnormality of any kind exists, it is sometimes wise, for the reassurance of the patient and/or parents, to insist that the patient have an evaluation by a cardiologist.

Extreme sensitivity must be shown to the issue of the so-called "sudden death" syndrome from desipramine which is mentioned in the *PDR* and in published papers. Reports by Riddle et al. [1] and Biederman et al. [2] cast doubt on the clinical significance of this syndrome, but present information does not allow physicians to totally disregard the possibility of sudden death from desipramine. This matter must be openly and frankly discussed when indicated because, ultimately, it is informed patients and/or parents who must assume final responsibility for medication risks.

During the first three months of treatment with desipramine, about 3% of individuals will develop an allergic drug rash. Most can be successfully given a substitute tricyclic medicine.

The Monoamine Oxidase Inhibitors

I favor Parnate (tranylcypromine) over Nardil (phenelzine) for the treatment of Adult Attention Deficit Disorder.

Approximately 70% of ADD adults can be treated successfully with Parnate. Its efficacy is comparable to that of the tricyclic medications, but it is clearly more tolerable for adults because there are no side-effects when it is properly dosed. Parnate should not be offered to adults unless they are responsible and medically compliant.

The warning in the *PDR* that Parnate should be a last choice medication refers to the treatment of depression. Appropriate warnings about the potential dangers of Parnate use must always be provided to patients.

For about 60% of ADD adults treated with Parnate, 10 mg a day is the correct dose. The "usual effective dosage" of 30 mg a day which is recommended in the *PDR* is not effective treatment for 90% of ADD adults. Doses of 20 mg a day are effective only about 30% of the time. The most common complaint of an excessive dose is significant sedation starting in the early afternoon. The sedation effect, by the way, is different from the tiredness that ADD adults often feel near the end of the afternoon. It is important to remember that the therapeutically effective dosage of Parnate can range from 5 mg up to 50 mg a day, and not infrequently patients strongly prefer to split their pills to provide intermediate doses such as 12.5 mg, 15 mg, 17.5 mg, or 25 mg a day to achieve maximum effectiveness.

Eldepryl (selegiline) is occasionally preferred and tolerated better than Parnate. The dosage range in 5 to 30 mg once a day. It is wise to issue the same warnings about diet and other medications as should be done for those taking Parnate regardless of the dose taken.

Prozac (Fluoxetine)

Over the few years since Prozac has been available, it has become the third most effective antidepressant for treating ADD after the tricyclics and Parnate. It is the drug of choice in 6% of ADD children and 15% of ADD adults.

Some psychiatrists argue that 40 mg should be an upper limit dosage, and the *PDR* says that the upper limit should not exceed 80 mg a day. In some instances, ADD individuals require 120 mg a day for maximum benefit and lower doses are not adequately helpful.

Prozac is an expensive medicine to buy at the local pharmacy. The cost of a 10 mg capsules is about the same as that of a 20 mg capsule. If cost is not a limiting factor, the starting dose should be a 10 mg capsule taken once a day. The dose can be increased in most instances by 10 mg each day with a pause for two to three days if there is uncertainty about the clinical effect. When the optimal dose has been exceeded, in the trial and error of trying to find the right dose, and needs to be reduced, Prozac should not be taken for two to three days and then the correct, lower dose can be started.

If cost is important, then it is not unreasonable to start with 20 mg capsules the first day and increase by 20 mg each subsequent day. This approach is less expensive and may reduce the time it takes to find the optimally effective dose, but it always runs the risk of passing over the correct dose which can be as low as 10 mg a day for people with ADD.

If splitting a 20 mg Prozac capsule is necessary, for example, to obtain a dose of 10 mg, it is possible to do at least one of the following: either, split the capsule into its two halves and seal the open end with peanut butter; or, empty the contents of a whole capsule into an acidic liquid such as grapefruit juice, to prevent it from losing potency, drink the dose wanted, and save the rest of the liquid in the refrigerator for use later. It is a bit tedious to do either of these maneuvers, and people tell me that the taste of Prozac in juice is not wonderful, but these approaches can save money.

There are four major therapeutic concerns that should be kept in mind for ADD individuals who take Prozac. One is that Prozac can flatten their emotions so that treated individuals do not "really care" about many of the stresses of their life. This is *not* a desirable effect, even if the individual likes the relief from discomfort that results, and it is a reason for stopping Prozac. Sadly, not knowing the clues to the diagnosis of ADD neurology, too many physicians and patients continue Prozac use when it is not proper treatment for ADD because the individual feels less stressed and "improved."

Some ADD individuals benefit dramatically from Prozac but lose their libido and/or ability to achieve a sexual orgasm. It is worth switching from Prozac to Paxil or Zoloft if this occurs, but the change may or may not eliminate the problem.

Still another major therapeutic concern is that an initially correct dose of Prozac will, in time, become excessive because of the long biological "half-life" of Prozac and its active metabolite, norfluoxetine. What this means is that Prozac and norfluoxetine are slowly released from the body and can build up over time and the blood level can become excessive for that patient. This can happen in adults and children and teenagers.

If anticipated, this problem can be easily recognized and dealt with. Just after the start of treatment when the ADD individual is maximally benefiting from Prozac, a blood level of fluoxetine and norfluoxetine should be obtained. Then, should the clinical response to Prozac change or the ADD individual stop doing well, the blood level of these substances can be measured again. If the blood level is different from what was obtained near the start of treatment, the reason for Prozac failure is immediately apparent and the dosage of Prozac can easily be readjusted.

A fourth potential problem with Prozac use to be aware of is that the concomitant use of Prozac with a tricyclic antidepressant will cause the latter medication to be higher in the blood for the same dose than it would be if used alone. In almost all instances, when tricyclic medication is started before Prozac is prescribed, that is, Prozac is added to an established regimen which includes a tricyclic medication, the dose of the tricyclic should be reduced by about 50% to ensure that the blood level of the tricyclic stays at the same safe and clinically effective level it had been. Measuring the blood level of the tricyclic medication before and after the addition of Prozac to the regimen can be extremely valuable.

Prozac has no significant cardiac effects at therapeutic levels and potentially may cause seizures only at doses that are far in excess of the therapeutic range.

Parents and guardians of children must be informed that Prozac is a drug approved by the FDA but that it is being prescribed for a nonapproved use.

Trazodone (Generic Name)

When Parnate, the tricyclics and Prozac are ineffective, the next antidepressant medication to try should be trazodone. 13% of ADD adults and 7% of children and teenagers with ADD can be successfully treated with this medication.

The greatest danger to the use of trazodone is to follow all of the *PDR* recommendations. These recommendations say, for example, that a proper starting dose is 150 mg, that is, three to six times the starting dose that I recommend. Moreover, doses of 150 mg and higher are effective in less than 10% of ADD individuals. The *PDR* also states that all of the trazodone dose need *not* be taken at bedtime even though trazodone almost always causes profound sedation for at least four hours after it is taken. In addition, the *PDR* recommends that trazodone be taken with meals, but, in my experience, it is not critical that it be taken with food.

In my experience, trazodone should be taken only at bedtime so that ADD individuals will be "sedated" while asleep. The starting dose should be 25 mg at bedtime and increased as needed by 25 mg increments on a daily basis. Typically, the effective dose is 50, 75 or 100 mg taken at bedtime. Very occasionally, a dose of 125 or 150 mg is better. Only rarely are higher doses needed and effective for the treatment of ADD.

It is extremely difficult to wake up during the four hours just after trazodone is taken. As a consequence, trazodone may be an undesirable medication for any one who does not want to or cannot safely be sedated during the first four or so hours of sleep.

Safety and effectiveness in children below the age of eighteen has not been established according to the *PDR* although the medication certainly can be a very effective treatment of ADD in children. Again, proper FDA warnings must be provided and informed consent obtained if trazodone is prescribed for young people.

Special attention must be given to providing a warning to male patients and/or their parents if they are minors about the possibility of priapism. In my experience, priapism has not been a problem when the starting dose of trazodone is no more than 25 to 50 mg. Of course, the *PDR* which warns about priapism also recommends an "initial starting dose of 150 mg/day."

When the dose of trazodone taken at bedtime is excessive, it typically causes profound sedation on awakening the next morning. This sedation is often described as "dopiness" or "grogginess." It is different from and usually more severe than the "tiredness" or coming-awake-slowly feeling that is common to people with ADD neurology. When experienced, it is one of the most important signs that the dose of trazodone is too high and needs to be reduced. Since trazodone has a short half-life in the blood and is clinically effective for only twenty-four hours, dosage adjustments can be made and accurately assessed on a daily basis.

Trazodone does not cause seizures and has no significant cardiac effects when taken in therapeutic doses.

Alprazolam (Generic Name)

In adults, if trazodone is not effective, the next choice of medication is alprazolam. I have never prescribed this medication for treating ADD children or teenagers. Alprazolam is dramatically effective but in only about 1% of ADD adults.

Alprazolam has a "bad reputation" for two reasons. First, it is often prescribed as a tranquilizer, a sleeping pill, and sometimes as an aid to escape from reality, thus sedating people who really should be alert. It is certainly not an effective ADD medication when this occurs. Second, withdrawal from even modest doses of alprazolam should be done very slowly to prevent withdrawal epileptic seizures.

The starting dose is comparable to that recommended in the *PDR*, that is, 0.25 mg nightly. Initially, the dose can be increased on a nightly basis by 0.25 mg a night to a total dose of 1.5 mg. Usually, some degree of positive or negative clinical effect will be evident by this dose even though some individuals do need much higher doses for full clinical benefit. This is a difficult medication to prescribe for the treatment of ADD because the effective dosage range can be as little as 0.5 to 1.0 mg or as much as 22-24 mg a day.

Moreover, the total effective dose may be different from day to day. Those who rely on alprazolam should always carry a supply with them each day. While the reason for variations in the daily dose is not always clear, it appears that ADD individuals are sensitive to daily variations in the intensity of adverse environmental and emotional stresses.

At what time each day should alprazolam be taken? The answer is dramatically different from one person to another. Alprazolam may be most effective for some when ingested only at bedtime. Others do better when they divide their dose between bedtime and daytime hours. A few do well taking all of their medication during the day in divided doses. Rarely, an individual does best taking alprazolam as a single dose each morning. For the prescribing physician, the only reliable guideline for the use of alprazolam is to be sure that the medication is correcting the neurological dysfunctions of ADD and to be flexible about dosing. Explain the possible dosing regimens to patients and help each patient search for what is the correct dose for that individual.

When alprazolam is properly helping ADD adults, they have more energy, are more functional at home and work, and are less tired during the day. Those with panic attacks stop having attacks, or the attacks become dramatically less intense and less often. Extra dosing is sometimes necessary to abort an incipient panic attack.

When it is an effective medication for the treatment of ADD, alprazolam is not sedating whether taken during the day or at night. ADD people may relax and sleep more easily after taking alprazolam at bedtime, but this is because they are more mellow, more relaxed, and not because they are sedated. Also, when alprazolam is acting as a proper ADD medication, ADD adults notice that they come awake more easily and function with more alertness and focus in the morning and during the day than they did before treatment.

Seeking Maximum Medication Benefit

For some with ADD, there is no one, single medication that is totally effective for their ADD symptom complex. They may do well, however, taking a combination of medications. This mixture might consist of two antidepressant or one or two antidepressants and a stimulant.

In those whose cognitive function responds to a tricyclic antidepressant but who remain emotionally negative and grouchy, mixing the tricyclic medicine with a selective serotonin reuptake inhibitor drug such as Prozac, Paxil or Zoloft can dramatically result in a happy, highly functional person. Keep in mind, of course, that the blood level of tricyclic medications will be significantly elevated by the concomitant use of Prozac or Paxil unless the dose of the tricyclic is reduced. Zoloft, at least in the short term, does not elevate tricyclic blood levels.

In patients who thrive emotionally with the tricyclic antidepressants, the selective serotonin reuptake inhibitors, or trazodone, but who do not adequately focus when doing mental or academic tasks, adding a stimulant may provide amazing benefit. Moreover, when a stimulant medication is added to an established antidepressant treatment regimen, in about 90% of cases Dexedrine Spansules in particular will have a 12-16 hour duration of action and *not* be followed by a "letdown." Normally, stimulants including Dexedrine Spansules have no more than a 6-8 hour action and, if taken in the morning, will be followed by a severe "letdown" or "crash" in the afternoon.

I no longer mix trazodone and tricyclic antidepressants, rarely mix Ritalin and Dexedrine, and have never found that mixing trazodone and a serotonin reuptake inhibitor is useful. Mixing Parnate and Dexedrine Spansules or Parnate and a serotonin reuptake inhibitor may be clinically very effective, but there is a warning against this mixture in the *PDR*. This mixing of drugs should be considered only if there is the full and informed consent of the patient, an obvious need for the benefit desired, other drug approach is effective, and the benefit clearly outweighs the potential risk.

FINAL COMMENT

When an antidepressant medication provides substantial but less than complete therapeutic benefit, it is wise to change first to another antidepressant within the same class rather than to a medicine of a different class.

For example, the tricyclic antidepressant, protriptyline, may be a suitable substitute for desipramine if this latter medication is not as effective as is desired or if an individual develops an allergy to it. Eldepryl and Nardil can sometimes substitute for Parnate if effectiveness is less than is desired. Paxil or Zoloft, serotonin reuptake inhibitors, are sometimes effective substitute medicines for Prozac if a side-effect of Prozac is intolerable.

Alternative medications are usually but not always available. I have not yet found a medication which substitutes for trazodone or alprazolam.

If changing from one antidepressant to another within the same class is not helpful, or if the response to the first medication is dramatically opposite to what is being sought, it is most appropriate to prescribe a medication from a different drug class. For example, if desipramine has only negative effects including worsening of tiredness and reduction in mental focusing, then changing to a different antidepressant class such as Prozac or trazodone is a logical next step.

Effective medication for most people with ADD neurology is now available. Unfortunately, there is still much too much confusion about how to use ADD medications. Hopefully, this situation along with the difficulty many professionals have diagnosing ADD and their lack of knowledge about the value of medication treatment will be less true in the future.

References

1. **Riddle, M.A., MD, B. Geller MD, and N. Ryan MD,** *Case Study: Another Sudden Death in a Child Treated with Desipramine.* Journal of the American Academy of Child and Adolescent Psychiatry, 1993. **32**(4): p. 792-797.
2. **Biederman, J., MD,** *et al., A Naturalistic Study of 24-Hour Electrocardiographic Recordings and Echocardiographic Findings in Children and Adolescents Treated with Desipramine.* Journal of the American Academy of Child and Adolescent Psychiatry, 1993. **32**(4): p. 805-813.

9

ATTENTION DEFICIT DISORDER AND CRIMINALITY

Criminality is the product of a complex interaction between biological and socio-environmental conditions. While individuals may be predisposed by genetic inheritance to behave in ways that ultimately become labeled as criminal, I believe that they are not genetically predetermined to be criminals.

In a free society governed by law such as the United States, a predisposition to dysfunctional behavior is not an excuse for being legally irresponsible nor is it a license to behave in a criminal manner. Experts have dealt with this issue by defining what are called the terms of "conditional free will" which postulate that: individuals choose a course of action within a preset, yet to some degree changeable, range of possibilities and that, assuming the conditions are suitable for rational thought, we are accountable for our actions [1].

ADD NEUROBIOLOGY IS A GENETIC RISK FACTOR FOR CRIMINALITY

Evidence that biological factors contribute to criminality comes mainly from family studies which "suggest that biological relatives of criminal or antisocial persons studied have a greater history of criminal convictions or antisocial behavior than the biological relatives of noncriminal control adoptees. In general, family environment, including such indices as social class, rearing styles, and parental attitudes, played a smaller role than did purported genetic effects [1]."

In particular, a study of Swedish adoptees showed an increased rate of criminality in the biological parents of petty criminals [2]. Also, adopted children who commit minor offenses are more likely to have natural fathers who have been offenders [3].

Genetic vulnerability to criminality is further supported by research which documents that Attention Deficit Hyperactivity Disorder, a genetically transmitted neurology, is found with a high incidence in the criminal population [4-7]. Hyperactivity and restlessness (fidgetiness), characteristics of the ADD syndrome, along with difficulty in the management of a child at age three, and the onset of behavior problems by the age of five, predict later antisocial outcomes [8]. It is now universally accepted by psychologists and other experts that the following neurological (see asterisks) and psychological dysfunctions, all of which are common to people with untreated ADD, are also related to criminality [9]:

1. *** Poor academic performance, or performance at levels below intellectual capability.
2. *** Impulsiveness, and nonpersistence at tasks assigned and coordinated by others.
3. *** Childhood hyperactivity.
4. General risk-taking and excitement-seeking.
5. Recreational drug use (especially chronic immoderate use of alcohol).
6. Preference for promiscuous and/or diverse sexual experiences.
7. Preference for active social interactions, often to the point of their being chaotic.
8. Resistance to conditioning, or defiance of punishment.

Learning disability, a problem which is very commonly due to ADD neurological dysfunction, is another biological problem that has strong links to delinquency and criminality. The likelihood of arrest and adjudication is substantially higher for teenagers handicapped by learning disabilities, and boys with learning disabilities have significantly higher rates of delinquent behavior than non-learning disabled boys [10]. Serial killers, especially persistent and dread criminals, are thought to have learning disability because they are often intellectually competent individuals who are "underachievers [11]." The important role of learning disability as a contributing factor to criminality is further illustrated by the fact that forty percent of juveniles who appear in New York Family Court are learning disabled. The majority, age seven to seventeen, have failed in and/or dropped out of school. These juveniles were found to have engaged in antisocial and criminal behavior from robbery to drug dealing to murder [7].

A history of primary nocturnal enuresis or bedwetting when five or older is virtually diagnostic of the ADD syndrome. Bedwetting past the age of twelve, along with a history of arson and cruelty to animals and people, is a clinical triad that the Federal Bureau of Investigation (FBI) identifies as consistent with their profile of serial murderers and indicative of future violent behavior [11].

Finally, my personal medical experience has shown that ADD neurology is a risk factor for alcoholism and problem drinking, both of which are associated with criminality [9]. In fact, it is not uncommon for violent crimes to be preceded by alcohol consumption even by those with other substance abuse and addiction problems [12, 13].

Socio-Environmental Factors Also Contribute to Criminality

There are various opinions about how specific biological and socio-environmental factors operate to promote criminality, but firm evidence is extremely limited.

One view, sometimes referred to as the *school failure hypothesis* [10], is that those with learning disabilities have poor academic achievement and generate negative attitudes toward themselves from relatives, peers and school officials. The individual with poor grades and about whom negative attitudes have developed is likely to develop associations with others who have similar problems having to do with school, including truancy and delinquency. Moreover, children with learning disabilities who are undiagnosed and untreated are more likely to get into trouble because they are unskilled, suffer from low self-esteem, and can be swayed easily by others [14].

Another postulate, sometimes called the *susceptibility hypothesis*, is that those with learning disabilities are also impulsive. Both dysfunctions are problems common to people with ADD. They also have "poor perception of social clues, irritability, suggestibility, and a tendency to act out." This concept suggests that certain characteristics make individuals susceptible to delinquency [10]. Impulsivity, along with these additional handicaps, are frequently associated with disruptive behavior in organized social settings such as school, the violation of rules, and delinquency.

An additional hypothesis linking criminality to ADD is that people with ADD neurology and difficulty with motivation often seek high adventure, excitement, and challenges which allow them to feel much more attentive, alive and energetic than they normally would on a typical school or working day. Thrill-seeking has been identified as one of the main motives for crime in juveniles who go on to adult criminal careers [13]. Similarly, risk-taking has been identified as a characteristic of youths involved in "extensive delinquency [15]." Consistent with this notion is the personality assessment study of a representative birth cohort of 862 male and female 18-year-olds which found that youths involved in extensive delinquency were uniquely characterized by feelings of alienation, lack of social closeness and risk taking [15]. These persons crave more than a normal level of sensory stimulation, quickly become habituated to incoming stimuli and feel bored in many ordinary environments. The theory is, therefore, that they are motivated to seek novel and/or intense sensory stimulation to a degree that most other people would choose to avoid [9].

Even the courts have recognized an important link between educational success and delinquency. In fact, courts are requiring equal funding of schools and probation orders requiring school attendance because of the strong inverse relation between education and the crime rate [16, 17]. These rulings are intended to help juveniles remain in school.

Performance in school is reasonably related to future criminality, both by deterring current delinquency, and by enhancing the ability to maintain prospective employment or to continue in advanced education upon graduation. A court may reasonably conclude a juvenile, without an adequate education, is more likely to resort to criminal activities [18].

The attitude of the courts reflects the belief that, with proper help, many learning-disabled young people are able to overcome their handicap enough to become good students and have socially acceptable behavior.

Learning disabilities contribute to delinquency [19], but a variety of environmental circumstances and factors such as acceptance in the school setting, remedial academic instruction, relationships with nondelinquent peers, and strong encouragement and support from the family contribute substantially to the prevention of antisocial and criminal adult outcomes.

Correcting ADD Neurological Dysfunctions will Reduce Recidivism

If ADD is not treated at an early age and criminality develops, rehabilitative programs during incarceration may provide help designed to return the person to open society, or the incarceration may be used merely to isolate the individual from society for as long as is legally possible.

The purpose of providing rehabilitation, of course, is not merely to return a person to society, but to return a person who will be productive and avoid future criminal behavior. By implication, if recidivism occurs, the released individual will have not only committed at least one additional crime but will return to an overloaded court system and an overcrowded prison system to the benefit of no one.

Individuals with ADD neurology are excessively impulsive, and impulsivity is linked to recidivism. The impulsive, ADD mind is mentally hyperactive, unfocused, and full of thoughts. ADD people move from one thought to another without apparent logic and without normal pauses for reflection and reconsideration. All too often, thoughts are acted upon without consideration for the consequences. Typically, impulsive behavior includes not finishing tasks, not finishing thoughts being expressed, and acting with prolonged indecisiveness. Impulsive people usually are very disorganized.

Impulsive behavior is an especially devastating handicap for individuals prone to criminality. Effectively socialized people have self-control and patience. While loved-ones and family may tolerate impulsive behavior in those close to them, the schools and society in general usually do not. Young people who blurt out answers, talk out of turn, and act without apparent consideration for others may be severely penalized both academically by teachers and socially by peers. Sometimes, they are even excluded from school activities and shunned. Similar and often worse consequences befall impulsive adults when at work or in other social settings.

Impulsivity can be dangerous, and being a criminal is often dangerous "work." Whether an adolescent or an adult, the impulsive individual tends to make poorly thought-out decisions and takes rash actions, and, unfortunately, may commit crimes on impulse without considering the consequences.

It is usually a mistake to attribute impulsivity to a lack of manners or maturity without first considering that the impulsive actions are more likely the expression of a neurological disorder, especially the ADD syndrome. Several recent studies have linked impulsivity to persistent, serious recidivistic delinquency [20-22]. "Violent recidivism, in particular, is strongly associated with the degree of impulsivity involved in crimes of killing and attempted murder [23]." According to the *DSM-IV*, impulsivity is common in people suffering from intermittent explosive disorder as well as kleptomania, pyromania and pathological gambling, many if not most of whom in my experience have ADD neurology.

Those with the impulsivity of ADD benefit dramatically when treated with medications that correct ADD neurological dysfunctions. To reduce the likelihood that an impulsive individual will return to crime, it is usually necessary to reduce impulsive tendencies.

Certainly, in established criminals who are to be returned to open society and in whom ADD neurology can be documented, medication treatment for Attention Deficit

Disorder problems should be a part of the total treatment approach to reduce recidivism.

What could be more to the point than the following letter:

(NOTE: The following letter to Dr. Gross was copied as typed.)

ADD Medical Treatment Center of Santa Clara Valley
Dr. Monroe A. Gross 2505 Samaritan Dr., Suite #402
San Jose, CA. 95124

May 22, 1995

Dear Dr. Gross,

Well I am sorry that I haven't written you sooner, but that is not because I haven't thought of you and the help that you provided me and many others.

I am sure that you remember me as the guy that came to your old office chained up but in good spirits. Well to bring you up to date. My Attorney (name omitted) and I are still working on the case and making some progress. The prison decided to treat me with Ritalin, Which I really didn't want to take, because of my prior problems with addiction (this is probably the same reason they decided to use it, I hate to say) but as you may remember I had worked real hard to overcome my addiction, anyway effect of the Ritalin was immediate and dramatic. Its been over a year know and My life is so much better it is hard to describe, but let me try.

The anger that use to explode out of me. Is now very much under control, that is not to say that I don't get angry or frustrated I do. It is now in my control and I choose not to lose control. The hyperactivity is also under control. I am still very active but I don't feel the need to pace and keep moving. The exercise that I do I do with other people and have fun doing it, not the driven way I use to. I am concentrating more, for longer periods of time. I am systematically studying some thing that I've always had some natural talent for, but could never get to the finer details that make for a professional. I really believe that I am now going to do the things that I always knew were in me, and that have so disappointed other that I didn't do. I sure wish my parents where alive, but my son will do. I'm not trying to put to much presume I could go on and on about all this but I think you know where I am coming from. I want to thank you and your staff for opening that door of trust enough to let me come in to your office. The help and encouragement that you gave me has been GRRRRRRRReat!! I don't think you know, but there was another guy there at the jail who I found Dead in his cell (suicide) he had ADD as well as his two brothers and mother. I still keep in touch with his mother and his brother I met here in prison. I want you to know that I am now not the only one being treated for ADD. There are at least 8 others and that's only the ones I know of. While there is problems with that treatment concerning my old problem (addiction) that need to be addressed. We have made enormous progress.

If there is anything that I can do for you, please don't hesitate to ask. If any researchers that could be helped by me or I could help by telling them about what I know about the problems with addiction in the treatment of ADD in this setting, please put me in contact with them.

Well Dr. Gross Thanks again for all the work you have done and the personal help you have given me.

PS 3 MONTHS AGO I COULDN'T TYPE!
LAST WEEK I HIT 37 W.P.M.
YEA, I KNOW I STILL MAKE
MISTAKES, BUT I'M GETTING BETTER!
I EVEN STARTED
WRITING A BOOK. GOT 70
PAGES SO FAR. ONE GOOD THING
ABOUT ADD'ERS. WE AREN'T AFRAID
OF GOING FOR IT.

Note: Sadly, by the time of publication of this book, San Quentin prison in California changed its policy and refused to allow the above prisoner or other prisoners in that institution to continue Ritalin treatment.

A Logical Conclusion: Identify and Treat ADD Neurology Early and Reduce Criminality

There is an important link between ADD and both delinquency and criminality. ADD has a very important biological effect on behavior and is very correctable with proper medication. It is essential, therefore, that school and law enforcement officials understand the nature of ADD and know to look beyond immediate antisocial behavior to see if ADD neurology exists. It is also critical that physicians improve their ability to diagnose ADD and sharpen their appreciation of the value of medication treatment for Attention Deficit Disorder in those who are established criminals or are heading toward being criminals.

The economic and social cost of preventing criminality is dramatically lower than the price paid for fighting crime and incarcerating criminals.

References

1. **Fishbein, D.H.**, *Biological Perspectives in Criminology.* Criminology, 1990. **28**(1): p. 27-72.
2. **Raine, A., P.H. Venables, and M. Williams**, *Relationships Between Central and Autonomic Measures of Arousal at Age 15 Years and Criminality at Age 24 Years.* Arch Gen Psychiatry, 1990. **47**(Nov): p. 1003-1007.
3. **McBroom, P.**, *Behavioral Genetics.* 1980, National Institute of Mental Health.
4. **Dizmang, L.H., M.D.**, *Use of the T.O.V.A. in the Diagnosis and Treatment of Attention Deficit Disorder in an Adult Inmate Population.* 1994, California Medical Facility.
5. **Dizmang, L.H., M.D.**, *Prevalence of Hyperactivity in Childhood in an Adult Inmate Population.* in press, California Medical Facility.
6. **Greenberg, L.M.**, *Attention Deficits in Incarcerated Youth --- A Preliminary Report.* 1995, Personal Communication.
7. **Zagar, R.**, *et al.*, *Developmental and Disruptive Behaviors among Delinquents.* J. Am. Acad. Child Adolesc. Psychiatry, 1989. **28**(3): p. 437-440.
8. **White, J.L.**, *et al.*, *How Early Can We Tell?: Predictors of Childhood Conduct Disorder and Adolescent Delinquency.* Criminology, 1990. **28**(No. 4): p. 507-533.
9. **Ellis, L. and H. Hoffman**, ed. *Crime in Biology, Social, and Moral Contexts.* ed. L. Ellis and H. Hoffman. 1990, Praeger Publishers: New York.
10. **Dunivant, N.**, *The Relationship Between Learning Disabilities and Juvenile Delinquency.* 1982, National Center for State Courts, Williamsburg, Virginia.

11. **Wilson, C. and D. Seaman**, *The Serial Killers: A Study in the Psychology of Violence.* 1990, London: W. H. Allen Publishing.
12. **Yarvis, R.M.**, *Patterns of substance abuse and intoxication among murderers.* Bulletin of the American Academy of Psychiatry & the Law, 1994. **22**(1): p. 133-44.
13. **Zawitz, M.W.**, *Report to the Nation on Crime and Justice.* 1988, U.S. Department of Justice.
14. **Morgan, T.**, *Learning Disabilities and Crime: New York Fights to Break Link,* in *The New York Times.* 1988, New York.
15. **Krueger, R.F.**, *et al.*, *Personality traits are linked to crime among men and women: evidence from a birth cohort.* Journal of Abnormal Psychology, 1994. **103**(2): p. 328-38.
16. Appeal, C.C.o., *Serrano v. Priest.* 1971, California Court of Appeal.
17. Appeal, C.C.o., *In re Robert M.* 1985, California Court of Appeal.
18. Appeal, C.C.o., *In re Angel J.* 1992, California Court of Appeal.
19. **Tremblay, R.E.,** *et al.*, *Early disruptive behavior, poor school achievement, delinquent behavior, and delinquent personality: longitudinal analyses.* Journal of Consulting & Clinical Psychology, 1992. **60**(1): p. 64-72.
20. **White, J.L.,** *et al.*, *Measuring impulsivity and examining its relationship to delinquency.* Journal of Abnormal Psychology, 1994. **103**(2): p. 192-205.
21. **Luengo, M.A.,** *et al.*, *A short-term longitudinal study of impulsivity and antisocial behavior.* Journal of Personality & Social Psychology, 1994. **66**(3): p. 542-8.
22. **Waldie, K. and O. Spreen**, *The Relationship Between Learning Disabilities and Persisting Delinquency.* Journal of Learning Disabilities, 1993. **26**(6): p. 417-423.
23. **DeJong, J., M. Virkkunen, and M. Linnoila**, *Factors associated with recidivism in a criminal population.* Journal of Nervous & Mental Disease, 1992. **180**(9): p. 543-50.

10

Clinical Findings and Analysis: A Study of 1377 Patients with Attention Deficit Disorder

Comments About Methodology

This clinical study of 1377 ADD patients from my private medical practice, on which the observations in this book are based, is not without its limitations. Subjects were not placebo controlled nor randomly assigned.

On the other hand, because the findings and analyses described are based on a very large number of patients who ranged in age from two to eighty-two at the time of diagnosis, they should not be dismissed out of hand. The data was collected in a medically sound manner and has been statistically analyzed.

Patient data was gathered over a period of approximately twenty-three years. During this time, my awareness and understanding of the nature of ADD grew. Every patient in this study was not asked all the questions that I now consider appropriate for investigating individuals suspected of having ADD.

Much of the information presented will be new to many of my readers whether they are professionals or nonprofessionals. I hope that the results are as exciting to you as they have been to me. But, the findings are just a beginning to our modern understanding of ADD. Hopefully, other practicing physicians and members of academia with its vast resources of talent and funds will be stimulated to confirm and extend the results of my study in the near future.

The diagnosis of ADD is now a positive process. ADD is no longer a disorder diagnosed by exclusion, lost in a haze of vague clinical findings, necessarily ignored until its adverse effects are severe, and invisible in adults some of whom try hard to mask their ADD neurology. The findings of this study show that a diagnosis can be made in young children as well as the many adults who slipped through the diagnostic cracks in childhood.

All of the individuals reported in my study, except four who received only stimulants, were treated successfully with antidepressant medication of one type or another. In view of this, doubt should be raised concerning the common claim that stimulant medications should always *initially* be prescribed to children, teenagers and adults in spite of their many disadvantages when compared to antidepressants. At the same time, there should be more awareness that, if stimulant medications are prescribed, they should be combined with antidepressant medication whenever possible to prolong the action of the stimulant and because once-a-day dosing is possible in about 90% of individuals so treated.

Whether or not individuals with ADD were feeling "depressed" or not never influenced my decision to use or not use antidepressant medication. Antidepressants are excellent medicines for treating people with ADD whether or not they are depressed. With rare exception, antidepressants are always given as a single-dose once each 24-hours, and they are the only drugs that can correct all ten neurological dysfunctions of the ADD syndrome. They are an extremely safe class of medication when blood testing and electrocardiographic monitoring is appropriately performed and properly interpreted.

For you to be comfortable with the point of view expressed in this book, I believe that you should have the primary data which support that ADD is a neurological problem, that the psychological consequences of living with ADD must be distinguished from the neurological dysfunctions that define the ADD syndrome, and that antidepressant medication should generally be the treatment of first choice for people with ADD.

I have tried to make the presentation of the scientific data in this chapter as readable as possible. It is of the utmost importance to me as a physician and scientist that the statements in this book are verified by more than anecdotal reports, case histories, or unquantified clinical impressions. Therefore, the data in this chapter has been statistically analyzed.

Since the ADD syndrome is a neurological disorder, all participants in this study were fully examined by the author, a medical doctor who is an internist and endocrinologist. Appropriate screening laboratory data was always collected prior to the start of treatment. See Appendix A. If medical abnormality was found that could significantly influence behavior, thinking or emotions, that abnormality was corrected before antidepressant medication was begun.

Only individuals whose treatment was successful as far as both they and I were concerned are part of the 1377 individuals in this study. ADD patients who, after being medically evaluated, refused medication treatment for whatever reason, or could not decide if medication was helpful, were excluded. ADD is a clinical syndrome. Proof of the diagnosis of ADD still cannot be confirmed by laboratory testing. Therefore, no diagnosis was considered documented until correction of the ADD complaints was achieved with medication. When necessary, medication treatment was started, stopped and restarted, and the cycle repeated if necessary until it became reasonably clear that the ADD complaints were indeed responding to medication and not incidental, unknown factors.

Each individual included in this study had several or all of the ten neurological dysfunctions of the ADD syndrome. Most, however, presented for treatment because of a single, chief complaint, such as being unfocused at school, feeling tired, chronically impulsive and mentally scattered, or episodically violent. Many were unaware of the diagnostic importance of their other ADD neurological dysfunctions nor aware that they were correctable. Some thought that they had to live with what turned out to be were ADD dysfunctions, believing that they had several, severe, permanent defects ingrained in their makeup. They often initially had great doubt, in fact, that medication could correct these problems which they had come to accept would be a permanent part of their nature. When medication was effective, it was often more a surprise than an expectation.

From a medical history-taking point of view, primary nocturnal enuresis (bed wetting), episodic explosiveness, waking slowly, falling asleep with difficulty and awareness of dyslexic reversals were not difficult to document clinically. Unexplained irritability and/or easy frustration were extremely common problems for ADD individuals and will be analyzed and reported on later.

Negativity is an ADD neurological dysfunction that is more difficult to evaluate and quantify than the other ADD dysfunctions. Not only is negativity present only some of the time, there is no easy way to define either how negative or how frequently a person must be negative to be labeled as "negative" or "not negative." Even though there are some individuals in whom negativity was so dramatically and chronically present that diagnostic controversy did not exist, the scientific approach of this study did not allow for the inclusion and analysis of only obvious cases which would then become anecdotal in nature. Accordingly, a precise incidence and severity of negativity was not defined in this study.

Inattentiveness, especially academic underachieving, along with impulsivity and hyperactivity were critical criteria for establishing the diagnosis of ADD although they may not have been the major reason why treatment was sought. A important purpose of this study is to show that more than just these three neurological dysfunctions belong to the spectrum of ADD neurological dysfunctions and that proper treatment should include medication that significantly corrects all ten areas of neurological dysfunction, if present.

A second purpose of this study is to document that ADD individuals are prone to a variety of psychological dysfunctions which usually have psychiatric names as if they were unique, isolated and independent disorders. Conversely, a number of people with major psychological dysfunction are shown to have a pattern of ADD neurological dysfunction that is identical to ADD individuals with classical *DSM-IV* criteria. These finds are interpreted to mean that people with ADD may or may not develop important psychological dysfunction, that a variety of psychological dysfunctions are a consequence, at least in part, of underlying ADD neurology, and that major psychological dysfunctions are not an inherent characteristic of the ADD syndrome.

Technical and Statistical Tools Used in this Study

Patient data was entered only by the author and stored in the AlphaFour (TM) database program, version 1.05a, which also was used for calculating incidence of occurrence. The computer program GB-STAT (TM), version 1.5, was used to obtain Chi-square values and probabilities through the CHI-SQUARE - INDEPENDENCE module in the nonparametric statistical analysis section of the program, and for performing 2-Sample T-test parametric statistical analyses.

Statistical significance required a probability level of .05.

Clinical ADD Research Caveats

There is no single medication that can effectively treat all ADD individuals, and, generally, only one medication or medication combination is dramatically effective and tolerated by any given individual.

It is impractical to try to run a placebo controlled study of private medical practice patients. They come for help, usually pay some money out of pocket for their medical care, and are very eager to receive treatment, if it is indicated. They cannot be expected to participate in a treatment protocol in which they may or may not receive effective medication. Also, they are especially reluctant to delay the relief of their very troublesome problems when, as is common for those who enter my medical practice, they are familiar with the possible benefits of treatment and with other individuals who have already been dramatically helped with medication.

While the lack of placebo control leaves open the issue of placebo effect, many of those in my study had previously received treatment by other physicians which included stimulant medications and antidepressants that were intolerable or ineffective. It is totally unreasonable to postulate that my possibly dazzling, hypnotic personality and treatment enthusiasm was the reason for clinical improvement of the patients reported in this study. I do accept, however, that academic studies in which the effects of a placebo are compared to a single study medication in randomly selected, age and sex matched individuals is a more ideal research approach.

Amelioration of psychological dysfunctions following medication treatment is desirable but is not the basis for evaluating medication effectiveness. ADD medication corrects neurological dysfunctions only. In some individuals, this is all that is needed to allow them to cope well enough to bring about important psychological changes on their own. For example, a young adult may continue to enjoy the thought of drinking alcohol even while taking medication for ADD, but thinking of this sort should not be interpreted to mean that medication is not effective. The critical issue for judging medication effectiveness should be, in this particular case, whether impulse control has improved to the point that the individual can focus and think about the possible consequences of excessive drinking and avoid the impulse to drink alcohol.

The high incidence of neurological dysfunction in ADD individuals is significant only if there is information about the likelihood of similar dysfunction in people without ADD. Therefore, the author collected data on a "normal" control group of nineteen adults without ADD whose ages range from 23 to 75 years old (mean age = 51) and who were originally examined because they had an endocrine disorder such as Hashimoto's Thyroiditis, Diabetes Mellitus (Type 1), a prolactin-secreting pituitary tumor, or Graves Disease. Each of these individuals underwent the same complete history, physical examination and basic laboratory study as did those who were seen by the author for ADD evaluation. Individuals in the control group had no ADD neurological dysfunction except for one woman, age 51 at the time of diagnosis, who had minimal difficulty with left-to-right discrimination and another woman, age 59 at the time of diagnosis, who had minimal verbal dyslexia. None of the control group could be given ADD medication because, practically speaking, there was not enough neurological dysfunction for judging the success or failure of treatment.

ADHD and ADD Individuals With No Major Psychological Dysfunction

Of the 1377 successfully treated individuals in this study, the presence or absence of hyperactivity was determined from the history or direct observation in 1173 people.

THE ADHD (HYPERACTIVITY) SUBGROUP SETS THE STANDARD

A subgroup of 375 Attention Deficit Hyperactivity Disorder individuals with hyperactivity, impulsivity, inattentiveness but none of the complaints of major psychological dysfunction listed below were identified from among these 1173 ADD individuals. The ratio of males to females in the subgroup was 2.7:1. Age at the time of diagnosis ranged from 2 to 59 years old.

None of these patients had any of the following thirteen psychological dysfunctions: (1) agoraphobia, (2) alcoholism, (3) anorexia nervosa, (4) binge eating, (5) bulimia, (6) chronic pain syndrome, (7) drug addiction, (8) major depressive episode, (9) panic syndrome, (10) sexual promiscuity, (11) suicide attempt, (12) tics, or (13) workaholic personality.

Graph I shows the frequency of ADD neurological dysfunctions in ADHD individuals with respect to waking slowly, going to sleep with difficulty, episodic explosiveness, enuresis, and spatial and/or verbal dyslexia.

GRAPH I

ADHD

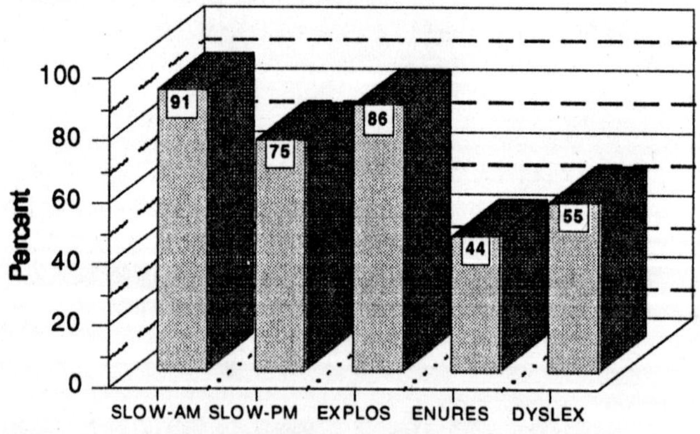

Of the 100% of this subgroup of ADHD individuals who were asked, 91% had a problem coming awake in the morning (AM-SLO). When analyzed by sex, 91% of males and 92% of females reported coming awake slowly in the morning, a difference that was not significant.

Of the 100% of this subgroup of ADHD individuals who were asked, 75% had difficulty falling asleep at night (PM-SLO). When analyzed by sex, 75% of males and 77% of females reported difficulty falling asleep at night, a difference that was not significant.

Of the 98% of this subgroup of ADHD individuals who were asked, 86% had episodic explosiveness (EXPLOS). When analyzed by sex, 88% of males and 79% of females reported episodic explosiveness. The incidence was high in both males and females. Statistically, males had a higher incidence that females (P=.03) for unknown reasons.

Of the 98% of this subgroup who were asked, 44% had a history of enuresis (ENURES). When analyzed by sex, 47% of males and 37% of females had a history of enuresis, a difference that was not significant.

Finally, of the 64% of this subgroup of ADHD individuals who were asked, 55% had dyslexia (DYSLEX). When analyzed by sex, 56% of males and 52% of females had dyslexia, a difference that was not significant.

Individuals in the ADHD subgroup fit the *DSM-III-R* and *DSM-IV* criteria for ADHD without psychological dysfunctions or so-called comorbidities. As such, the subgroup is ideal to serve as the "gold" standard for drawing comparisons between individuals with "pure" ADHD and two subgroups:

1. A subgroup of Attention Deficit Disorder individuals *without* major psychological dysfunction and without documented hyperactivity ("pure" ADHD v "pure" ADD).
2. A subgroup of Attention Deficit Disorder individuals *with* major psychological dysfunction some of whom had a history of hyperactivity and some of whom did not.

These comparative studies document:

First, there is a very high incidence of five additional ADD neurological dysfunctions which should be considered as an integral part, not just comorbidities, of the clinical picture of the ADD syndrome.

Second, individuals with a variety of psychological dysfunctions have the same pattern of neurological dysfunctions that is present in ADHD individuals without psychological dysfunctions.

Third, individuals with Attention Deficit Disorder with or without a history of hyperactivity are at high risk for developing serious psychological dysfunctions because they have ADD neurology.

Describing the ADD Subgroup

The subgroup of Attention Deficit Disorder individuals without hyperactivity and without major psychological dysfunction consists of 149 individuals. 52% are males and 48% are females. The members of this subgroup fit the criteria defined in the *DSM-III* for Attention Deficit Disorder without hyperactivity. The age of individuals in this study at the time of diagnosis ranged from 6 to 63 years old. Attention Deficit Disorder is more commonly diagnosed in males when only children and teenagers are studied, but it is diagnosed equally in females and males when ADD adults, teenagers and children are analyzed as one group.

Graph II shows the frequency of ADD neurological dysfunctions in this subgroup with respect to waking slowly, going to sleep with difficulty, episodic explosiveness, enuresis, and spatial and/or verbal dyslexia.

GRAPH II

ADHD v ADD

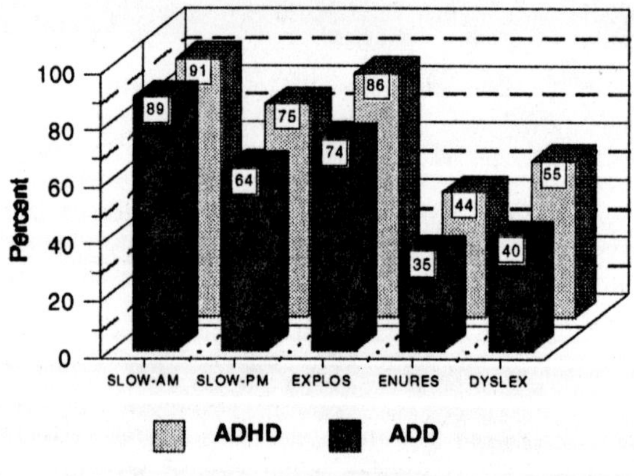

Of the 100% of this subgroup of ADD individuals who were asked, 89% came awake slowly in the morning (AM-SLO). When analyzed by sex, 88% of the males and 89% of the females came awake slowly, a difference that was not significant.

Of the 99% of this subgroup of ADD individuals who were asked, 64% had difficulty falling asleep at night (PM-SLO). When analyzed by sex, 69% of the males and 57% of the females had difficulty falling asleep, a difference that was not significant.

Of the 97% of this subgroup of ADD individuals who were asked, 74% had episodic explosiveness (EXPLOS). When analyzed by sex, 80% of the males and 68% of the females had episodic explosiveness, a difference that was not significant.

Of the 97% of this subgroup of ADD individuals who were asked, 35% had a history of enuresis (ENURES). When analyzed by sex, 47% of the males and 22% of the females had enuresis. This difference between the sexes only was highly significant (P=.002), and the reason for the difference is not known.

Of the 72% of this subgroup of ADD individuals who were asked, 40% had spatial and/or verbal dyslexia (DYSLEX). When analyzed by sex, 45% of the males and 35% of the females had dyslexia, a difference that was not significant.

Comparing the ADHD and ADD Subgroups

The incidence of the five ADD neurological dysfunctions, waking slowly, falling asleep with difficulty, episodic explosiveness, enuresis, and dyslexia is high and very similar in both the ADHD and ADD subgroups.

Nevertheless, there is a small but statistically significant difference but only with respect to women in the ADHD and ADD subgroups concerning two dysfunctions: (1) the incidence of falling asleep with difficulty at night is significantly lower in females (57%) in the ADD subgroup compared to females (77%) in the ADHD subgroup (P=.006); and, (2) the incidence of enuresis is lower in the females (22%) of the ADD subgroup compared to females (37%) in the ADHD subgroup (P=.04).

Since the incidence of these dysfunctions in the males without hyperactivity in this subgroup was not significantly different from that in the males and females in the ADHD subgroup who had a history of hyperactivity, it is unlikely that the presence of hyperactivity *per se* is a factor contributing to these differences.

ADHD and ADD Individuals with Major Psychological Dysfunction

Individuals with the Attention Deficit Disorder syndrome often get into personal and social trouble of one sort or another because of psychological dysfunctions. Commonly, they seek help for the specific behaviors that caused their trouble and not because of their underlying ADD neurological dysfunctions.

Certain psychological disorders occur very commonly in untreated ADD people who have lived with their ADD neurological dysfunctions for long periods of time. To document that they have underlying ADD which may well be playing a significant causative role in why these individuals develop various psychological dysfunctions, it follows that the observable frequency of ADD neurological dysfunction in these individuals should be the same as that found in the ADHD subgroup without psychological dysfunctions. The following data document that this is true for both males and females.

Agoraphobia Compared to the ADHD Subgroup

Agoraphobia was a problem in five males and sixteen females with ADD. Graph III shows that the incidence of coming awake slowly, falling asleep with difficulty, episodic explosiveness, and enuresis was not significantly different between the sexes nor between the ADHD and agoraphobia subgroups. Only between females with agoraphobia (92%) and ADHD females (52%) was the incidence of dyslexia significantly higher (P=.01).

GRAPH III

ADHD v AGORAPHOBIA

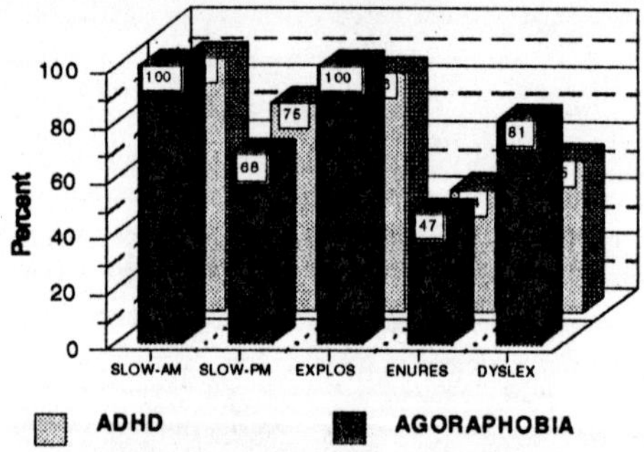

Alcoholism Compared to the ADHD Subgroup

Alcoholism was documented in 145 males and 106 females with ADD. Very few were actively drinking at the time of their diagnosis when treatment for ADD was started. In Graph IV, the incidence of coming awake slowly, falling asleep with difficulty, episodic explosiveness, and enuresis was not significantly different between the ADHD and alcoholism subgroups nor between the sexes. Only the incidence of dyslexia in the alcoholic females (79%) was significantly higher than that in the females (52%) of the ADHD subgroup (P=.002).

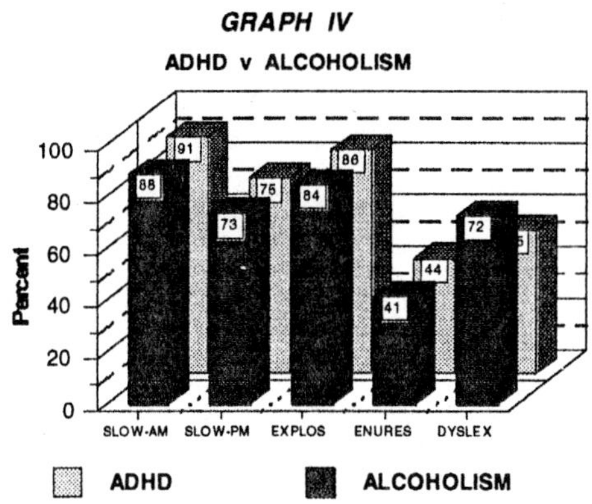

Anorexia Nervous Compared to the ADHD Subgroup

Anorexia nervosa was documented in the history of twenty-two females with ADD. In Graph V, the incidence of coming awake slowly, falling asleep with difficulty, episodic explosiveness, and enuresis was not significantly different between the females in the anorexia nervosa subgroup and females in the ADHD subgroup. The incidence of dyslexia in the anorexia nervosa females (78%) was significantly higher than that in the females (52%) of the ADHD subgroup (P=.05).

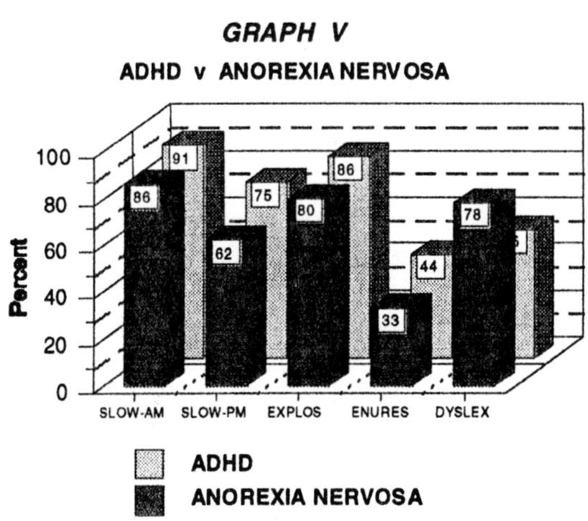

Binge Eating Compared to the ADHD Subgroup

Binge eating was documented in the history of forty-two males and seventy-eight females with ADD. In Graph VI, the incidence of coming awake slowly, falling asleep with difficulty, episodic explosiveness, enuresis, and dyslexia was not significantly different from that in the ADHD subgroup.

GRAPH VI

ADHD v BINGE EATING

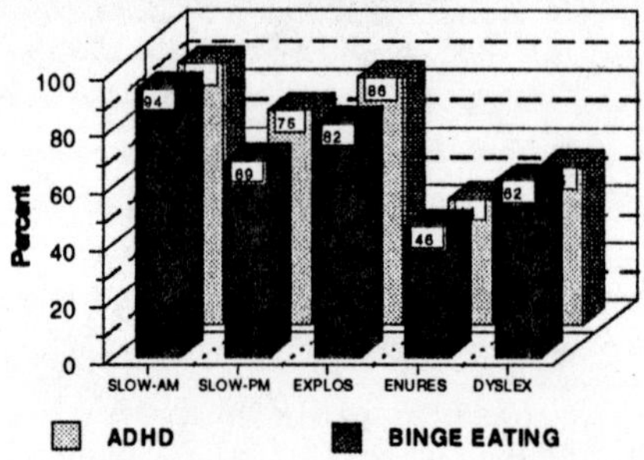

Bulimia Compared to the ADHD Subgroup

Bulimia was documented in the history of three males and fifty-eight females who were diagnosed to have ADD. In Graph VII, the incidence of coming awake slowly, falling asleep with difficulty, episodic explosiveness, and enuresis is not significantly different between the anorexia nervosa subgroup and the ADHD subgroup. The incidence of dyslexia in the bulimic females (78%) is significantly higher than that in the females (52%) of the ADHD subgroup (P=.004).

GRAPH VII

ADHD v BULIMIA

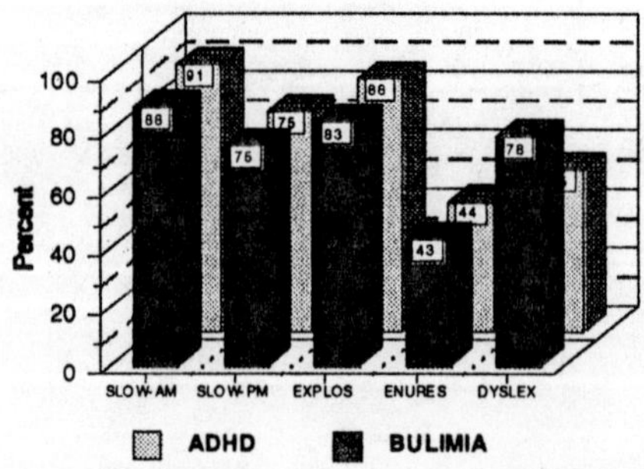

Chronic Pain Syndrome Compared to the ADHD Subgroup

Pain consistent with a diagnosis of the chronic pain syndrome was documented in eighteen males and twenty-three females who were diagnosed to have ADD. In Graph VIII, the incidence of coming awake slowly, falling asleep with difficulty, episodic explosiveness, enuresis, and dyslexia was not significantly from that of the ADHD subgroup.

GRAPH VIII

ADHD v CHRONIC PAIN SYNDROME

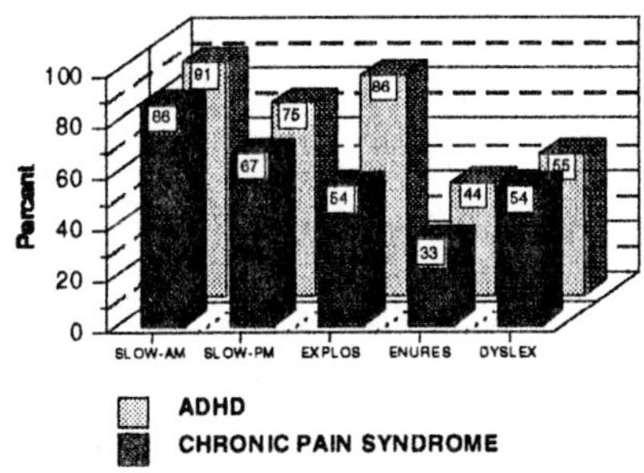

Depression Compared to the ADHD Subgroup

Serious depression was documented in 123 males and 255 females who were diagnosed to have ADD. In Graph IX, the incidence of coming awake slowly, falling asleep with difficulty, episodic explosiveness, and enuresis was not significantly different between the depression subgroup and the ADHD subgroup. The incidence of dyslexia in the depressed females (70%) was significantly higher than that in the females (52%) of the ADHD subgroup (P=.02).

GRAPH IX

ADHD v DEPRESSION

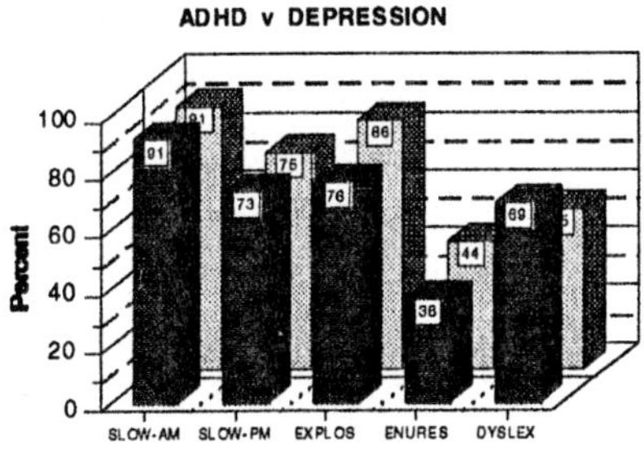

Drug Addiction Compared to the ADHD Subgroup

Addiction to illicit drugs was documented in the history of thirty-seven males and 32 females who were diagnosed to have ADD. In Graph X, there is no significant difference between each subgroup. However, males in the drug addiction subgroup had significantly less difficulty waking in the morning (78%) than males in the ADHD (91%) subgroup (P=.01). And, females in the drug addiction (41%) subgroup had significantly less difficulty with falling asleep at night than females in the ADHD (77%) subgroup (P<.0001), a difference that is possibly related to the use of illicit drugs. There was a significantly higher incidence (87%) of dyslexia in females in the drug addiction subgroup than in the females (52%) of the ADHD subgroup (P=.003).

GRAPH X

ADHD v ILLICIT DRUG ADDICTION

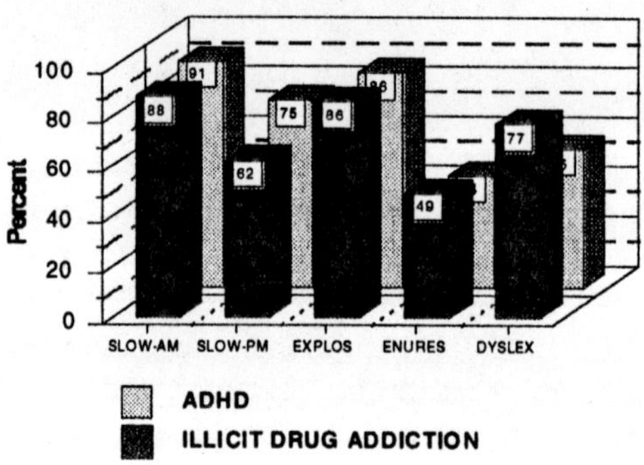

Panic Syndrome Compared to the ADHD Subgroup

Severe recurrent panic attacks consistent with the diagnosis of panic syndrome were part of the history of eleven males and thirteen females who were diagnosed to have ADD. In Graph XI, the incidence of coming awake slowly, falling asleep with difficulty, episodic explosiveness, enuresis, and dyslexia was not significantly different between the depression subgroup and the ADHD subgroup. Males (57%) in the panic syndrome subgroup had significantly less episodic explosiveness than males (88%) in the ADHD subgroup (P=.02).

GRAPH XI

ADHD v PANIC SYNDROME

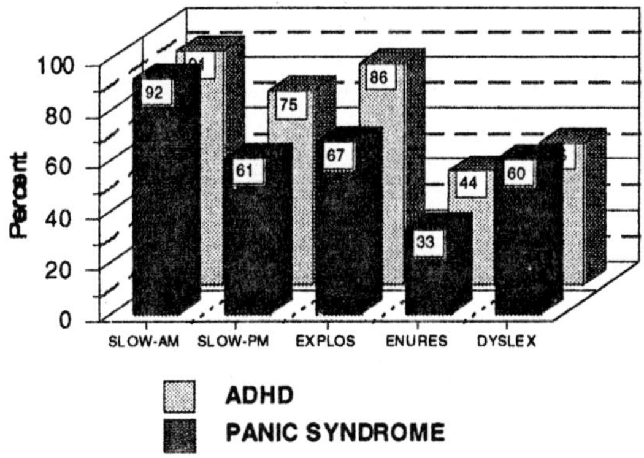

SEXUAL PROMISCUITY COMPARED TO THE ADHD SUBGROUP

Recurrent, poorly controlled sexual acting-out problems were noted in the history of nine females who were diagnosed to have ADD. In Graph XII, the incidence of coming awake slowly, falling asleep with difficulty, episodic explosiveness, enuresis, and dyslexia is not significantly different between the sexually promiscuous female subgroup and females in the ADHD subgroup.

GRAPH XII

ADHD v SEXUAL PROMISCUITY

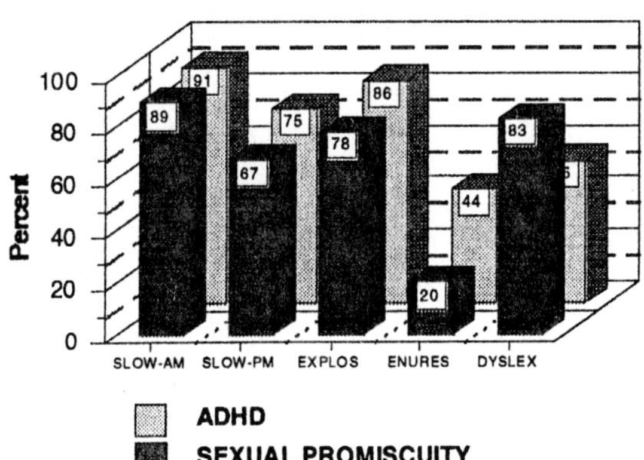

The Attempted Suicide Subgroup Compared to the ADHD Subgroup

A subgroup of individuals who were diagnosed to have ADD, each of whom had made a suicide gesture that was serious enough to require immediate medical attention, consisted of twelve males and thirty-four females. The incidence of coming awake slowly, falling asleep with difficulty, episodic explosiveness, enuresis, and dyslexia in males is not significantly different between those who attempted suicide and the ADHD subgroup. The incidence of dyslexia in the females who attempted suicide (80%) is significantly higher than that in the females (52%) of the ADHD subgroup (P=.02).

GRAPH XIII

ADHD v ATTEMPTED SUICIDE

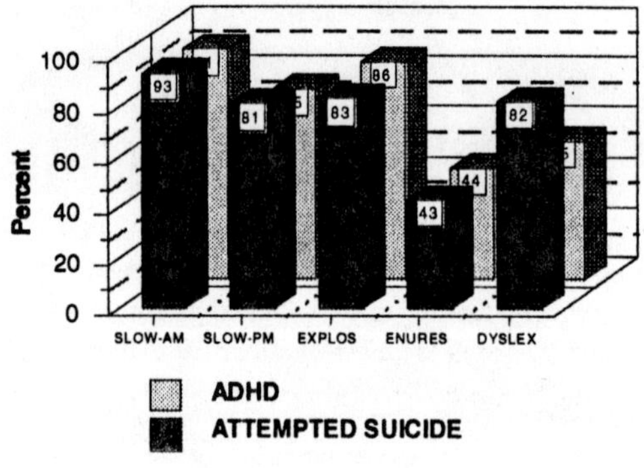

Individuals With Tics Compared to the ADHD Subgroup

Obvious and troublesome tic behavior was present in twenty-two males and six females who were diagnosed to have ADD. In Graph XIV, there is no significant difference between the two subgroups . Moreover, the incidence of falling asleep with difficulty, episodic explosiveness, enuresis, and dyslexia in males is not significantly different between the those with tics and the ADHD subgroup. Only the incidence of coming awake slowly in males with tics (77%) is significantly lower than that in the males (91%) of the ADHD subgroup (P=.03). The incidence of coming awake slowly, falling asleep with difficulty, enuresis, and dyslexia in females is not significantly different between these two subgroups, but the incidence of episodic explosiveness in females (33%) is significantly lower in those who had tics compared to females (79%) in the ADHD subgroup (P=.01).

GRAPH XIV

ADHD v TICS

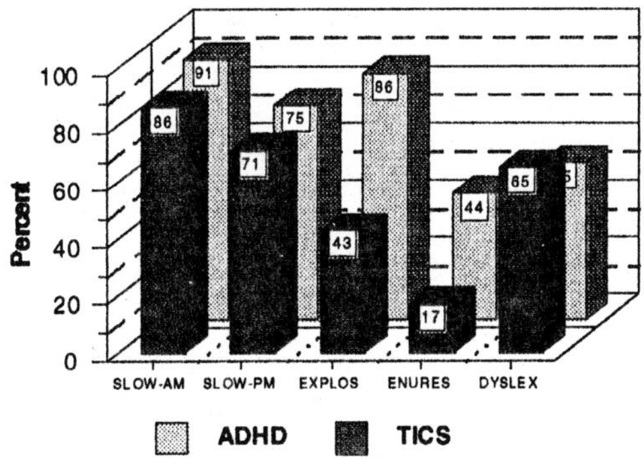

WORKAHOLICS COMPARED TO THE ADHD SUBGROUP

Forty-one males and twenty-one females with ADD were diagnosed to have workaholic personality. In Graph XV, there is no significant difference in the incidence of coming awake slowly, falling asleep with difficulty, episodic explosiveness, enuresis and dyslexia in the subgroups or in the female workaholic subgroup compared to the female ADHD subgroup. In workaholic males, however, the incidence of coming awake slowly (50%) is significantly lower (P<.0001) than it is in males in the ADHD subgroup (91%) and falling asleep with difficulty (49%) is significantly lower (P=.001) than in males in the ADHD subgroup (75%).

GRAPH XV

ADHD v WORKAHOLIC PERSONALITY

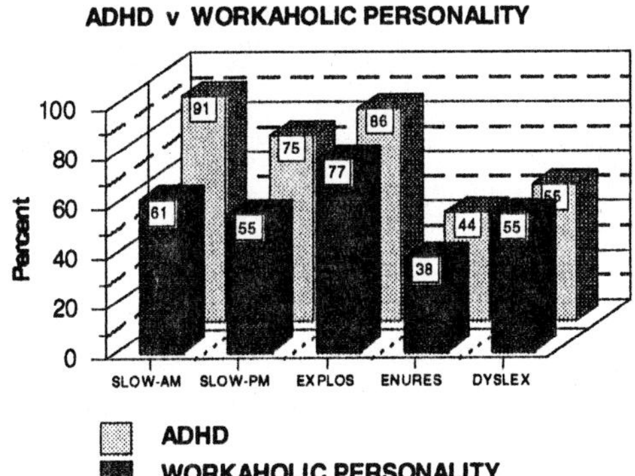

ADD and Other Health-Related Problems and Issues

What is the pattern of neurological dysfunctions in ADD women who also have PMS (Premenstrual Syndrome)? How can PMS be distinguished from the ADD syndrome?

Is there an association between the incidence of smoking cigarettes and psychological dysfunction in ADD males and females?

Which of the psychological dysfunctions common to ADD individuals are associated with an increased use of caffeine, especially caffeinated coffee, to promote wakefulness?

Are ADD males more likely to undergo surgical procedures or have more broken bones from accidents than ADD females? Let's look at data concerning these matters.

ADD and the Premenstrual Syndrome (PMS)

PMS is not an uncommon syndrome in women with ADD. Of the 437 women asked, 52% had a history of PMS symptoms including feeling irritable, tired, depressed and explosive prior to most menstrual periods. These symptoms are very much like the symptoms that ADD individuals experience all month long and not just before the start of menses.

If PMS-like symptoms are present all month long, it is more likely that they are a consequence of ADD than of the premenstrual syndrome. What if, however, PMS-like/ADD-like symptoms are present all month long but are worse just before the menstrual period? Is this ADD *and* PMS, or is it merely ADD with an exacerbation of ADD prior to the start of menses?

It is now possible to diagnose with accuracy the ADD syndrome in women. But, it is not easy to diagnose PMS which has no reasonably unique clinical clues other than acute onset hours to days prior to menses. One diagnostic approach to this dilemma is to assess the response of ADD and PMS to what is now established medical treatment of each syndrome.

If PMS-like symptoms stop occurring after a woman with ADD takes nonsteroidal anti-inflammatory medication or birth control pills, medications that do not eliminate ADD complaints but often relieve the symptoms of PMS, it is reasonable to believe that she does have PMS as well as ADD.

If a woman takes antidepressant medication for her ADD neurology and PMS-like symptoms fail to develop near the time of her menses, it is reasonable to think that she does not have PMS but only ADD.

One caveat. If PMS symptoms disappear for a while then return while a woman is taking ADD medication, would she be wise to believe that she now has

PMS or that her ADD medication treatment is inadequate or no longer effective? I would recommend that her ADD medication treatment be reevaluated.

Women who feel dramatic improvement only when taking medicine for both ADD and PMS probably have both disorders and should be treated for both disorders if they are severe enough to warrant treatment. Some women who have a mild form of PMS may not need and may refuse medication treatment. Unfortunately, others have a form of PMS which is severe and can lead even to suicide. When severe, all women should have the opportunity of knowing about the possibility that they have PMS and be offered appropriate medication.

Graph XVI shows the in the incidence of coming awake slowly in the morning (93%), going to sleep at night with difficulty (74%), episodic explosiveness (84%), and enuresis (31%) in 227 women with both PMS and ADD. There is no significantly different between the subgroup of women with ADHD and the subgroup of men with ADHD, no psychological dysfunctions and of course no PMS, the "gold" standard ADHD subgroup.

GRAPH XVI

ADHD MEN v WOMEN WITH PMS

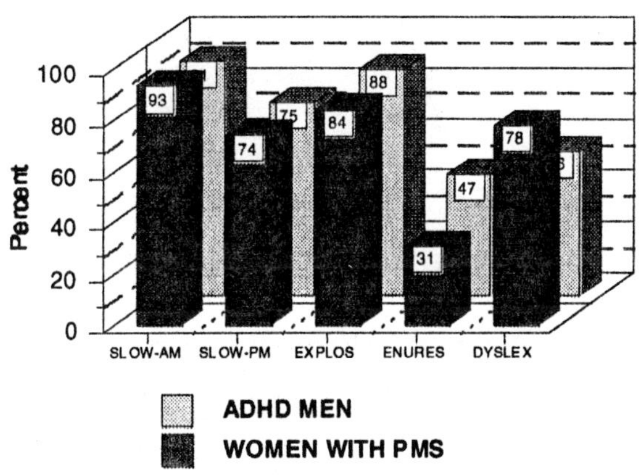

In addition, in Graph XVII the incidence of coming awake slowly in the morning (90%), going to sleep with difficulty (66%), and enuresis (29%) is no different the 227 women with both PMS and ADD when compared to women who did not report PMS problems. However, the women without PMS do have a significantly lower incidence of episodic explosiveness (73%) (P=.006) and dyslexia (63%) (P=.001) when compared to ADD women with PMS.

GRAPH XVII

ADD WOMEN WITH PMS v ADD WOMEN WITHOUT PMS

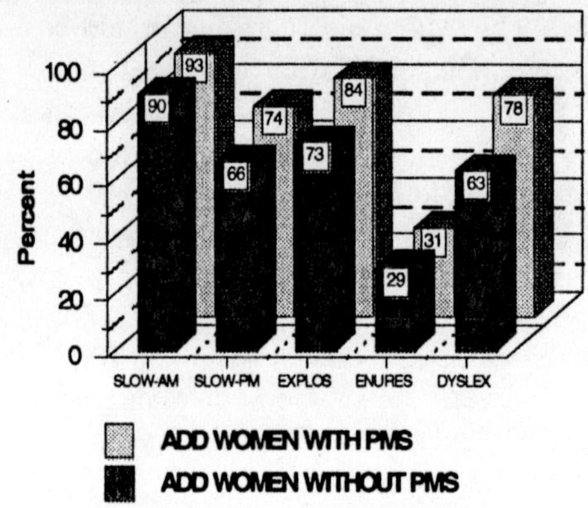

ADD and Cigarette Smoking

Of the 733 individuals with a history of hyperactivity (ADHD), 25% had at some time in the past or still were cigarette smokers on a regular basis. The incidence of cigarette smoking in ADD individuals without a history of hyperactivity is 31%, a value that is not significantly different from that of the ADHD individuals. These frequencies are similar to the incidence of cigarette smoking in general in the United States [1].

The following ADD individuals with a variety of psychological dysfunctions are not more likely to be smokers because of their dysfunctions. See Table 1.

Table 1

PSYCHOLOGICAL DYSFUNCTIONS THAT ARE NOT ASSOCIATED WITH AN INCREASED INCIDENCE OF SMOKING

- Anorexia Nervosa
- Bulimia
- Binge Eating
- Chronic Pain Syndrome
- Attempted Suicide
- Tics
- Workaholic Personality
- Premenstrual Syndrome (women)
- Sexual Promiscuity (women)

The following ADD individuals with psychological dysfunctions are more likely to be cigarette smokers than ADD individuals in general. See Table 2.

Table 2

PSYCHOLOGICAL DYSFUNCTIONS THAT ARE ASSOCIATED WITH AN INCREASED INCIDENCE OF SMOKING
Depression (P=.05)
Agoraphobia (P=.003)
Illicit Drug Addiction (P=.0001)
Panic Syndrome (P=.03)
Alcoholism (P=.0001)

It is unclear why an increased incidence of cigarette smoking is associated with the psychological dysfunctions noted in Table 2, except perhaps for those with alcoholism. In humans, nicotine from cigarettes causes the release of antidiuretic hormone from the pituitary gland in the head, a hormone that reduces the amount of urine released by the kidney. In contrast, drinking alcohol, a chemical which inhibits the release of antidiuretic hormone, leads to the production of increased amounts of urine and the need to urinate frequently. People who drink alcohol and do not smoke will urinate more often than those who drink alcohol and do not smoke cigarettes while drinking. Individuals who like to socialize while drinking will have more time to do so if they smoke cigarettes. This is not, by the way, a recommendation that people smoke cigarettes under any conditions. Whether or not the hormone effects of alcohol and cigarettes on urine production is scientifically understood by people who drink, drinkers may have learned of this physiological phenomenon from experience and therefore be inclined to smoke if they are alcohol drinkers.

Why ADD people with depression, agoraphobia, illicit drug addictions, panic syndrome and sexual promiscuity smoke more than other ADD individuals is unclear.

ADD and Surgical Procedures

Of the total study group of 1377 cases, 99% were asked about past surgical procedures. 44% of the males and 25% of the females had no history of surgical procedures. The incidence of surgeries performed in ADD males compared to ADD females is not significantly different.

ADD and Bone Fractures Due to Accidents

Of the total study group of 1377 cases, 99% were asked about bone fractures due to accidents (not spontaneous fractures). 59% of the males and 63% of the females had no history of accident-related bone fractures. The difference in the incidence of accident-related bone fractures in ADD males compared to ADD females is not significant.

Conclusion

Data in this study documents that a substantial number of individuals with significant and often harmful psychological dysfunctions have extremely similar patterns of ADD neurological dysfunction when compared to ADHD individuals without psychological dysfunctions. This data strongly suggests that people with a variety of psychological dysfunctions are likely to have ADD neurology. Even though ADD neurology is almost certainly not the sole cause of these psychological dysfunctions, it should be recognized as such and treated with medication along with any other forms of treatment that may be rendered.

Whether the psychological dysfunctions analyzed in this study are labeled as "mental disorders" as the *DSM-III*, *DSM-III-R* and *DSM-IV* psychiatric guides have done, or as psychological dysfunctions which are very likely to occur in individuals with ADD neurology, as the data in this book purports to show, is to some degree a matter of ones personal choice and professional preference at this point in time. In my opinion, however, the concept of recognizing that a variety of psychological dysfunctions are related to underlying ADD neurology is the approach of greatest value. The reduction or elimination of ADD neurological dysfunction requires proper ADD medication treatment, not psychotherapy. And, psychotherapy, if indicated, will only be more effective if the underlying ADD neurology is corrected.

Moreover, the identification of one individual with ADD neurology should encourage the search for ADD in other family members, especially if there is substantial dysfunctional psychological behavior in the family. Treating risk factors can only improve the overall success rate and outcome. Early medication treatment of ADD neurology is even likely to help prevent my psychological problems from ever developing.

REFERENCES

1. **Schnabel, R.A., J.A. Villamil, and B.E. Bryant**, *Statistical Abstract of the United States 1992*. 112 ed. ed. U.S. Department of Commerce, *et al.* 1992, Washington, D.C.: U.S. Government Printing Office, p 128.

Appendix "A"
Medical Evaluation of Each Study Patient

HISTORY:

A full internal medicine history was taken from each patient. This includes a chief complaint, present illness, review of all systems, habits including the use of caffeine, cigarettes and alcohol, injuries, operations, allergies as well as a family and work history.

In addition, the neurological dysfunctions of ADD were evaluated.

PHYSICAL EXAMINATION:

Each patient had a comprehensive physical examination by the author which excluded a genital and rectal examination in those with a primary care physician.

LABORATORY TESTING:

The initial evaluation of each patient included a CBC, Chemistry Panel, Urinalysis, Sedimentation Rate, Total T4, Total T3 and TSH. Additional testing was done, when appropriate, for other conditions that could cause symptoms and signs that might be confused with those of the ADD syndrome such as FSH testing for the menopause.

Index

E

F

H

I

K

L

M

N